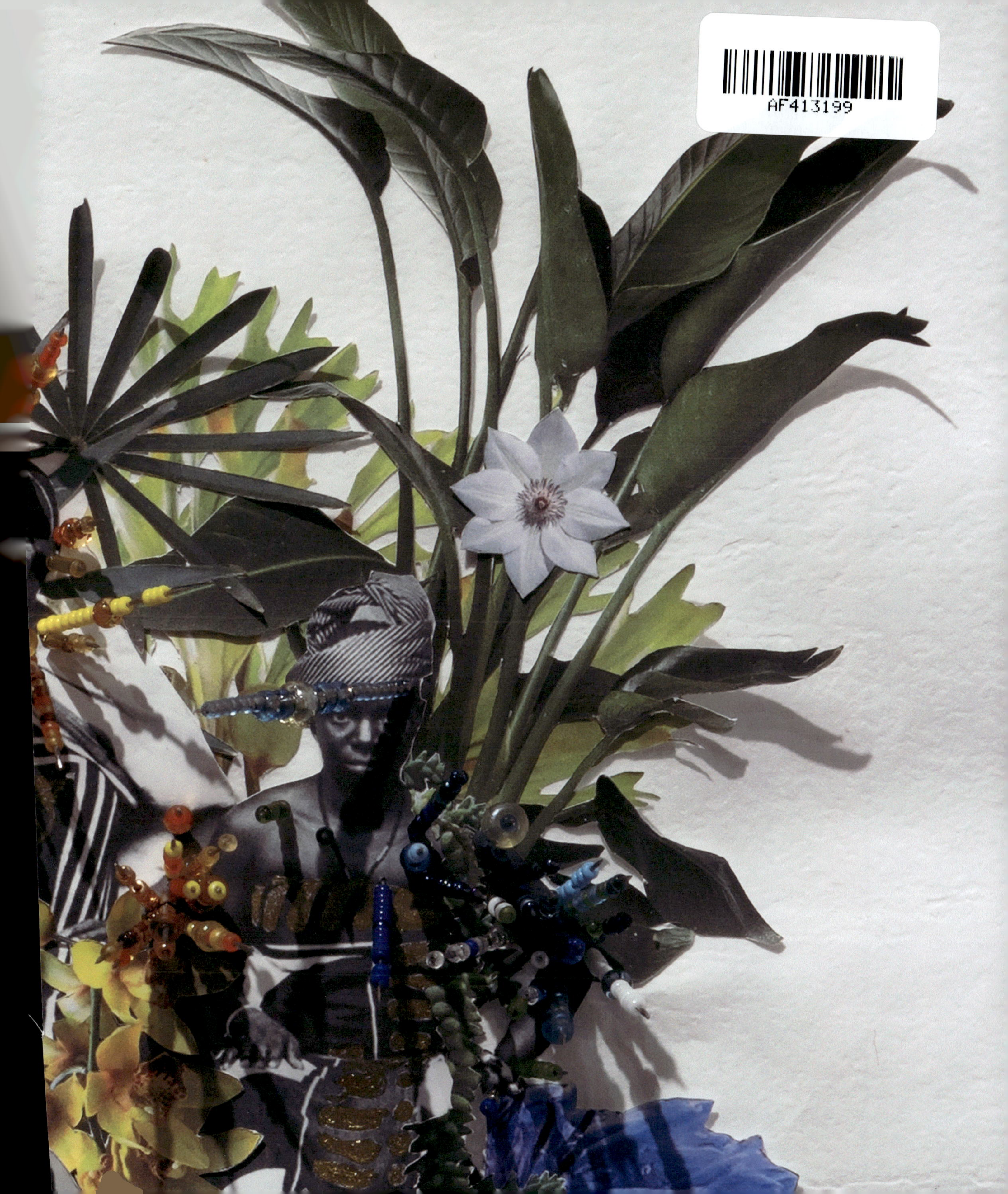

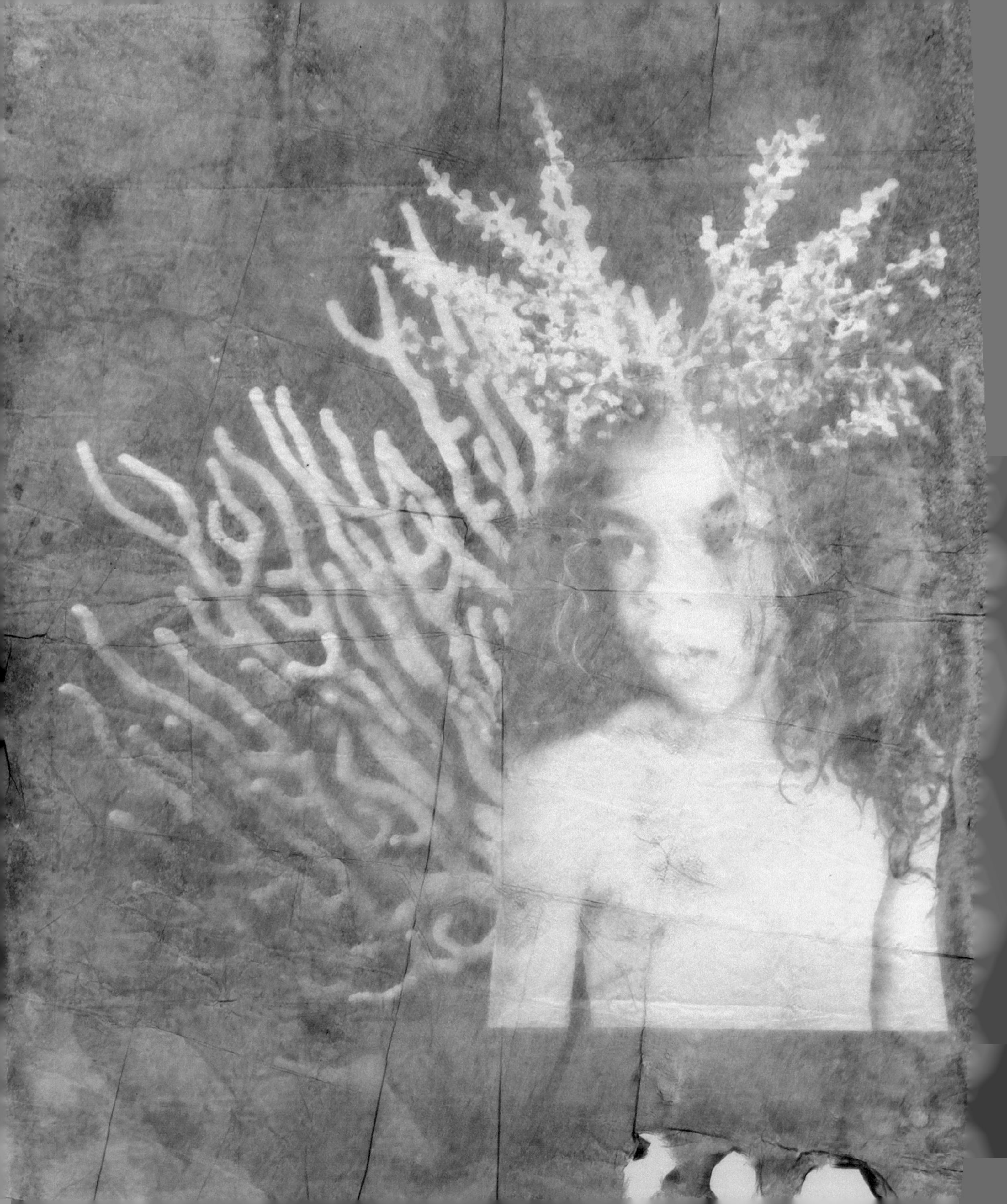

Andrea Chung

Andrea Chung

Between Too Late & Too Early

Curated by Adeze Wilford

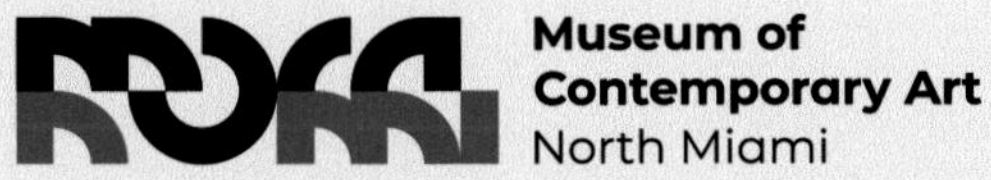

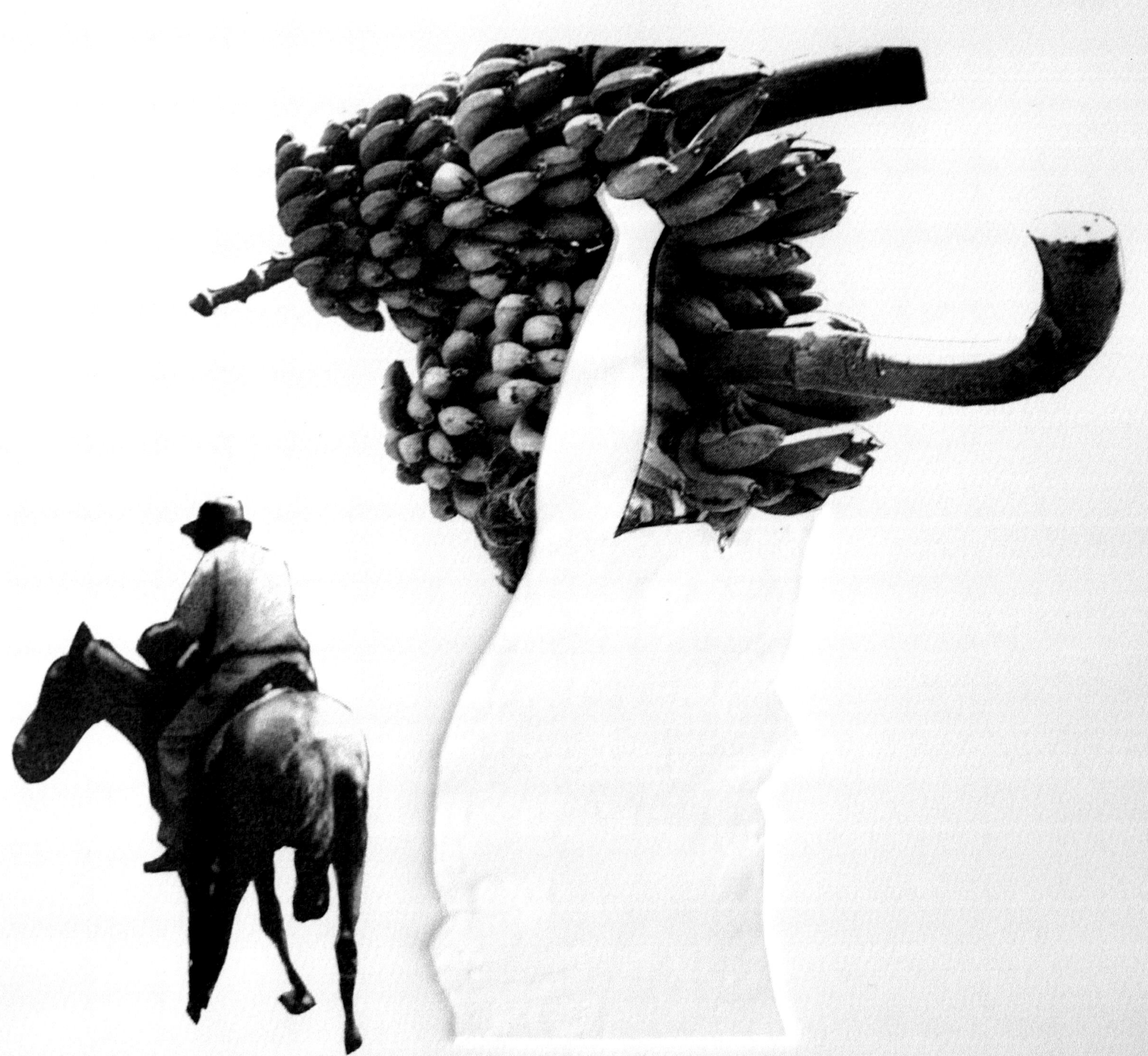

Contents

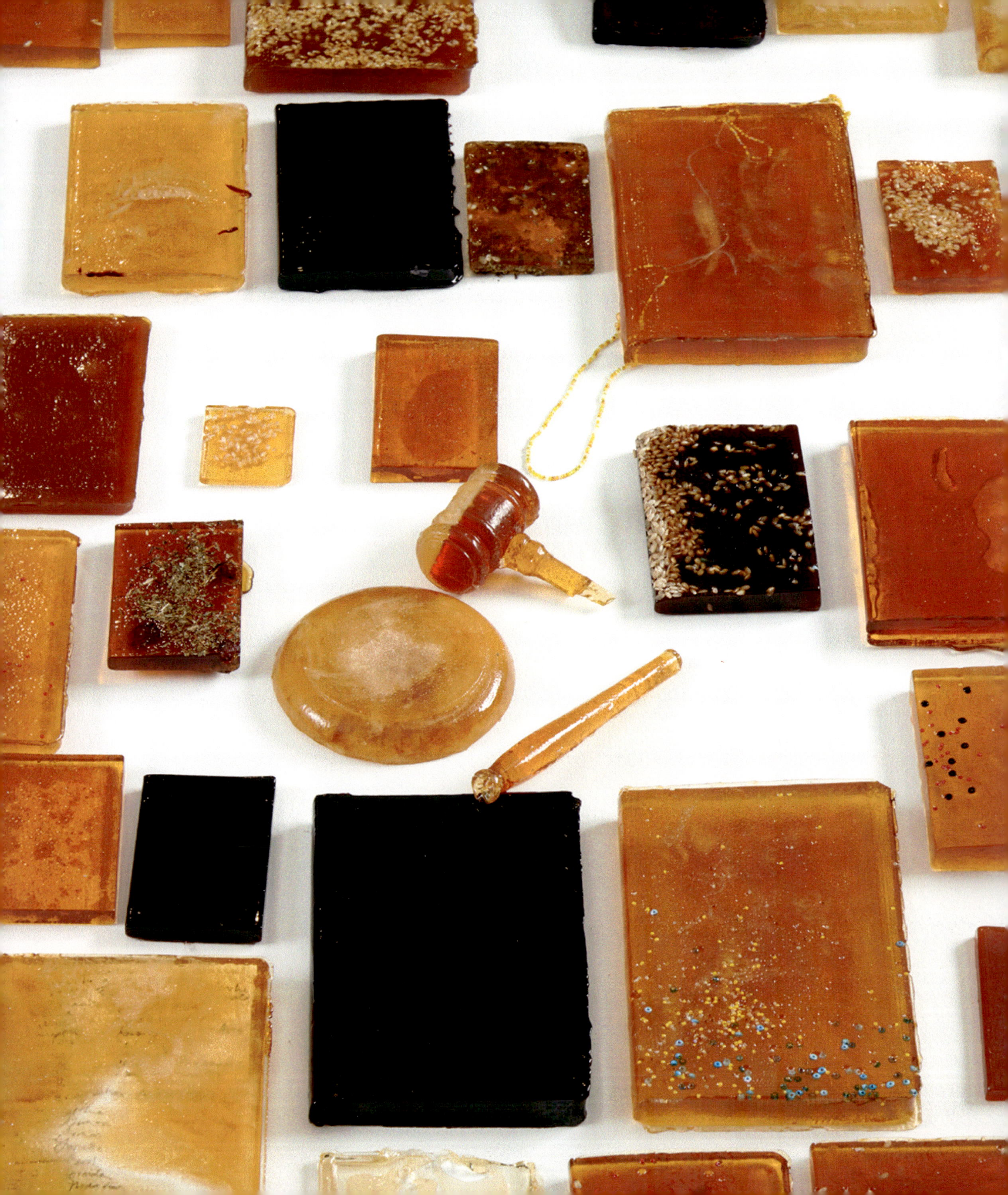

Chana Budgazad Sheldon

Foreword

At MOCA, we deeply value artists and their power to create works that are relevant in the present moment and resonate into the future. As an institution that has been the site where many emerging artists have gone on to storied careers, it is important for us to highlight and support artists at all moments of their practice. When we first began conversations for this exhibition with Andrea Chung, we discussed her keen ability to bring lessons from history to the present day as a meaningful aspect of her work that made her survey exhibition feel vital to this moment.

As a museum that seeks to be a space where artists can experiment, expand their practice, and share ideas, our commission program has become a key part of our work. We are grateful to Andrea for realizing two new commissions as part of this exhibition. The first commissioned work, "...*there is no me. There is I and I, which is you too. You and I intertwined.*" welcomes visitors into the space and sets the tone for the experience of the exhibition. The other, *The Wailing Room*, is a large-scale multimedia installation that the artist was able to create in Miami through a wonderful partnership with the residency space at El Espacio 23. We are thrilled to be able to support artists in realizing their ideas and are proud to be able to bring this work and other collaborative efforts to South Florida.

At a time when cultural institutions have a tangible impact on how we navigate the world and can shift ideas and open minds, MOCA is rooted in bringing these renowned projects to our community. As we approach our thirtieth anniversary and celebrate the legacy of MOCA as an innovative site for artists to shape their practice and impact our area, we continue to be a welcoming space that allows for nuanced and complex conversations. My heartfelt appreciation to Adeze Wilford for her leadership in envisioning this exhibition that inspires critical conversation while furthering the goals of the museum to be a vessel for diverse stories and experiences. I deeply appreciate the hard work of our entire MOCA team that does so much to ensure the museum can continue to support artists and bring powerful work to North Miami.

left
Proverbs, 12:22, 2018. Detail

This exhibition is made possible with support from the Funding Arts Network. MOCA North Miami is generously funded by the Miami-Dade County Department of Cultural Affairs and the Cultural Affairs Council, the Miami-Dade County Mayor and Board of County Commissioners; and the John S. and James L. Knight Foundation. Founding support for the MOCA Sustainability Fund provided by the Green Family Foundation Trust. Major support provided by Shirley and William M. Lehman, Jr. Thank you to Rosie Gordon-Wallace and Roy Wallace for their support of this publication.

My deepest thanks and appreciation to MOCA's dedicated board of trustees. Led by it chair, Dr. Rudy Moise, the board's support has been and continues to be critical to the success of our institution. I sincerely thank the City of North Miami Mayor and Council and the North Miami Interim City Manager, Anna-Bo Emmanuel, Esq., FRA-RA, for their continued partnership and support.

Finally, thank you and congratulations, Andrea. I am grateful for your trust and your thoughtful collaboration with MOCA. It is our honor to host your work at the museum.

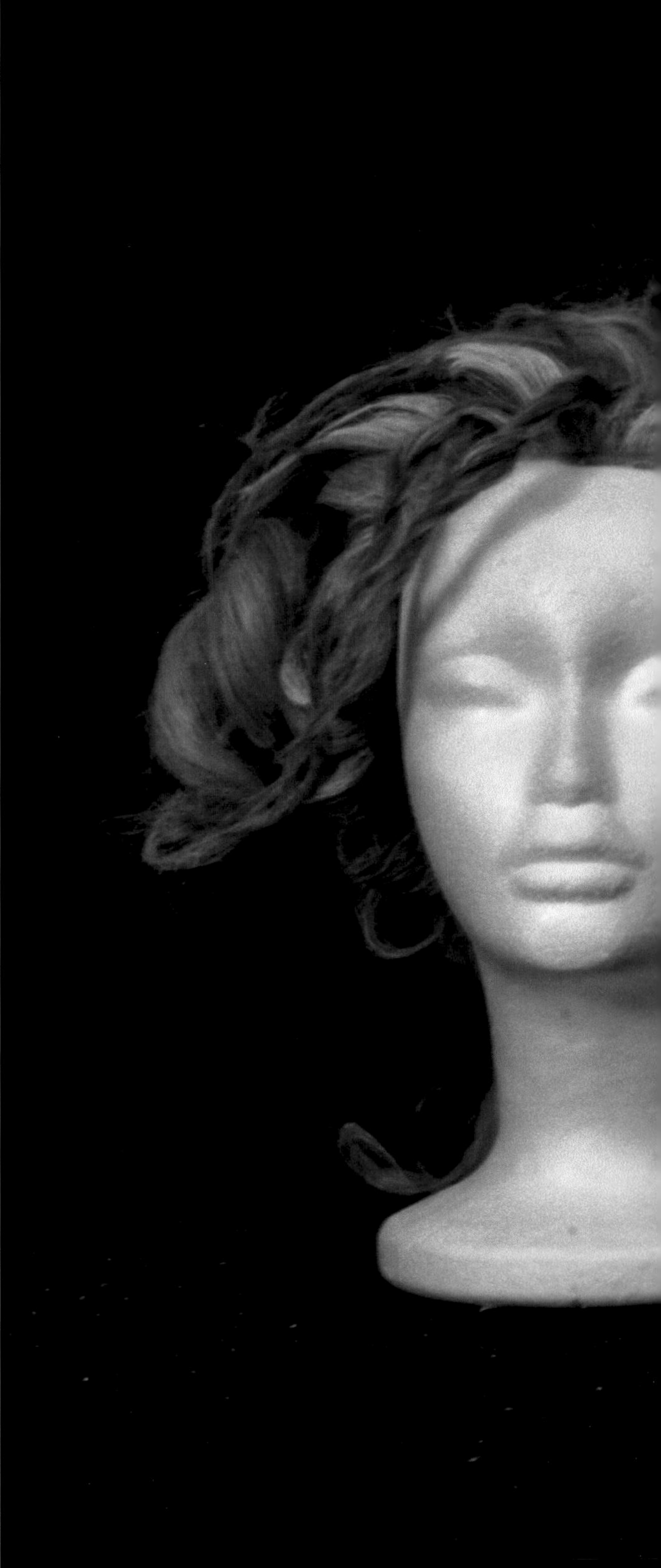

An Unrequited Love, 2019. Detail

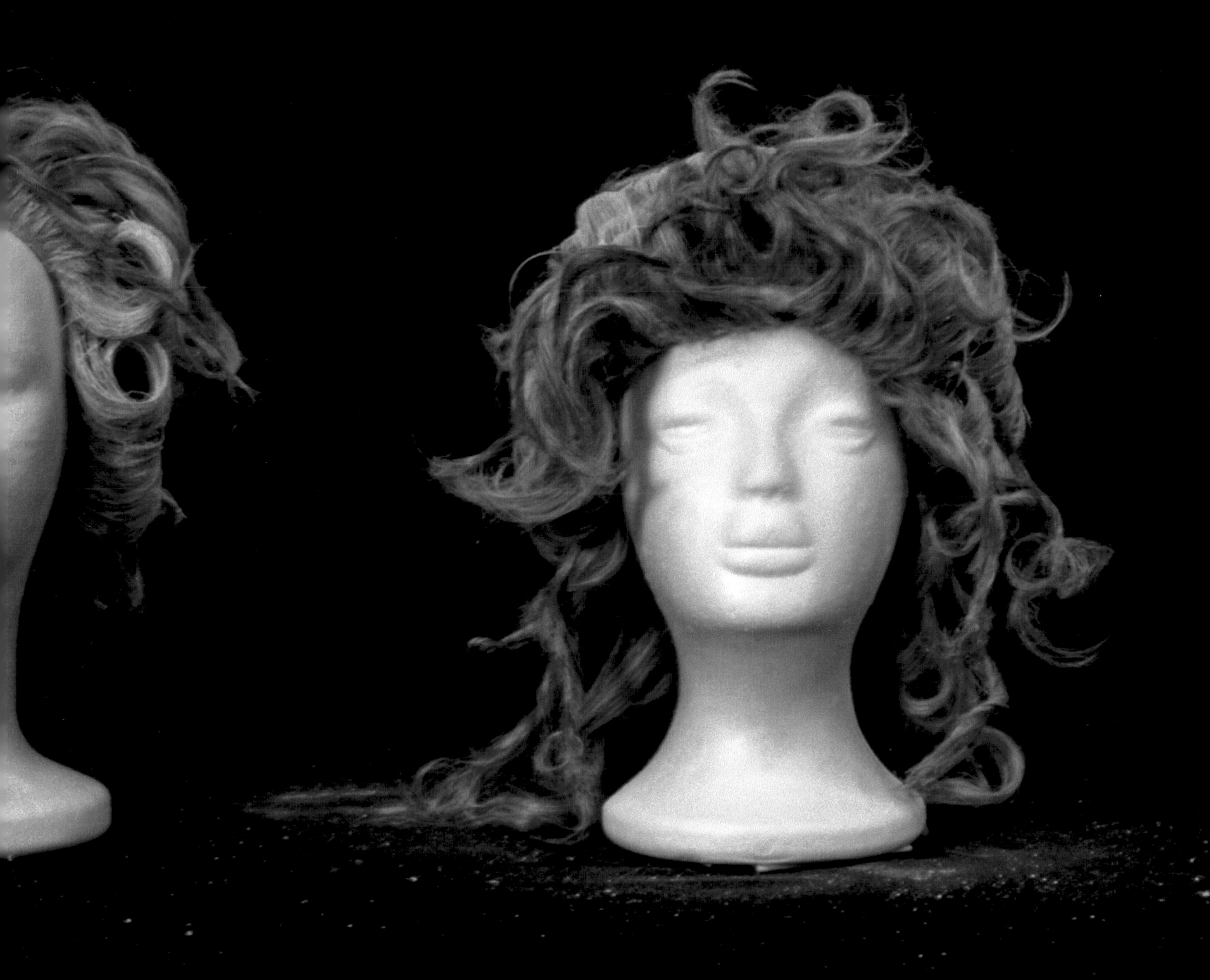

Adeze Wilford

Sweet/Bitter

———————

And I offer my love to your nails and your secrets, your teeth and technology, your heaviness of your hair, your float and your leap. I can hardly believe that the waves did not break you. And your scream? It is scripture and wall. It is map . . . And my scream too a scripture as sacred as love. And my choice.

—Alexis Pauline Gumbs[1]

WHEN CONSIDERING multihyphenate artist Andrea Chung's practice, the guiding concept that one can return to is subversion. The obvious, overt, intentional beauty of the work acts as a Trojan horse to bring in the dark histories and painful truths Chung aims to excavate. Her work spans countries, concepts, and time frames all with a unified effort to move toward and consider Black liberation. Deeply rooted in a Black feminist framework, her collages reclaim exploitative photographs and adorn the sitters with lush surroundings that act as a counterpoint to the original archival image. The luminous cyanotype installations absorb the viewer while simultaneously delving into the deeply insidious nature of colonialism and the Caribbean through the metaphor of the increasing invasive lionfish populations in the Atlantic. Through sound, smell, and scale, the work seduces the viewer. It demands attention and suddenly one is left to consider the *why* of the work: why systems such as chattel slavery were permitted to exist, why the cruelty of the absence of bodily autonomy often leads to unthinkable choices, why certain power dynamics persist, and what is our collective role in perpetuating them? Most importantly her work invokes the question of what next? Now that we've established the impact of trauma, the wrongness of subjugation, what are *we* collectively, for this kind of change cannot occur singularly, going to do for a better now and more importantly for a better future?

Throughout the making of this exhibition, much of our communication has been through sharing texts, mostly written by Black women scholars. A great deal of the work, both from an ideological and conceptual framework, for *Between Too Late and Too Early* has been reflecting on the words of these brilliant minds that mirror an immediacy represented in Andrea's artwork. Mining the past has long been a technique used by many artists seeking to make political or social commentary about the present. Texts that do similar work have been integral to the creation of Chung's artwork. The exhibition takes its title from a passage in Saidiya Hartman's essay "Venus in Two Acts," in which she ruminates on time, our relationship to history, and the desire to humanize figures from the past. She discusses how this excavation often leads to more labor from these figures, now doing the work of carrying our imagined sentiment and dreams for them, and whether this impetus to engage with the historical in this way is helpful or harmful to the lives we learn about.[2] The inclination to give a moment of respite to the troubled life of young kidnapped and enslaved girl of whom Hartman discovered a record is something the scholar grapples with in the text. An imagined friendship between the two young girls on the ship seems to be more for the author's sake than the truth of what could have potentially happened within "Venus's" short and tragic life, and Hartman argues that the archive instead requires us to sit with the painful parts of the past and leave them laid bare. Chung seems to take this work on as well, especially in her series May Day, where the figures themselves are excised from the image. In a conversation about the ways women of the diaspora were positioned in photographs historically, the artist notes that, "Many stereotypes that come from the Caribbean are of exoticized women, or market women, who are often pictured in subservient positions— laying down or bending over or sitting with another figure, usually a white person, standing above them. I wanted to change the way we read these image and question who took those images and why."[3] The desire to trouble the archive, to question the record, for its sparseness or the lens through which a history is manipulated to tell one narrative, becomes a crucial way to understand how Chung's practice deftly engages with the authority of image makers and is able to recontextualize how we determine truth.

While Hartman's position regarding the historical record is a necessary stance in regard to particular scholarship, the beauty of an artistic practice is at the moment of slippage between what is known fact and imagination. In the text *Undercurrents of Power*, an exploration of water and the African diaspora, Kevin Dawson posits, "Waterscapes are also challenged racial perceptions, values, and hierarchies in other ways. For example, they provided captives with a medium for defying white claims to their bodies. Women used waterways to prevent white men from sexually abusing them. Simultaneously, men and women used water to steal their bodies when they swam to freedom."[4] This concept of water being a source of physical escape is centered on freedom and bodily autonomy while alive. It is well documented that in lieu of being enslaved, some kidnapped Africans chose to commit suicide during the Middle Passage. This ultimate act of rebellion also counterbalanced those who were thrown overboard for various reasons including health or in some cases, the slave ship captain's desire for profits via insurance claims. This level of dehumanization, the literal reduction of human life to property, is irreconcilable. Rooted in the ideas of these circumstances, the myth of Drexciya was born.[5]

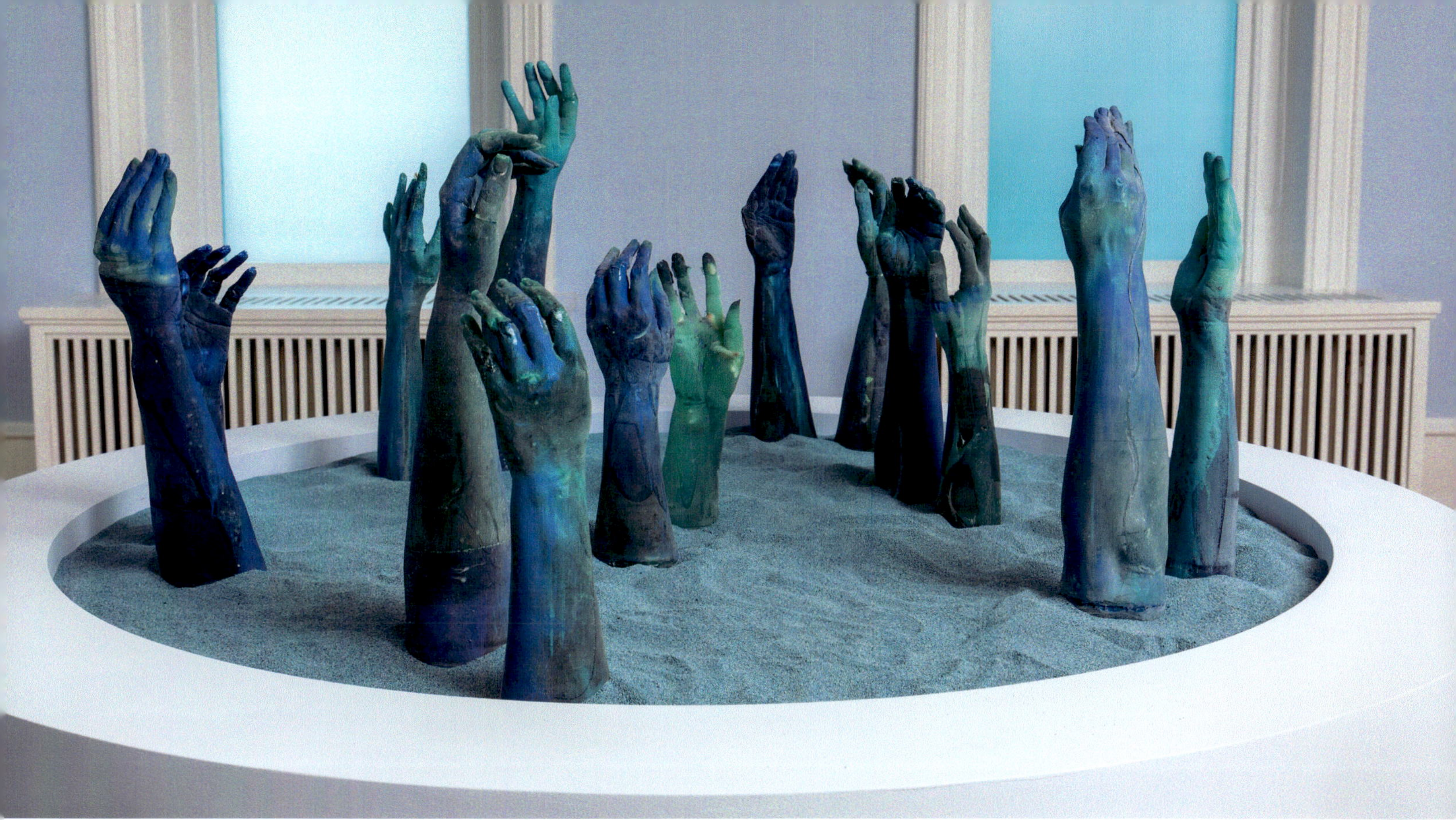

"if they put an iron circle around your neck I will bite it away", 2022.
Resin, dimensions variable
John Michael Kohler Arts Center

In 1992, a Detroit underground techno duo created a mythology exploring the concept that the children of pregnant kidnapped Africans who were tossed overboard evolved to be able to breathe underwater and would go on to create an underwater civilization. Drexciya has been a focal point for several artists because it represents such a keen understanding of a particular kind of hope in the face of such deeply traumatic circumstances. In this mythological space, autonomy and self-determination were snatched back; a watery burial ground becomes a new world order, and this type of fantasy becomes all the more alluring as vestiges of the transatlantic slave trade continue to have seemingly unending effects on the world today even centuries later.

In Chung's installation *"if they put an iron circle around your neck I will bite it away,"* first staged in the historic home at the John

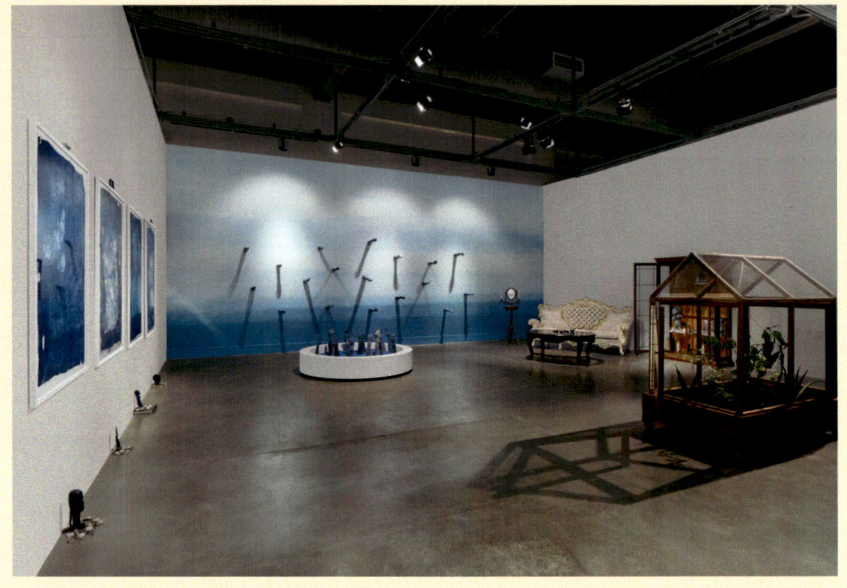

Michael Kohler Arts Center in Sheboygan, the artist directly references a passage from Toni Morrison's novel *Beloved* that grapples with the repercussions of a mother making the shocking choice of infanticide to prevent her child from experiencing enslavement. The installation is explored again in a restaging in her survey at MOCA North Miami. The room is filled with furnishings meant to recall the markers of colonialism, counterbalanced with tools for healing, like herbs, and for agency, such as crystals and spices, that act as a tether to the spiritual similar to the spectral-like figures on printed fabric and the disembodied hands reaching up and out throughout the room. These arms recall ancestors reaching out from the deep as a welcome, a safe harbor from the trauma of the choices (are they choices really?) created by the circumstances.

This work reflects our current political climate. When the Supreme Court overturned 50 years of precedent on June 22, 2022, the ramifications for the loss of constitutional rights were immediately made clear. While the conditions of women in the United States are leagues away from the harrowing positions of women in the antebellum South, there is an underpinning of fear, loss, and surveillance that is now an unavoidable facet of life. Just as Sethe, the protagonist of *Beloved*, began to lose herself to paranoia and repress her actions and past, we are seeing a rise in women making unfathomable choices or being forced to suffer with delayed medical care. In some cases there is even a complete lack of obstetrics access in more strict states as doctors flee areas that impede their ability to uphold the Hippocratic oath without fear of legal prosecution. This return to the past is also seen in a rise of community care networks, including a renewed interest in homeopathy and knowledge of herbal remedies, referenced in the greenhouse featuring plants that are facilitators of women's healthcare, ranging from plants to help with lactation, assist with menstrual cramps, and yes, family planning. The reality of the world is that since time

Between Too Late & Too Early

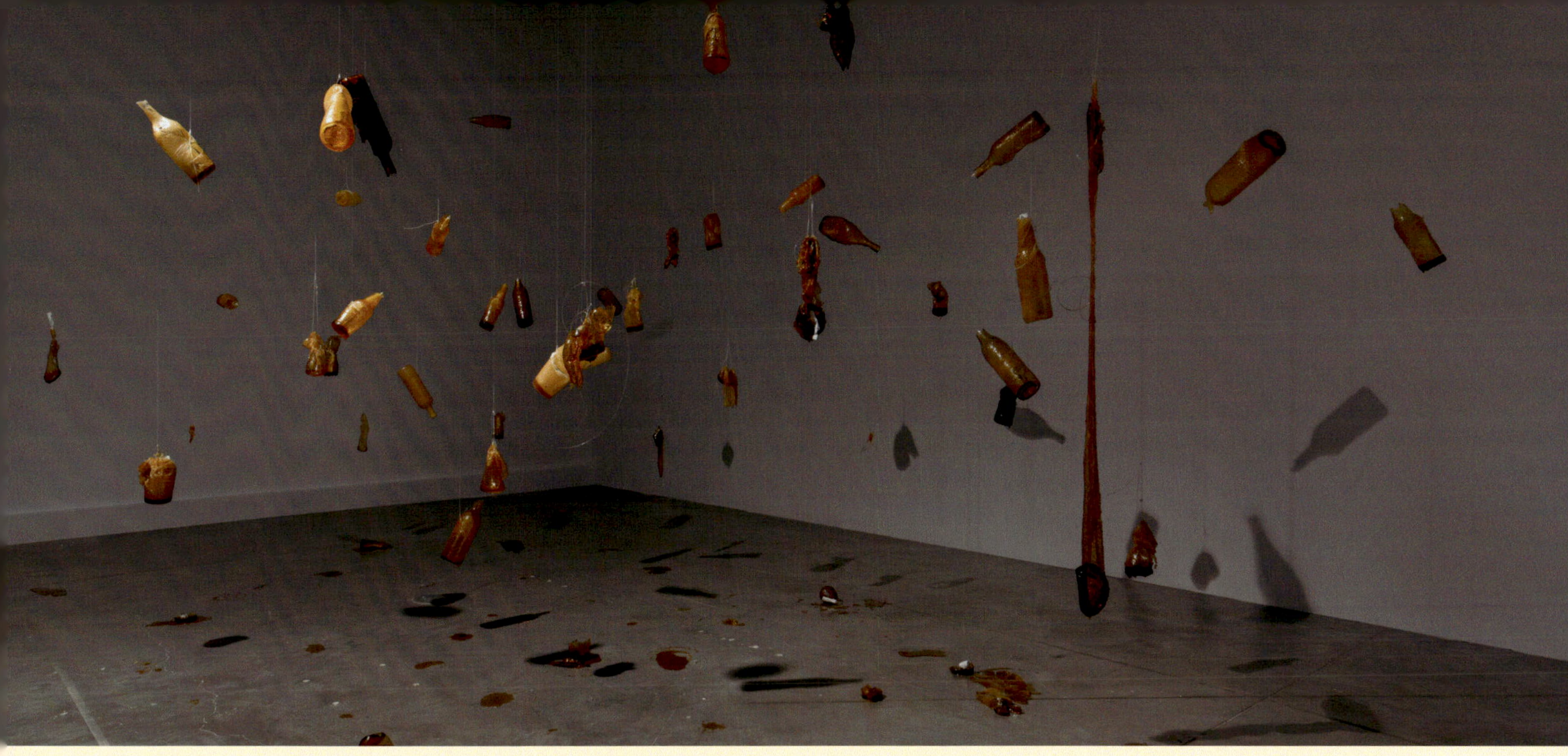

immemorial, women have relied on knowledge frequently passed through intimate spaces in order to provide for others and themselves. The state's involvement in women's bodily autonomy has never caused these tools or information to go away, instead it has only caused women to be at a disadvantage, Black women doubly so. What could Sethe and Denver, her daughter, have become had they not been plagued by the vestiges of the decisions made in reaction to their lack of freedom? What are we as a society losing as we restrict women to stay in situations that are harmful, no longer serve them, or are the result of the unfathomable? Are we then not creating a circumstance that leaves a swath of the population hobbled, stunted, and never truly free?

Autonomy by any means is also the core feature of Chung's new commission *The Wailing Room*. Building upon her investigations of sugar as a temporal medium rooted in an imperial-colonial framework, the work is encapsulated in a room. Dozens of bottles cast from molds of various liquor bottles are suspended from the ceiling including rum, which is connected to the Caribbean on multiple levels from sugar plantations to use in spiritual practices. These bottles recall the Kongo tradition of bottle trees that spread throughout the American South. The meaning of these botanical interventions is largely rooted in invocations of ancestral protection. Scholar Farris Thompson makes the connection of these traditional art forms being carried on in the twentieth century Yard artist output and how spiritual practices and symbolism have been passed down despite the trauma of enslavement.[6] Farris saliently observes that the contemporary bottle tree practice in West Africa near gravesites acts as a way to keep or invoke the power and talents of the dead in this realm. He writes, "Lifting up their plates on trees or saplings also means 'not the end', death will not end our fight."[7] By this reading, the viewer can also infer that Chung's bottles are manifestations or declarations that slavery and infanticide are not a means of separation, but rather an attempt to commune with the spirits of lost lives. There is a desire to keep some part of the relationship on this plane. Enclosed in several bottles are letters to these children lost to infanticide, imagined conversations, pleas for forgiveness, and explanations. Impermeable, the bottles allow for privacy in the public sphere: the mourning is on display, but the details remain between mother and child. The bottles hang at different heights creating an environment that is equal parts magical and disconcerting, intriguing, and ominous. Adding to the visual is the smell. The work is made of cheaply processed, readily available white sugar that is slowly heated from granules to a molten liquid and poured into molds. As the cooking happens the material is transformed. The sweet smell becomes more prominent. When the bottles dangle en masse, the scent is overwhelming, the sweetness taking on a sickly quality that becomes ominous. Overtime, as is common and intended with Chung's sugar work, the objects begin to transform. The shape becomes less and less legible as the environment of the space impacts the composition of the sugar. In *The Wailing Room*, this serves the additional purpose of locking in the letters, making them even more for the private audience, only between mother and child.

Another aspect of the work is the haunting soundscape that further activates the senses. Black women laughing and crying are layered over each other and on a loop. Deep, full-throated chuckles slowly descend into sobs. The sound evokes the idea of release the work is meant to offer for those who made an unimaginable choice. Chung recognizes that such a drastic choice, as deftly explored in Morrison's *Beloved*, could only have been made under duress and only causes deep psychological harm. There is double suffering here, and the laughter slips into a mania that illustrates how the impossibility of true bodily autonomy leads to the ultimate loss of both sound body and mind. As Sethe sorrowfully notes in *Beloved*, "It ain't my job to know what's worse. It's my job to know what is and to keep them away from what I know is terrible. I did that."[8] There is an understanding of that the role of a mother is to keep their child safe and to nurture them to adulthood. This novel and this installation investigate the horror of the knowledge that perhaps the life of being enslaved was one too terrible to be experienced, and instead a harrowing decision was made. The difficulty of this work is approached with care as the artist images the sorrow these women must have felt and, in turn centuries later, creates a space for them to make penance, a place for their anguish to finally be heard.

A reoccurring theme in Chung's practice is a notion of care as a network, from her work in *We Was Girls Together* to her collage series Vex and Colostrum that are meditations on the tradition of midwifery, from both a personal legacy within the artist's family but also the necessity of women banding together in support to bring a child into the world, or not, and to providing the tools of choice when they have been systematically removed. The artist turns her focus to the support networks that existed before formal concepts relating to feminism were created in lecture halls, an engagement of operating outside of the system in the margins and the power that has in the most practical sense. For all of the luminous ideas of radical Black imagination, there is also a deep consideration

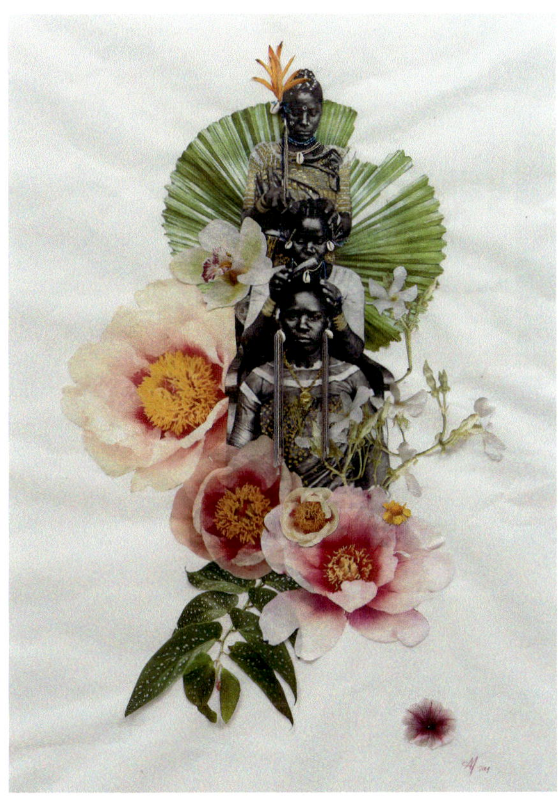

Sula Never Competed; She Simply Helped Other Define Themselves, VII, 2021. Collage, gold ink, shells, pins, and beads on paper handmade from traditional birthing cloth, framed: 55¼ × 35¼ × 2¾ in.

that veil" off of subjects that have long been considered too much to talk about freely[9] and by doing so creates a space of confrontation that by necessity will pull us forward, much like the legacy of the many women writers, scholars, artists, healers, and laborers who came before her.

of pragmatism within Chung's investigations. It allows for a suspension of time, a pause to consider those who came before her while still recognizing the toiling, the growing, and the yearning that was present in the lives of those throughout the diaspora reconciling an existence under colonialism. This balance of both daring to dream and doing the tangible tasks for obtaining freedom is the crux of the success of her work. Her art seeks to "rip

---

ENDNOTES

[1] Alexis Pauline Gumbs, *Undrowned: Black Feminist Lessons from Marine Mammals* (AK Press, 2020), 152.

[2] Saidiya Hartman, "Venus in Two Acts," *Small Axe* 26, vol. 12, no. 2 (June 2008): 1–14.

[3] Nicole J. Caruth, "Black Birth Matters – A Conversation with Andrea Chung and D'Yuanna Allen Robb," *Black Matrilineage, Photography, and Representation: Another Way of Knowing*, ed. Lesly Deschler Canossi and Zoraida Lopez-Diago (Leuven University Press, 2022), 184–185.

[4] Kevin Dawson, *Undercurrents of Power: Aquatic Culture in the African Diaspora* (University of Pennsylvania Press, 2018), 19.

[5] Mike Rubin, "Infinite Journey to Inner Space: The Legacy of Drexciya," Red Bull Music Academy Daily, June 29, 2017, https://daily.redbullmusicacademy.com/2017/06/drexciya-infinite-journey-to-inner-space.

[6] Robert Farris Thompson, *Flash of the Spirit: African & Afro-American Art & Philosophy* (Random House US, 2010), 146–147.

[7] Thompson, *Flash of the Spirit*, 144–145.

[8] Toni Morrison, *Beloved* (Vintage Books, 1987), 194.

[9] Toni Morrison, "Site of Memory" in *Inventing the Truth: The Art and Craft of Memoir*, 2d ed., ed. William Zinsser (Houghton Mifflin, 1995), 90.

Eddie Chambers

Between Too Late & Too Early: Some Considerations

TO BE IMMERSED in the artistic practices of Andrea Chung is to be immersed in the worlds of geography, history, identity, ecology, and resistance. Her work has multiple resonances within each of these nouns, and consequently, the viewer experience is both profound and nuanced. Though she was born in the US, there is no doubting the degree to which the multiple resonances alluded to have a distinctly international (or perhaps more accurately, diasporic) dimension. This diasporic perspective is not only born of Chung's strong and unwavering commitment to social justice, it also, inevitably, emerges from her own biography. Chung was born to parents of Jamaican, Chinese, and Trinidadian descent, meaning her heritage is not only Caribbean but, on account of the approximately two thousand kilometers that lie between Jamaica in the west and Trinidad in the east, pan-Caribbean. This sense of Chung's pan-Caribbean heritage is further enriched by her connection to multiple diasporas, namely African and Chinese.[1] Again, though Chung was born in the US, her work speaks to the sense of unbelonging experienced by many people within the US for whom Blackness is a mark not only of difference but, more crucially, of otherness. Gender is a distinct and recognizable thread that runs through much of Chung's work, accentuated by the current reactionary climate typified by the recent Supreme Court reversal of women's autonomy over their bodies. Ecological concerns also resonate through her pieces, and it's not difficult to appreciate the varied reasons for this. After all, not only does her work speak to global concerns, it does so in large part through the prism of her

Caribbean heritage and the ways in which the poorer people of the region are particularly vulnerable to climate change and the reckless ecological damage wrought by global capitalism and mass tourism.[2]

There is a wonderful and pronounced oscillation between the historical and the contemporary in Chung's work giving rise to graphic understandings of the ways in which historical events have such a pronounced bearing on the here and the now. Typical in this regard is her Colostrum series, in which Black women with their babies (represented by photographic depictions, drawn from colonial-era archival images) are collaged with flora, generating multiple readings that empathetically speak to the gendered and racialized experiences of such women. A consistent feature of Chung's practice is the wonderful titles she assigns to her pieces and her series, titles that offer multiple points of access. Typical in this regard is colostrum, a sixteenth-century word, Latin in origin, which refers to the first secretion from the mammary glands after giving birth, rich in antibodies. By applying such an original and deliberate title to this series, Chung opens up a world of considerations of the abuses heaped on the Black woman (and more specifically, the Black woman's body) during slavery, the ensuing colonial era, and on into present times.

First, Colostrum obliges us to consider the difficult historical experiences of Black women as wet nurses. The dictionary might, rather innocuously, have the term as meaning a woman employed to suckle another woman's child, but in reality, Black women's experiences of wet-nursing are, as reflected in Chung's series, infinitely more loaded and complex than this. As articulated by Emily West and R. J. Knight, in

"Mothers' Milk: Slavery, Wet-Nursing, and Black and White Women in the Antebellum South,"

> *Wet-nursing is a uniquely gendered kind of exploitation, and under slavery it represented the point at which the exploitation of enslaved women as workers and as reproducers literally intersected. Feeding another woman's child with one's own milk constituted a form of labor, but it was work that could only be undertaken by lactating women who had borne their own children. As a form of exploitation specific to slave mothers, enforced wet-nursing constituted a distinct aspect of enslaved women's commodification. The evocative image of an enslaved wet nurse, carefully holding a white child to her breast in order to provide sustenance through her own milk, therefore holds much resonance for historians interested in gender, slavery, and relationships between black and white women in the antebellum South . . . [U]ltimately, white women used wet-nursing as a tool to manipulate enslaved women's motherhood for slaveholders' own ends.[3]*

Within Colostrum, Chung draws sobering and visually engaging attention to the dehumanization and trauma of enslaved African women in the Caribbean forced to wet-nurse the babies of slaveholders, even as these women were cruelly stripped of their autonomy and ability to provide nourishment for their own children. Rendered on handmade paper that has the look and resonance of historic parchment, Colostrum in effect bears witness, bears testament, to aspects of Black women's dehumanization and trauma not widely recognized, particularly by a dominant culture quick to practice a selective amnesia vis-à-

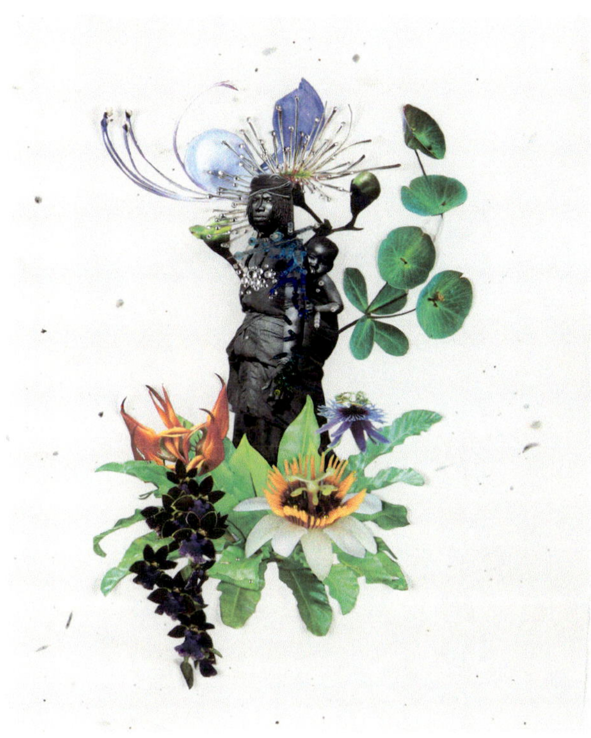

Colostrum VII, 2020.
Collage, ink, rhinestones, pins, and beads on paper handmade from traditional birthing cloth, 17 × 13 in.

vis historical cruelties and injustices visited upon Black people during enslavement and its colonial aftermath. But the most remarkable aspect of Colostrum, which marks Chung as a unique and noteworthy artist, is the arresting beauty of the series. It's as if these women (whose names and identities we invariably do not know, on account of the dehumanizing inferiority assigned to them) are rescued from raced obscurity, and their humanity, personhood, and autonomy restored through the manifestation of these collages. There is a deliberate, pointed beauty and attractiveness in these images. A visual restitution that, in marked contrast to the degradations and violations of slavery, becomes life-affirming in its restorative impulses.

As much as the Colostrum series is rooted in historical resonances, the work has enduring and ongoing application to the visualization of the Black woman. There is a deliberate, pronounced, and joyous decorative adornment to the women depicted. Over the course of centuries, the dominant culture has pictured Black women in the sparsest, basest, and most degenerate and reductive of ways. But the floral adornments that figure so tellingly in the collages speak to a sustaining layering of beautification by Chung. While artist Mickalene Thomas has tended to use multiple fabrics, patterns, cloth, and soft furnishings to reinscribe Black women's rightful but historically withheld proximity to beauty, Chung has pursued this strategy by way of exquisite arrangements of nature's bounty of flora (the women further embellished with opulent and indulgent decorations, including necklaces of rhinestones and beads). In so many respects, the Caribbean orientation of Chung's practices are discernible at every turn, and the viewer may well designate the flora embellishments as emanating from or resonating with distinctly Caribbean zones.

What some of us might perceive as a distinct Caribbean orientation in Chung's work is cogently and creatively reinscribed by the artist's critical spotlight on the mass tourism with which the region is associated. It's now beyond dispute that many parts of the world—such as Barcelona, Venice, Berlin—are, for a variety of reasons, suffering the consequences of mass tourism. But the Caribbean may well be unique in the *raced* dimensions of tourism whereby, in essence, Black and Brown workers in the tourism sector are required to serve white vacationers and to do so in particularly obsequious ways that represent an umbilical cord stretching back to the racial politics of enslavement. The ecological damage wrought by mass tourism is thrown into sharp relief by way of the Caribbean's dependence on the tourist dollar and the accommodations to obsequiousness on the part of Black and Brown workers in the tourism sector. Chung's multiple series that date from the first decade of the twenty-first century undertake and achieve wonderful work by turning a critical spotlight on the mass tourism the region attracts (aided, in no small part, by a dominant perception that the Caribbean is little more than a region of the world in which to take a holiday). This work by Chung is measured, precise, and poignant in its impulses.

Pieces such as *Dexter is Trained With Uncompromising Standard of Excellence* draw bitter and caustic but necessary attention to the mannered culture of subservience and servitude that is indelibly a part of Caribbean tourism. The work in question features an enlarged image of a couple, circa the 1980s, sitting in deck chairs on a beach facing the deep blue and tranquil waters of the Caribbean sea. As if to underline the recreational nature of the tropical paradise they occupy, a small motorboat rests in shallow water a few meters away from where they sit raising a glass to each other, about to enjoy their beverages of choice. What gives the extremely happy, peaceful, and picturesque scene its sharpness and potency (and indeed, its pathos) is the outline of the Black man (Dexter) who has been excised from the picture by Chung, remaining only in blank outline. It is of course Dexter who has brought the couple their beverages, going to the otherworldly trouble of bringing them their drinks by use of the speedboat. Upon arrival, Dexter must take off his shoes and socks, roll up his trousers, and wading through the water, carry a tray of drinks to the deck-chaired couple. Not only must he do this but equally as important (or more), he must render service with a smile.

Time and again within Chung's work, the conjoined yet oppositional notions of absence and presence are central. We are obliged to ask ourselves pertinent questions: *Who* is absent? *Who* is present? In other pieces by the artist, related questions of absence and presence emerge. *What* is absent? *What* is present? Perhaps Chung has spared the blushes of the Dexters of the Caribbean, obliging us to put ourselves in the position of a man who can only attend to the welfare of his family by pampering those more economically and racially privileged than he. Not only that, but Dexter must go to near-theatrical lengths to serve those on whom he is economically dependent. Dexter's dignity is absent even as racial privilege is present. Dexter himself and Dexter's individual identity are absent—after all, he could be any one of a number of waiters employed by the couple's hotel. The white

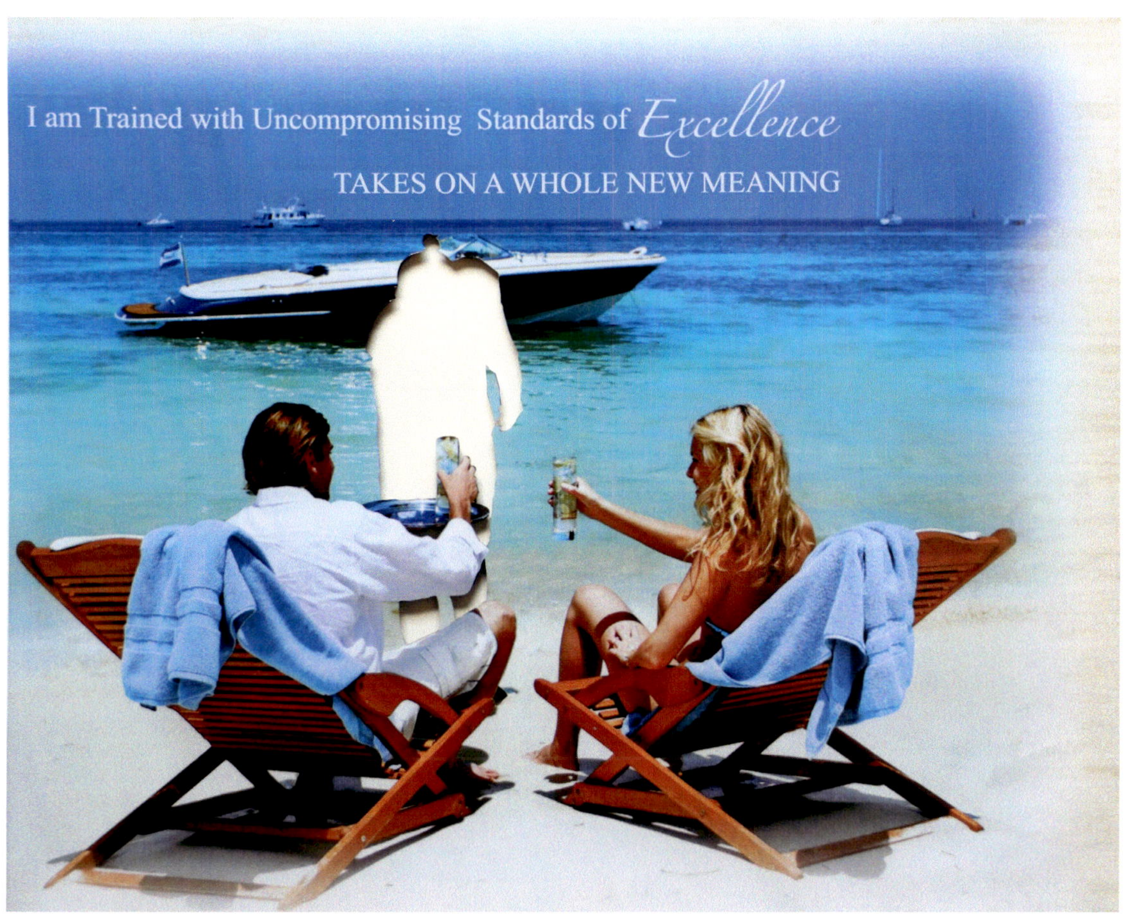

Dexter is Trained With Uncompromising
Standard of Excellence, 2008.
Photo cutout, 15¾ × 13 in.

couple are present because they represent the be-all and end-all of tourism in the Caribbean.

In conclusion, I want to draw attention to another fascinating dimension of Chung's practice—her use of patois to title a number of her pieces. Chung's use of the common dialect of different regions of the Caribbean is hugely important, in part on account of the ways in which Caribbean or nation-specific patois differs in various respects from the standard language of the dominant culture. Much work has been done by Caribbean-born scholars of English and linguistics to draw attention to the raced dimensions of speech patterns, whereby patois is invariably regarded as less than, and occupying a lower status than, the King's or the Queen's English. As much as Chung blithely disregards these problematic hierarchies, she also draws important attention to language's countercultural potential through works that have titles such as *Daylight Cum An' Mi Waan Guh Home* and *'Im Hole 'Im Canher.*[4] Both of these works—*Daylight Cum An' Mi Waan Guh Home* and *'Im Hole 'Im Canher*—speak to the notions of absence and presence referred to

earlier. The former is an archival photograph of a banana cutter standing with a formidable limb of a banana tree laden with multiple bunches coming up to the banana cutter's waist. As evidenced in so many other pieces by Chung, the central figure is there in outline only, leaving us with a somewhat anonymized silhouette. *'Im Hole 'Im Canher*, on the other hand, is a group portrait of what we might take to be a group of colonial-era cane field-workers. Again, the figures have been carefully excised by Chung, leaving only their multiple outlines. It's worth reiterating the wonderful and pronounced oscillation between the historical and the contemporary in Chung's work, which, as mentioned earlier, gives rise to graphic understandings of the ways in which history has such a pronounced bearing on the here and the now. The twenty-first-century manifestations of agrarian work in the Caribbean (as referenced in respect of Chung's Colostrum series) represent something akin to sharecropping, as mentioned earlier, an umbilical cord stretching back to the racial politics and economies of enslavement. In so many respects, the lives of modern-day plantation workers have much in common with the lives and constraints of plantation workers during the colonial era. In works such as *Daylight Cum An' Mi Waan Guh Home* and *'Im Hole 'Im Canher*, Chung, in remarkable fashion, makes these truths known. At every turn Chung animates the multiple worlds of geography, history, identity, ecology and in so doing, gives us multiple narratives of resistance.

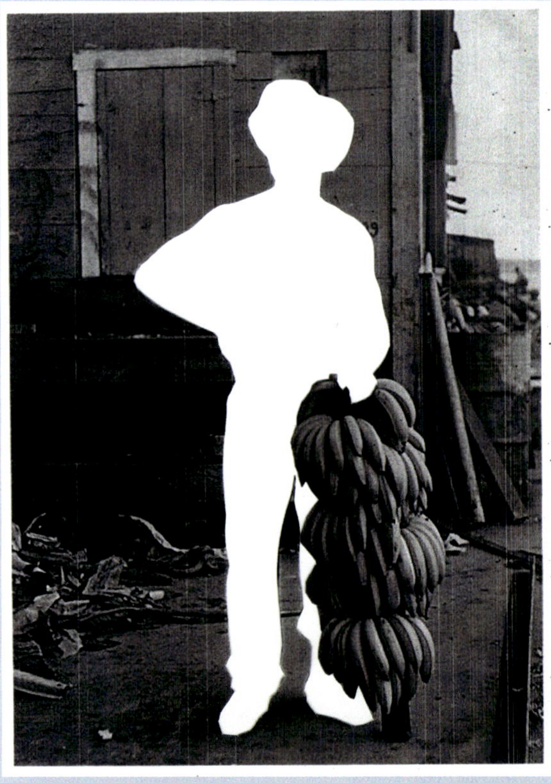

Daylight Cum An' Mi Waan
Guh Home, 2007.
Photo cutout, 15 × 13½ in.

ENDNOTES

1   Chung's African Chinese heritage meant that she was an important inclusion in the Chinese American Museum and California African American Museum (Los Angeles) exhibition of 2017–2018 *Circles and Circuits II: Contemporary Chinese Caribbean Art*. This exhibition brought together the works of artists of color who challenge the perceived binaries of ethnicity to which so many people are thoughtlessly and needlessly wedded. The Caribbean is home to multiple diasporas, leading to a history of racial mixing and blending that was accentuated within *Circles and Circuits II*. Chung's work in this wonderful exhibition appeared alongside as well as in dialogue with other contemporary artists of Black Caribbean and Chinese heritage, including Albert Chong and María Magdalena Campos-Pons.

2   In July 2024 Hurricane Beryl tore through parts of the Caribbean, bringing death and extensive destruction in its wake. As is so often the case with violent tropical cyclones in the Caribbean, it's the poorer, most socially and habitat-challenged people whose lives are laid waste by hurricanes. Such death and destruction visited upon the region is made all the more difficult by the fleeting attention of the world's mainstream media, already disinclined to regard the Caribbean as more than a tropical destination for tourists and vacationers.

3   *Journal of Southern History* 83, no. 1 (February 2017): 37–68. For a related study, within a Brazilian context, see Kimberly Cleveland, *Black Women Slaves Who Nourished A Nation: Artistic Renderings of Black Wet Nurses of Brazil* (Cambria Press, 2019).

4   *Daylight Cum An' Mi Waan Guh Home* comes from a famous refrain in a song popularized by Harry Belafonte, "Banana Boat (Day-O)." The song originated as a Jamaican dockworkers' work song, with the refrain "daylight come and me wan' go home." A remarkable elasticity and multiplicity of meanings exist in a phrase like "'Im hole 'im canher." It could be taken as an expression of admiration for someone who, in the face of adversity, with fortitude and perseverance, holds his corner, or stands his ground, maintains his sense of self, and so on. But 'Im hole 'im canher (which might also be written as Him hole him cahna) can also be taken as an expression that someone has been put in their place, as a result of a rebuke or an adverse change of fortune or circumstances.

Aruna D'Souza

Labor

———————

I believe that I must include within my work an element of my own labor. It is not my intention to compare or equate my labor with the subjects in my pieces. Rather, I find that if I make a conscious decision to use a laborious process to cast objects in molten sugar or create elaborate cyanotype installations, then my labor itself becomes a medium.

—Andrea Chung [1]

IT'S ALL TOO EASY to get lost in the gorgeous elegance of Andrea Chung's work, whether it's the limpid blues of her mural-sized cyanotypes of lionfish, an invasive species that has destroyed the Caribbean's aquatic ecosystems, much like the colonizing Europeans did; or the delicate, transparent ambers of the hanging cast-sugar bottles, each filled with cast-sugar nuts and bolts, that make up *Sink or Swim* (2013), a piece which emerges from the history and aftermath of plantation economies and enslavement in Mauritius, a sugar-producing colony in the Indian Ocean; or the delicacy of beadwork and embellishment in her recent collages centered around ethnographic photographs of Black women. [2]

This beauty is strategic: it seduces the viewer to face what are often horrifying realities of the histories of colonization and imperialism, especially as it has shaped the lives of women of African and Asian descent in the Caribbean, the American South, and other parts of the world. But this close viewing opens up another aspect of Chung's practice, one that is as integral to its conceptual import as its subject matter and its material inventiveness, and that is the sheer labor that goes into every one of her projects. That effort is a necessary interpretive lens for understanding the work, given that so much of it revolves around the exploitation of people through the European institutions of slavery and indentured labor, as well as the often-overlooked work of Black women in their own communities.

The theme of labor has had a long presence in Chung's oeuvre. Her May Day series, photo cutouts from 2007–2008 including *All Fruits Ripe*, *'Im Hole 'Im Canher* and *Daylight Cum An' Mi Waan Guh Home*, begin with photographs

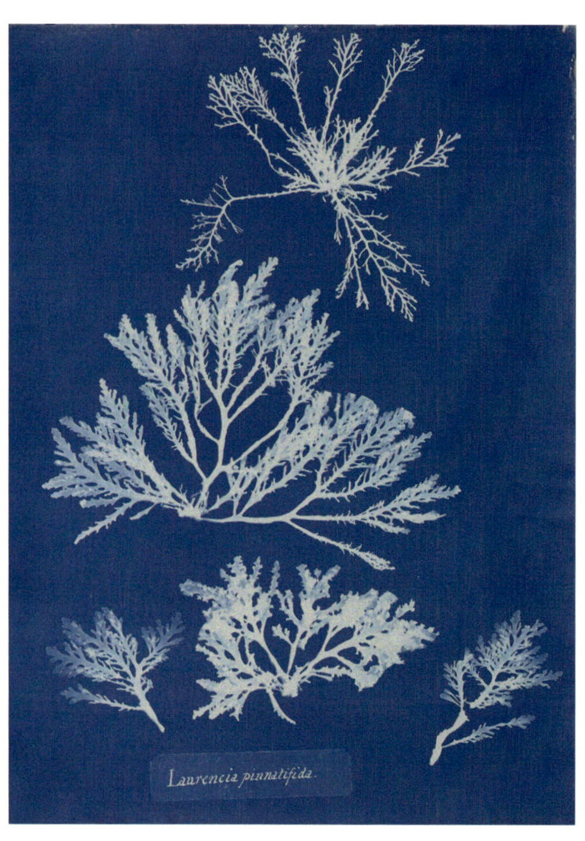

Anna Atkins (British, 1799–1871),
Plocamium coccineum, 1846–47.
Cyanotype, 10⅜ × 8¼ in. The J. Paul Getty
Museum, Los Angeles, 84.XA.1107.9

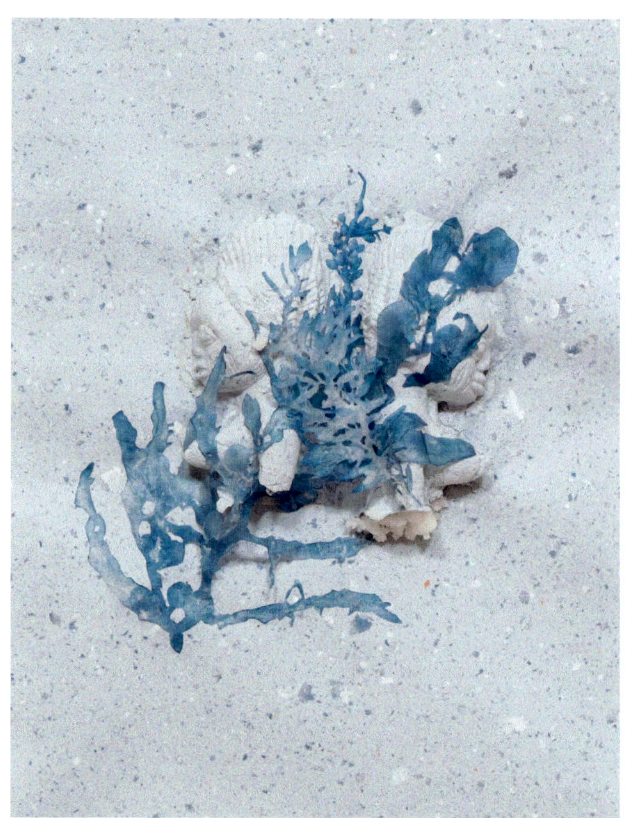

However The Image Enters Its Force
Remains Within My Eyes V, 2023.
Cyanotype, framed: 28.5 × 22.75 × 3 in.

of plantation laborers in cane fields or banana groves. Because the original pictures were made as tourist collectibles, the figures are shown happily posing—a careful erasure of the conditions under which they must have been working and the histories that brought them to the islands in the first place. To remedy this, Chung performs another act of erasure that, paradoxically, sheds light on what is suppressed: she carefully cuts out the figures, leaving them as silhouetted absences in the scenes. Chung has said the gesture was meant to give the workers a day off—an act of restitution, at least in the space of the image. (The series title, fittingly, refers both to an international celebration of workers and a cry of distress.) These same sorts of photographs appear, in other instances, juxtaposed with contemporary tourism advertisements, drawing attention to the ways in which the pleasures of the Caribbean being sold to people abroad even now are dependent on the aestheticization of the labor of Black- and Brown-skinned people—their toil both creates and becomes part of the picturesque landscape.

But labor surfaces in other ways in Chung's work too. However the Image Enters Its Force Remains within My Eyes, a series of works on paper from 2020, emerges from Chung's research into Anna Atkins (1799-1871), a British botanist and photographer who is thought to have been the first person who included photographs in a book and may have been the first woman to produce a photograph. Atkins used the cyanotype process to make images of algae, ferns, and other botanical specimens, placing the plants directly on light sensitive paper to generate the image. Her first book, on types of British seaweeds, was published in 1843, only a year after the invention of

cyanotypes; another, on ferns from both Britain and other parts of the world—including Jamaica and other parts of the Americas—was published in 1853.

While Atkins may have broken significant gender barriers to be taken seriously as a scientist and a photographer, she was able to do so because of her status and wealth, a status and wealth secured by the proceeds of the slave trade—her husband and father-in-law owned at least eight plantations in Jamaica.

In order to excavate this history, to make it palpable, Chung undertook the laborious process of turning Atkins's prints and words—in this case, taken from a recent deluxe publication of her cyanotypes—into handmade paper. She used the paper to cast West African fertility figures in relief, so they can only be seen when you view the pieces from an angle. Chung then used the same method to reproduce Atkins's images of Jamaican botanical specimens on Japanese kozo paper, a tissue so ethereal and delicate that it threatens to dissolve with the merest touch. These she draped over the sculptural reliefs.

The fertility figures function as metonyms for the people who carried them, in actuality or in memory, to Jamaica—that is, for the African people who were brought against their will to work on the plantations owned by those like Atkins's relatives. They are what lurk behind the benign beauty Atkins's taxonomies. Chung's exacting process of fashioning her pieces is her way of ensuring that these human presences remain palpable in the pages of Atkins's book. The title of the series speaks to this idea that vision is inextricable from memory, even if that memory comes in the form of ghosts: it is a line

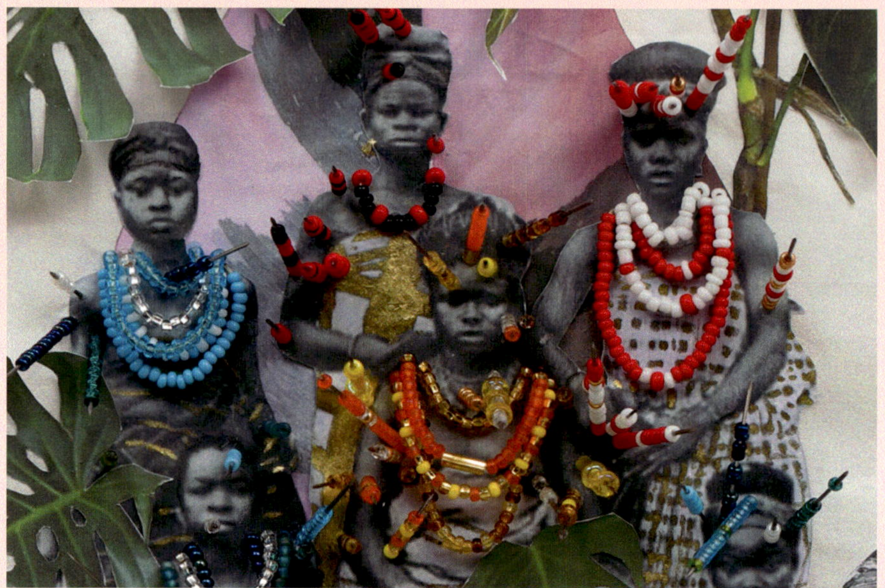

Vex VII, 2020. Collage, ink, and beads on paper handmade from traditional birthing cloth, 22 × 16½ in. Detail

from Audre Lorde's "Afterimages," a poem that evokes the painful and necessary job of bearing witness to anti-Blackness.

For her collage series Colostrum (2020-21), Sula Never Competed; She Simply Helped Others Define Themselves (2021), Vex (2020), and The Load is Heavy, and My Back is Tired (2023), Chung has again created paper, this time out of handkerchiefs, often used as birthing cloths by Black midwives in the Caribbean and the American South. The process involved macerating the fabric, beating it, then combining it with cotton, abaca, and red raspberry tea (an herbal solution for speeding up childbirth). She uses the paper as surfaces on which to collage ethnographic photographs of African-origin women from throughout the diaspora (the Caribbean, the US, but also Brazil, Madagascar, Nigeria)—photographs, that is, that served the same purpose as Atkins's reproductions of botanical specimens, namely

the categorization of all the flora, fauna, and human life in the colonies. But Chung refuses the reduction of the women to mere types in an ethnographic taxonomy, honoring their work, their relationships, and their capacity for survival by adding pointed elements: flowers and foliage specific to the places the photos were taken surround and protect the women, small strings of impossibly tiny beads, often in the colors of Orishas (divine spirits from the Yoruban tradition) adorn them, gold ink embellishes them. Small pins protrude from the collages; at first they seem to emulate the nails often seen hammered into Congolese *nkisi* figures, but upon closer look one finds that the pins are not driven into the collages but protrude like porcupine quills, a gesture that Chung describes as protective:

> *I wanted to make these women into the nkisi, except I decided to use needles . . . . What I liked about it was that you have to get close and intimate with it in order to see*

all the detail, but you can't get too close. You're not allowed to look past a certain point, because you can be stabbed by the needles. I saw it as a form of protection and guarding, and also being able to remain private and take your subjectivity for yourself, not allowing anyone to turn you into that object. It makes the viewer understand their place in looking at the images of these women.[3]

The references to motherhood and midwifery in Chung's oeuvre—in her collages, but also in complex installations such as *"If they put an iron around your neck I will bite it away"* (2023)—raise the impossible-to-miss connection between the two senses of the word labor: physical toil and the process of giving birth. For Black women living in conditions of enslavement, those two meanings merged into one—they were forced to bear children, many conceived through rape by their captors, in order to create a larger workforce for the plantation. Colostrum, the title of one of her collage series, is the breast milk produced in the immediate aftermath of childbirth, known to be especially nutritious, even vital, for infants. Enslaved women were often impregnated at the same time as plantation mistresses so they could be available to provide the precious fluid to slaveholders' children. After the abolishment of slavery, Black women servants were called upon still to nurse the children of white elite families, often at the expense of their own. Chung honors such work and recognizes the injustice that make it necessary by offering up her own labor as recompense at the same time as she images freedom from that work—by showing us instead images of Black women breastfeeding their own children (as in Colostrum) or, in the case of *"If they put an iron around your neck I will bite it away"*, by referring to a contemporary

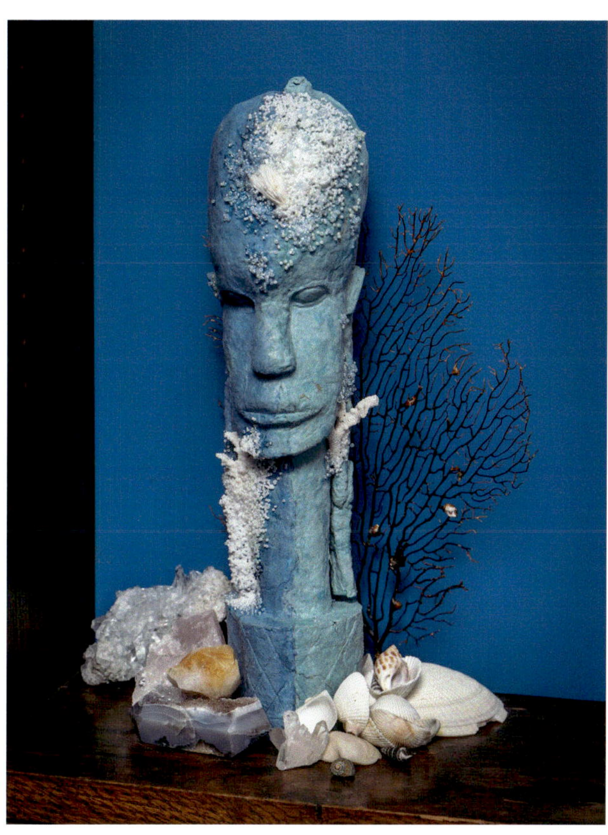

Untitled, 2022. Pulped paper, sugar, crystals, shells, 14 × 5 × 3 in.

fantasy of Drexciya, an underwater realm where the children of pregnant women who threw themselves or were thrown off slave ships became amphibious and thrived in the depths of the ocean.[4]

While Chung's approach to artmaking can be understood as a form of restitution to the people who have been exploited, abused, and destroyed by colonial frameworks, she does not

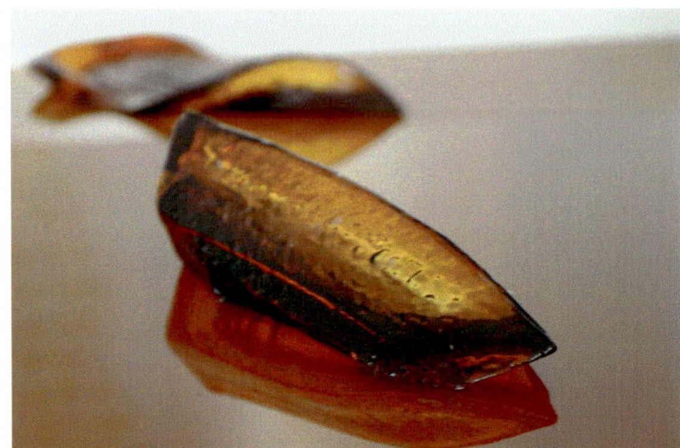

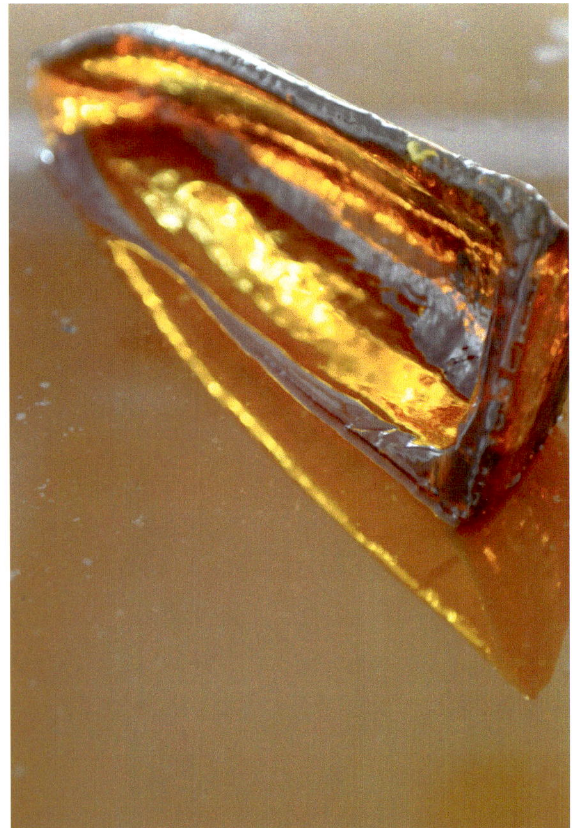

Bato Disik, 2013. Site-specific
installation. Sugar, resin, saltwater.
Variable dimensions. Details

quite memorialize such labor. Memorialization suggests permanence, and the artist's choice of material—friable, delicate, ephemeral—is often anything but. This is especially true of her work with sugar. The piece *Bato Disik*, for example, was made to honor the stories of people who escaped slavery and hid out on a mountainside in Mauritius for many years, surviving as fisherpeople. When Britain abolished slavery in the early nineteenth century, a group of armed soldiers were sent to the village to inform the refugees that they could come out of hiding. The villagers, seeing the approaching soldiers, threw themselves into the ocean rather than face the terrors of the plantation again. Chung's large-scale work consists of small, simple boats ("bato" in Mauritian creole) cast from pure cane sugar; they sit in a shallow bath of amber colored water, into which they slowly melt over time. The boats, and their imagined occupants, cannot be captured, cannot be held, cannot be forced to labor against their will.

Chung steps in to carry their burden in a way: every time the piece is shown, she has to begin again, undertaking the casting of each element anew. This repeated effort, a Sisyphean task, is part of her understanding of the problematics of ownership—the ownership not only of things, like artwork, but of people too and their labor. "With the sugar pieces, I've had people ask me 'How do you even sell that?'" she explained in an interview, "and I [respond], 'Do you even care what the work is about, or do you just want to possess it?' . . . I don't want you to be able to own everything, and I like that it will self-destruct on its own."[5] Though it took a collective act of self-destruction, the escapees in Mauritius freed themselves from what they believed was their future of forced labor—and through her canny use of process and materials, Chung frees them again.

ENDNOTES

[1] Andrea Chung, "Artist Statement," *Biomythography: Reflexive Remix* (2018), https://www.biomythart.com/andreachung.

[2] Here, I will admit to directly contradicting Chung's own take on beauty: "I really don't think about beauty when I'm making work. Beauty is overrated and not always honest. I think more about refinement. How can I make a concise statement? I do try to make the work elegant, but not necessarily in an aesthetic way. I think elegant in a conceptual way." AM DeBrincat, "Labor, History, Power," *ArtFile Magazine*, accessed September 5, 2024, https://cargocollective.com/artfilemagazine/Andrea-Chung.

[3] "Andrea Chung with HereIn," *HereIn*, October 16, 2020, https://www.hereinjournal.org/conversations/andrea-chung-with-herein.

[4] For an overview of the myth, see Helen Scales, "Drexciya: How Afrofuturism is inspiring calls for an ocean memorial to slavery," *The Guardian*, January 25, 2021. A number of artists, including Chung, Firelei Báez, and Ayana V. Jackson, have made work on this theme lately.

[5] Hope Nardone and Simi Gandhi, "Artist Andrea Chung Embraces the Natural Lifecycle of Artwork," *Phillipian*, April 9, 2021, https://phillipian.net/2021/04/09/artist-andrea-chung-embraces-the-natural-lifecycle-of-artwork/.

overleaf

Andrea Chung, **Vex XI**, 2020. Detail

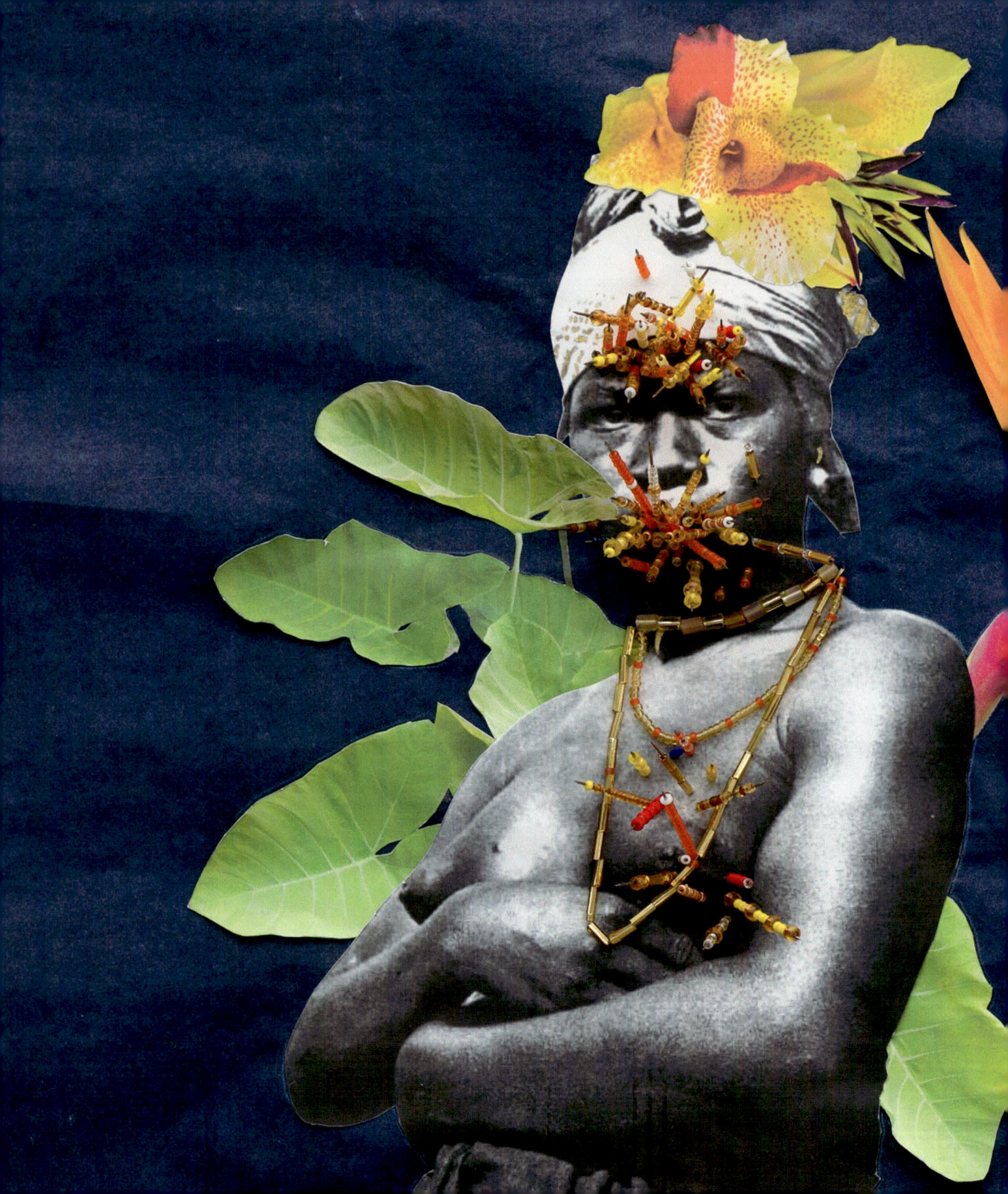

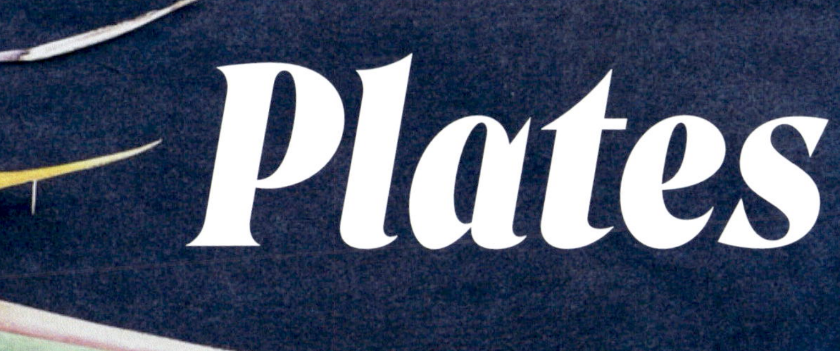

Plates

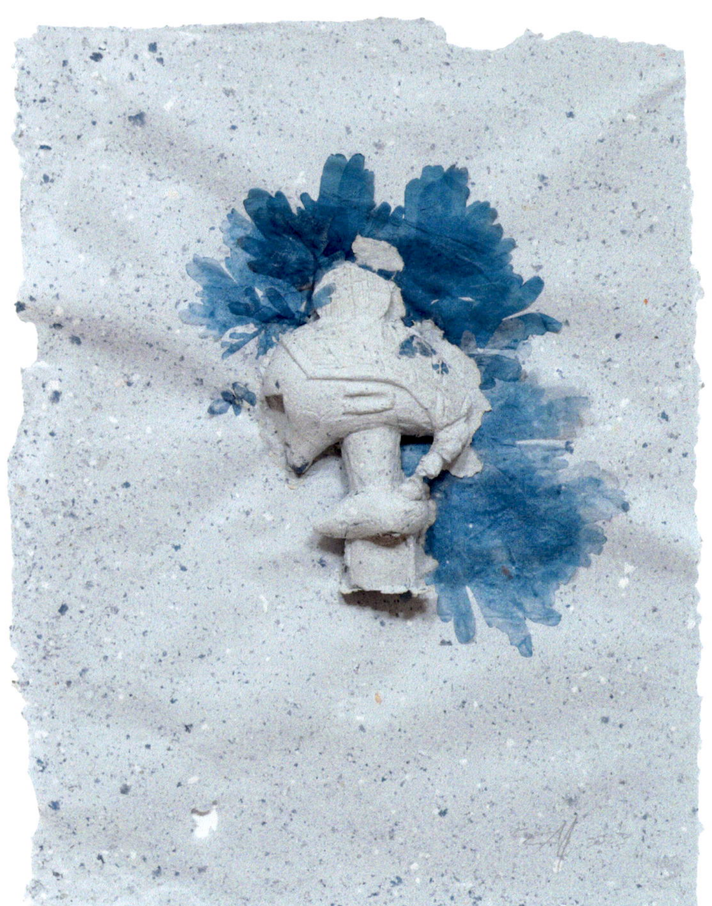

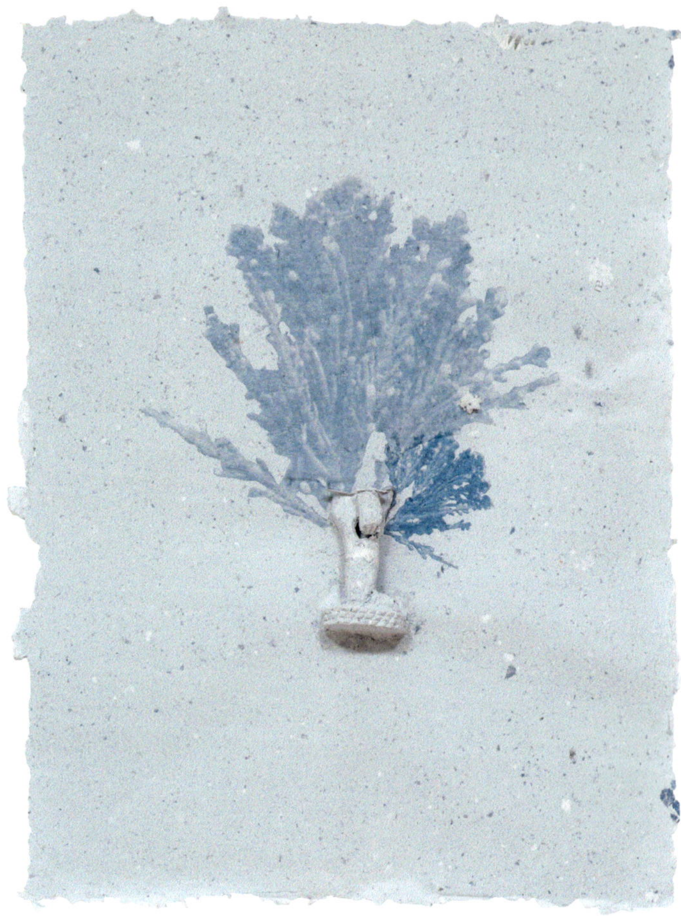

However The Image Enters Its Force
Remains Within My Eyes, VIII, 2023
Paper made from **Anna Atkins:
Cyanotypes** book published by
Taschen, methyl cellulose, and
cyanotypes on kozo paper
24½ × 18¾ × 2¼ in.

However The Image Enters Its Force
Remains Within My Eyes, VII, 2023
Paper made from **Anna Atkins:
Cyanotypes** book published by
Taschen, methyl cellulose, crystallized
sugar, and cyanotypes on kozo paper
29½ × 22¾ × 2½ in.

However The Image Enters Its Force
Remains Within My Eyes, VI, 2023
Paper made from **Anna Atkins:
Cyanotypes** book published by
Taschen, methyl cellulose, crystalized
sugar, and cyanotypes on kozo paper
29½ × 22 × 2½ in.

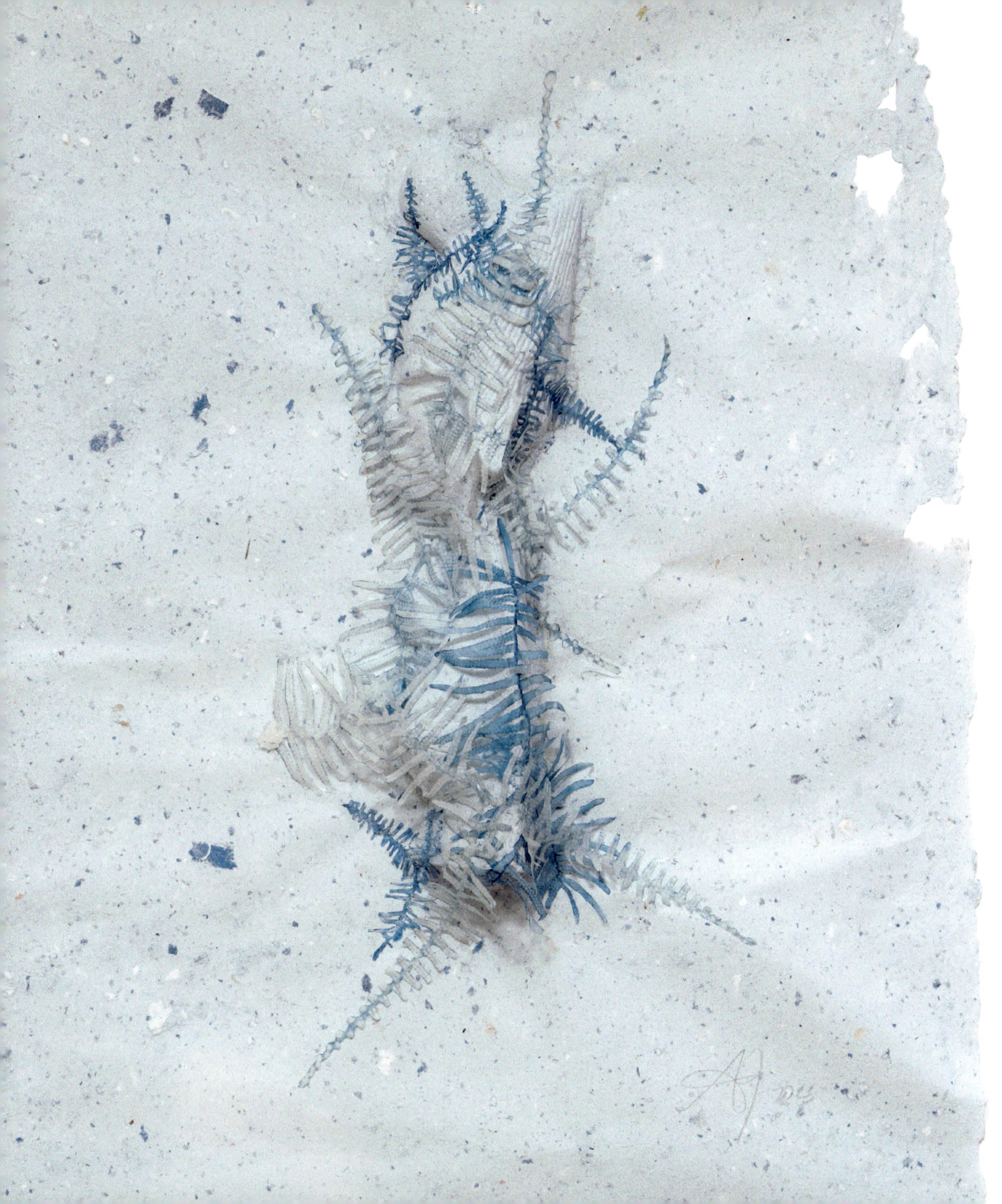

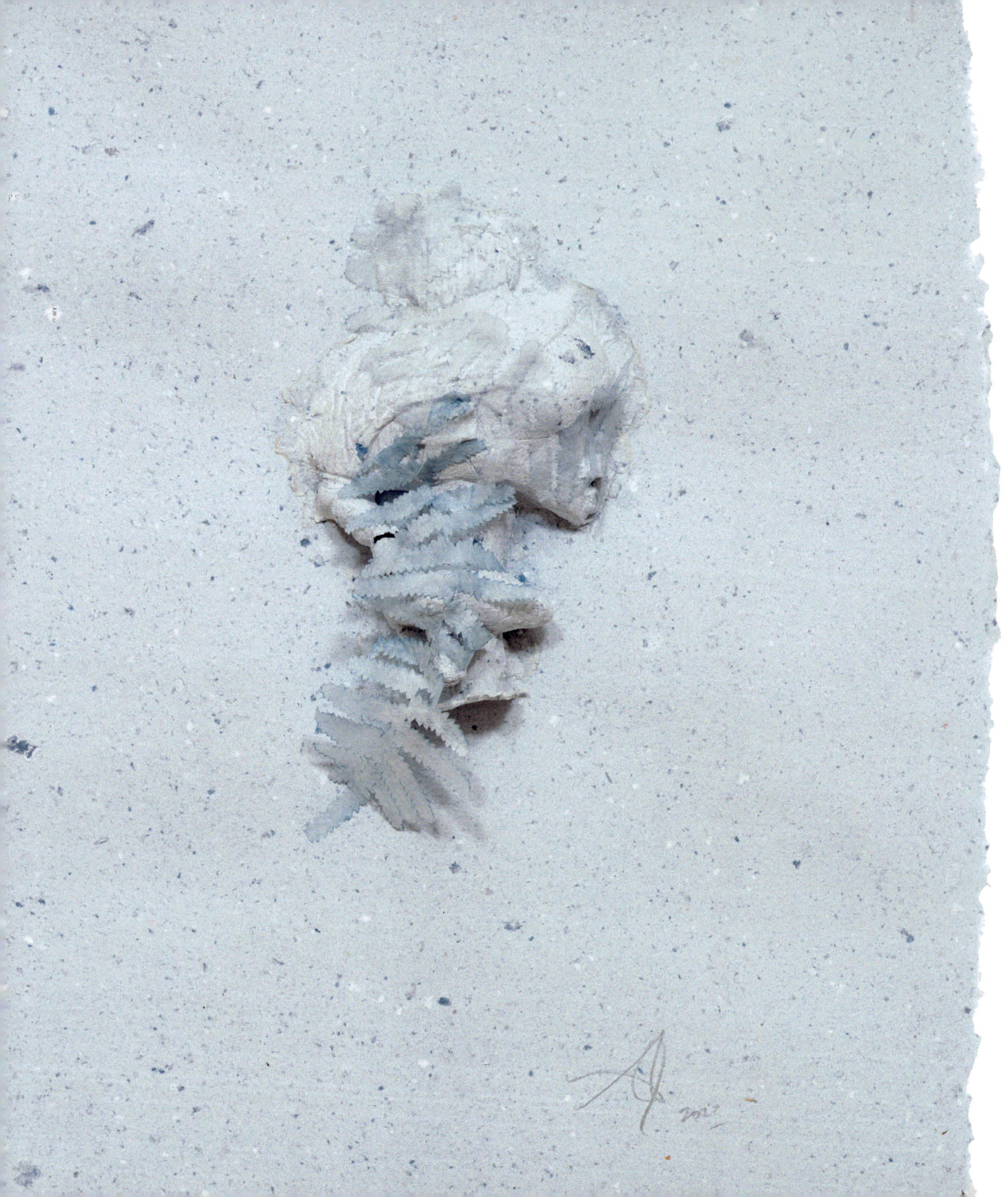

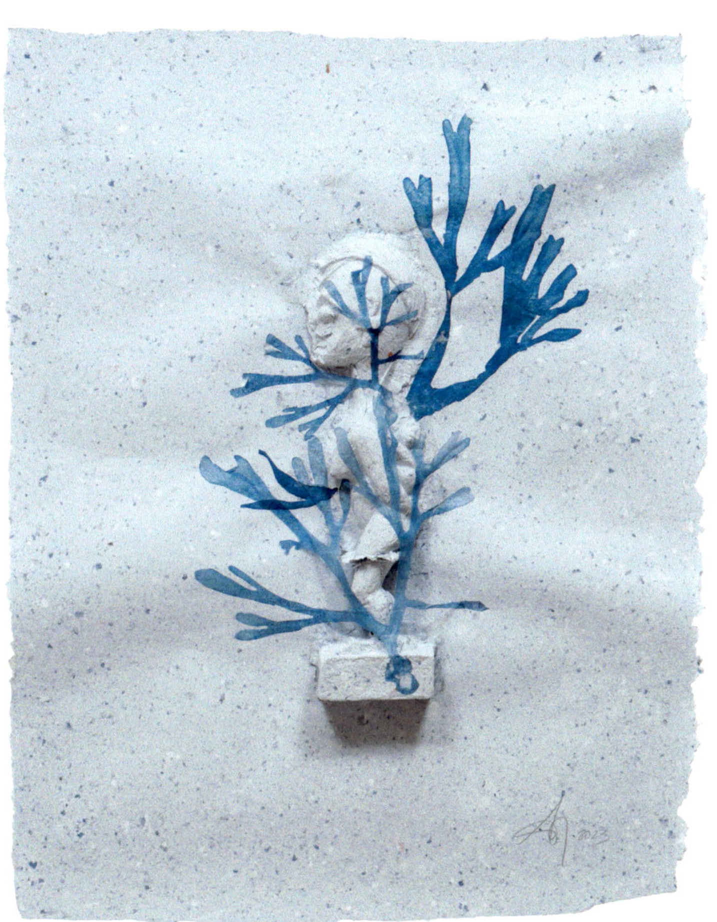

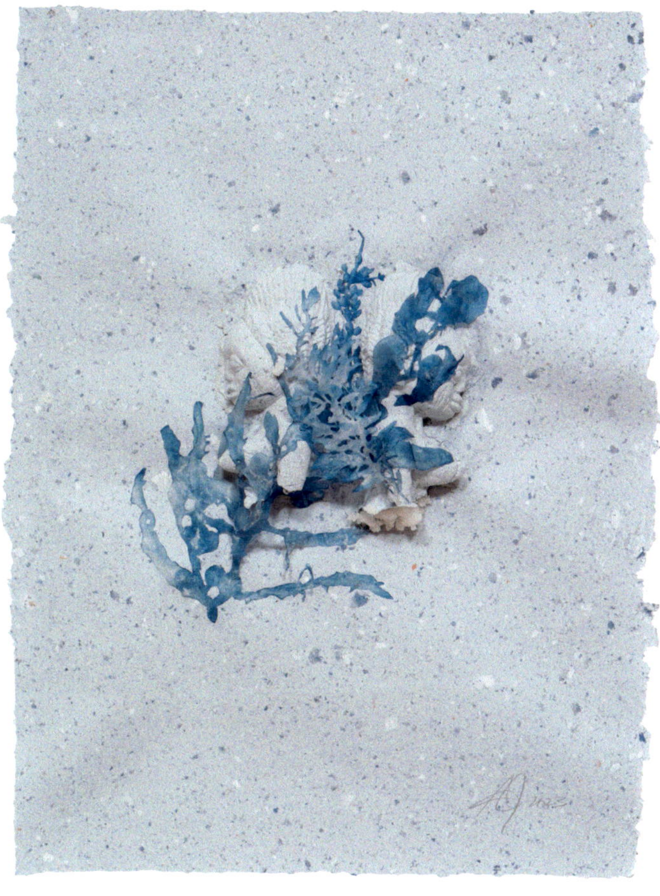

However The Image Enters Its Force
Remains Within My Eyes, V, 2023
Paper made from **Anna Atkins:
Cyanotypes** book published by
Taschen, methyl cellulose, and
cyanotypes on kozo paper
24 × 19 × 2¼ in.

However The Image Enters Its Force
Remains Within My Eyes, III, 2023
Paper made from **Anna Atkins:
Cyanotypes** book published by
Taschen, methyl cellulose, and
cyanotypes on kozo paper
24½ × 19½ × 1½ in.

overleaf

Sea Change, 2017
Cyanotype on watercolor paper,
site-specific installation
Wall 1: 221 × 164 in.; wall 2: 212 × 164 in.;
wall 3: 221 × 164 in., wall 4: 157 × 164 in.

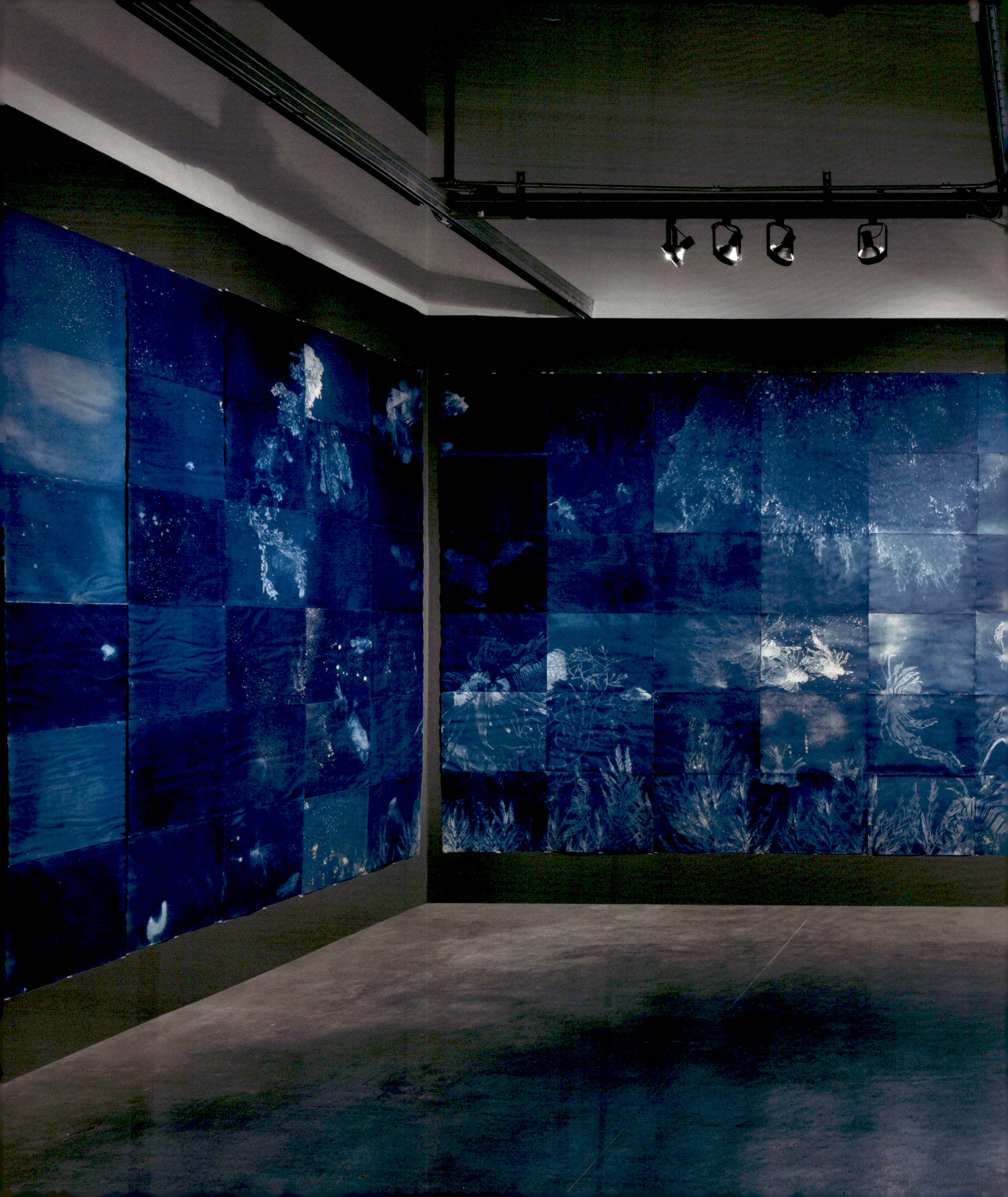

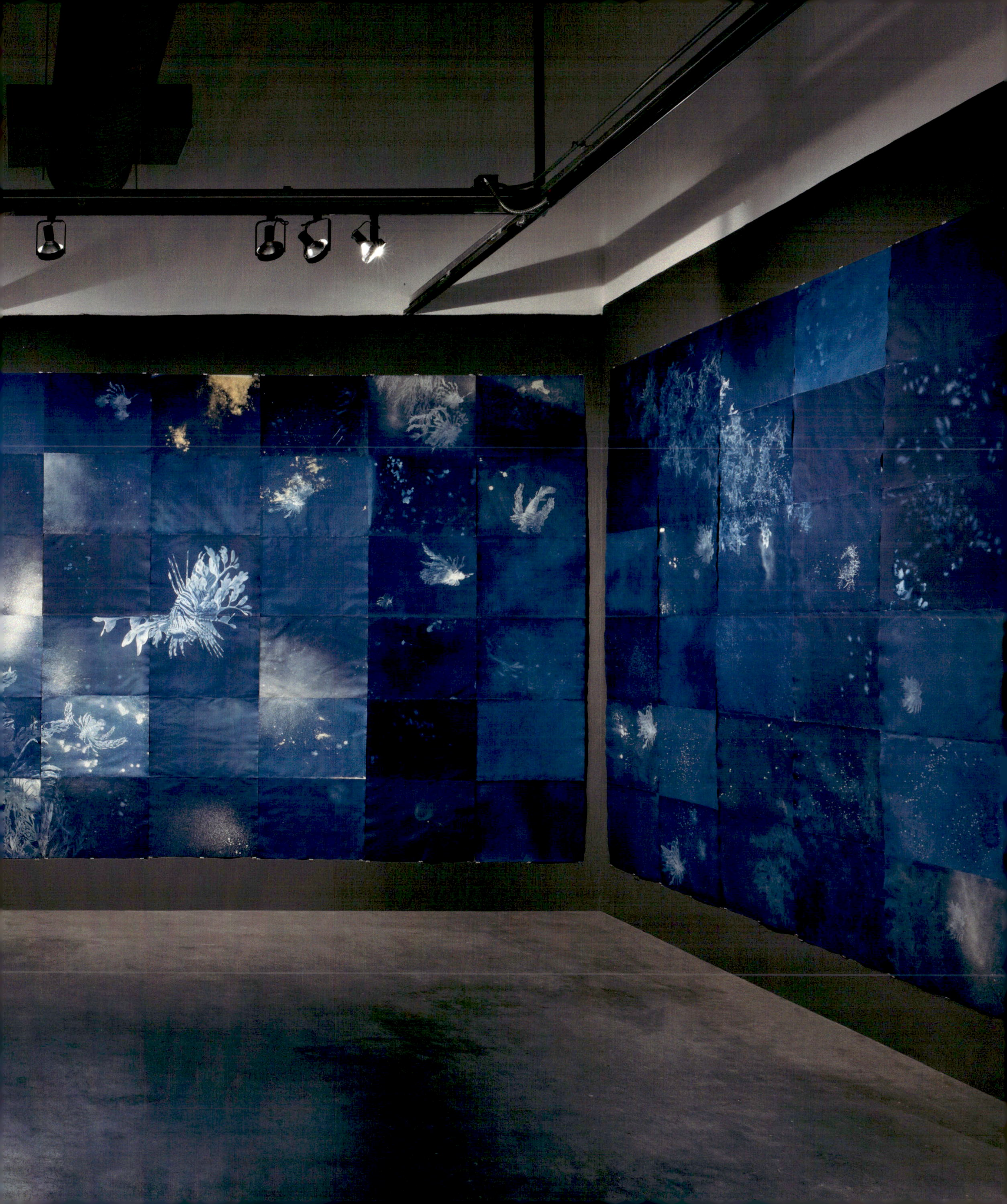

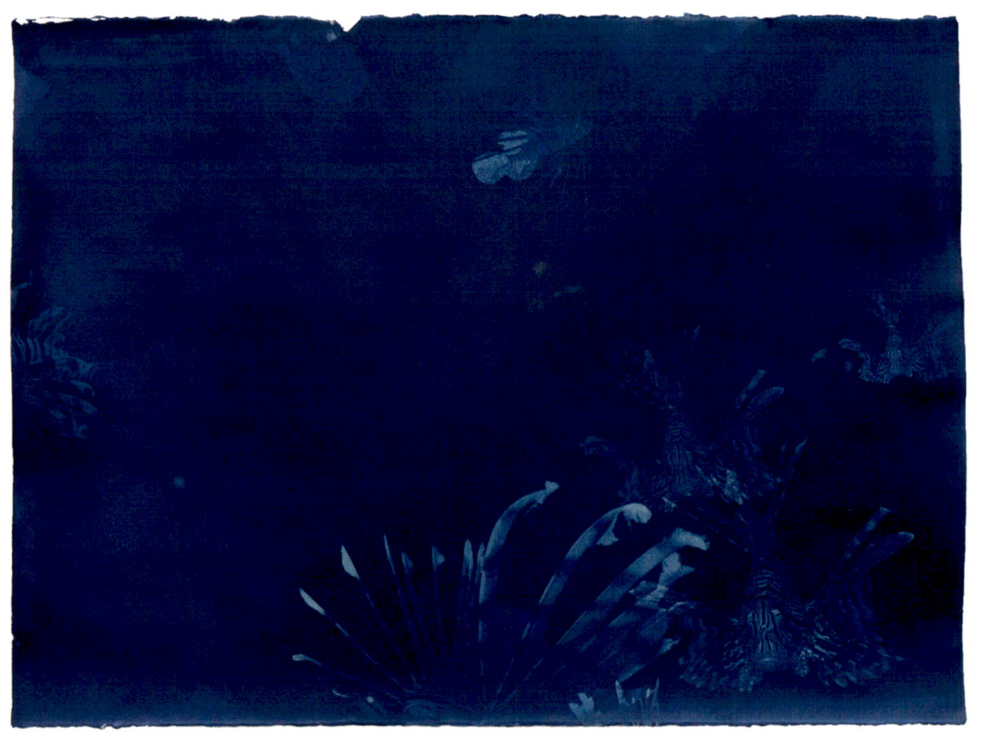
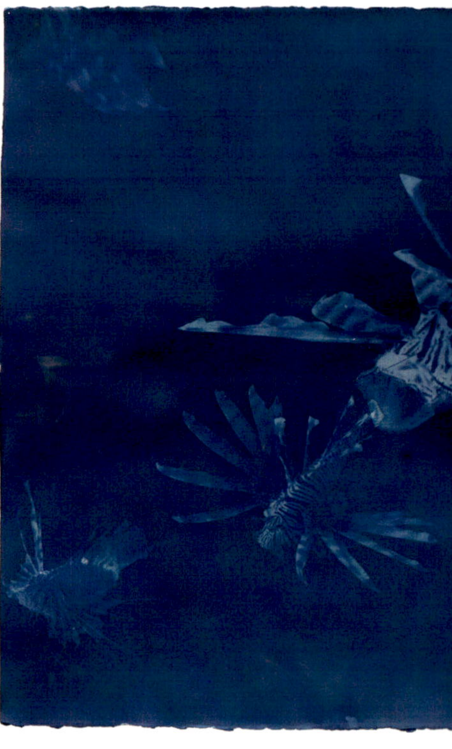
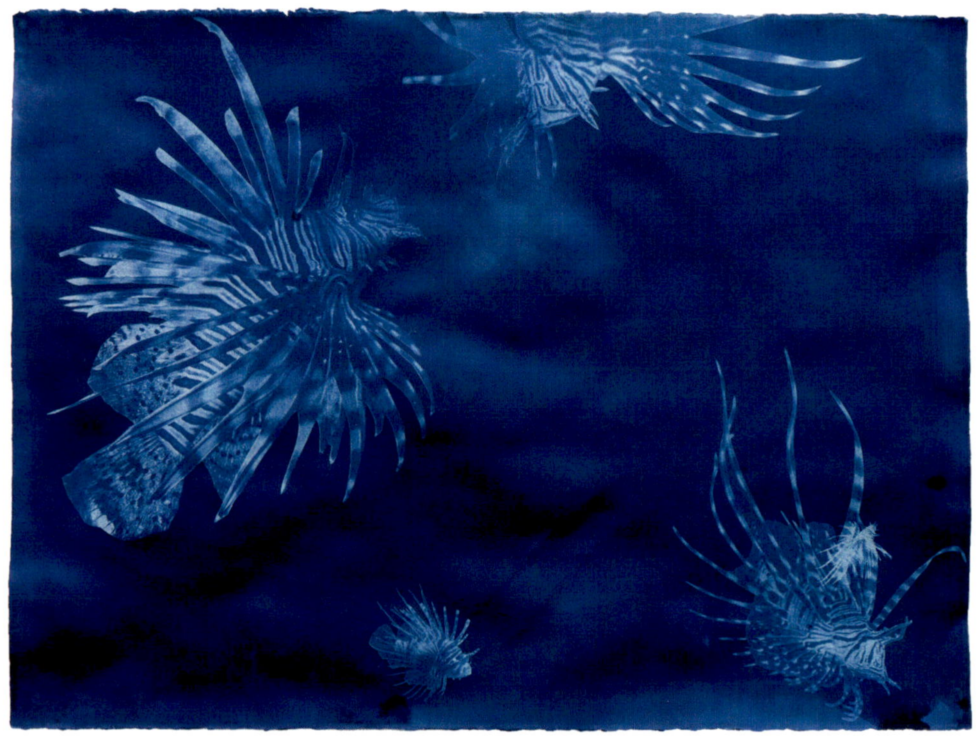
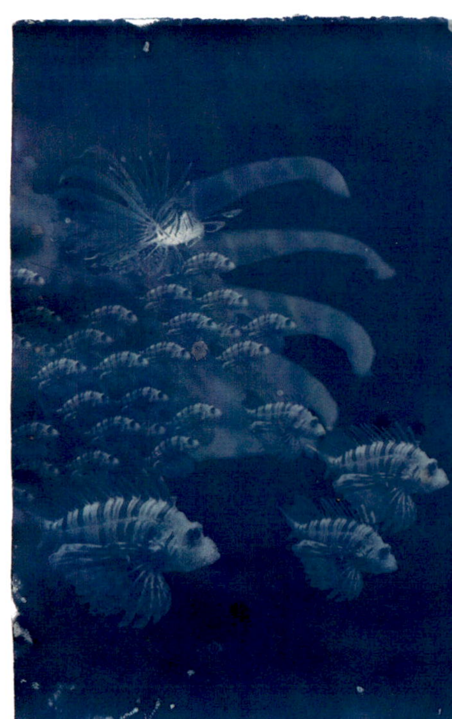

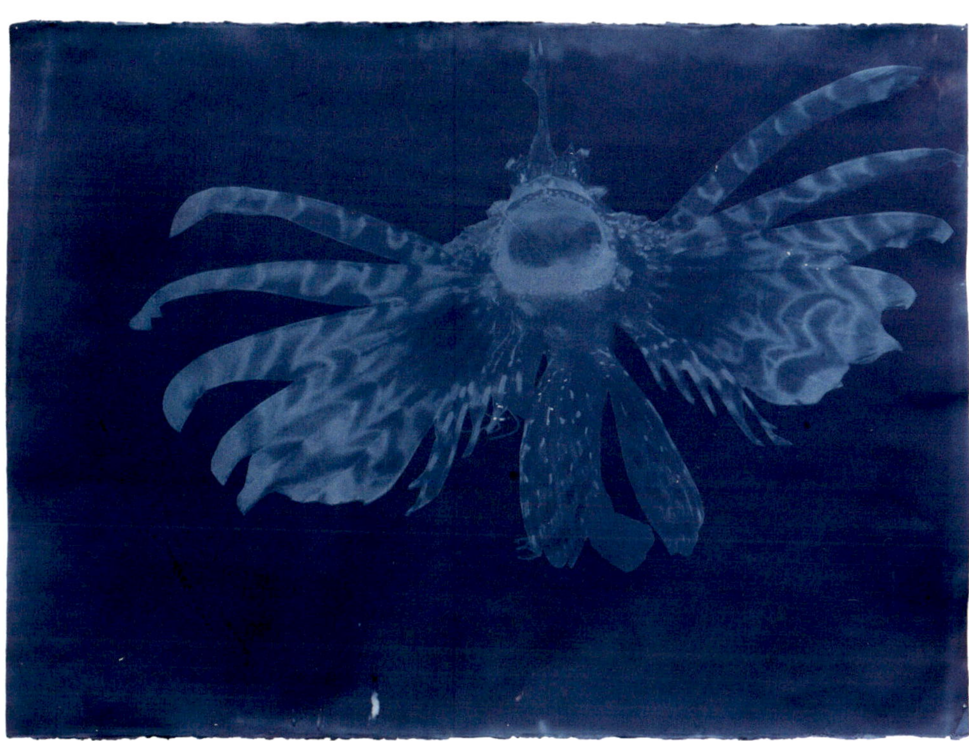

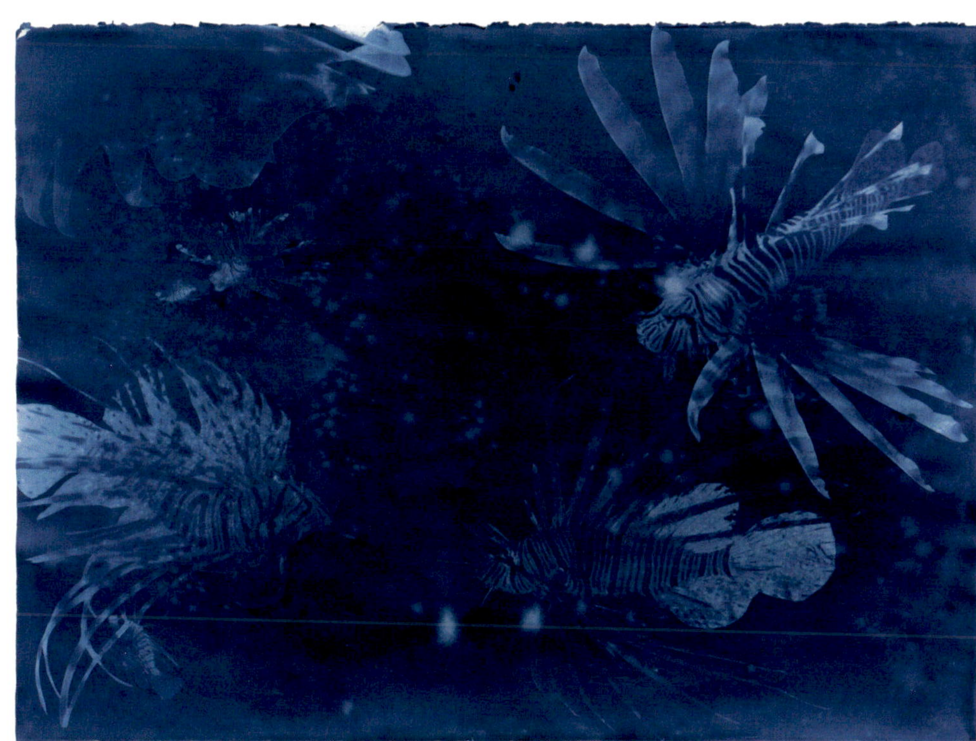

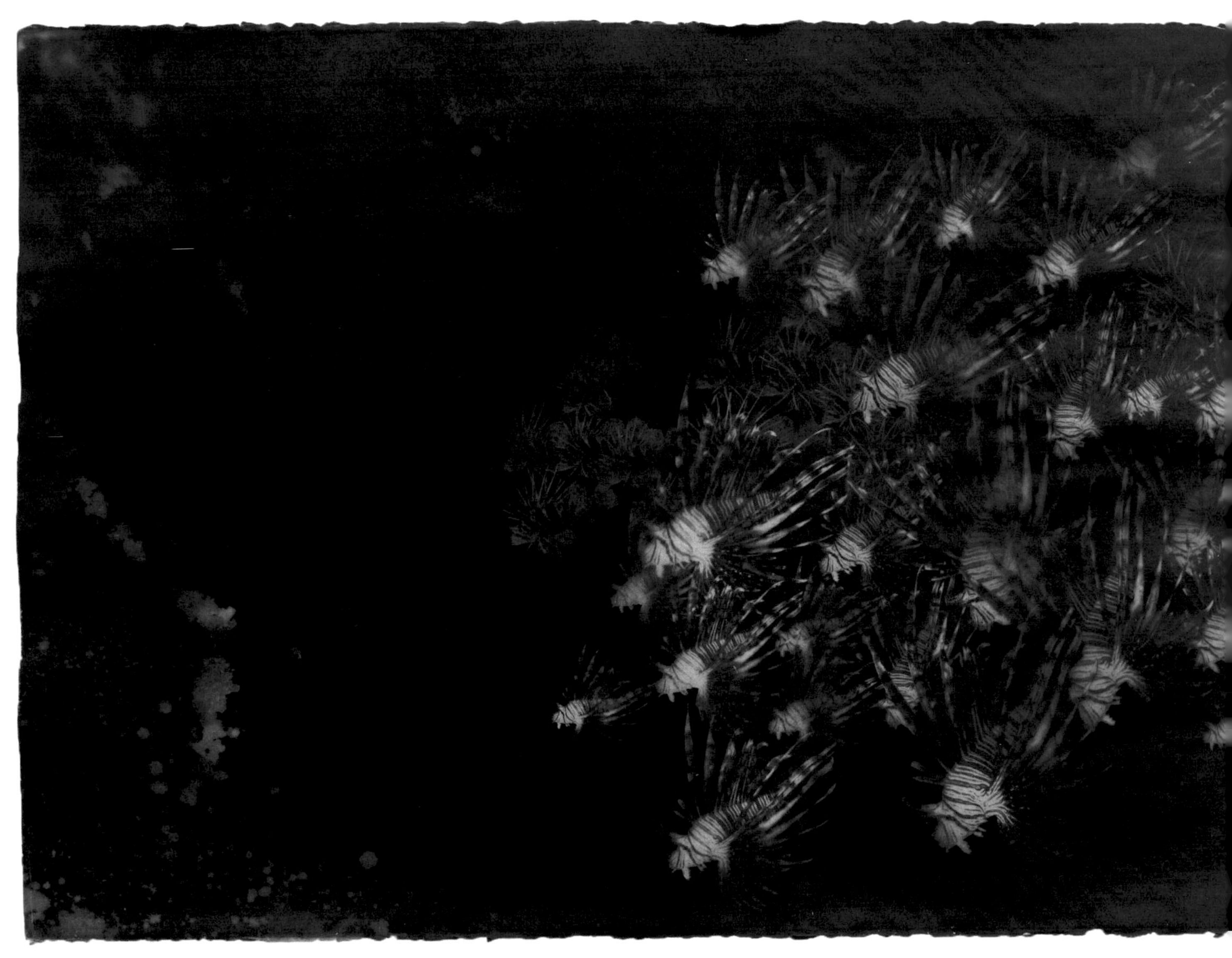

Each work on the previous spread,
clockwise from top left

Untitled, 2016
Cyanotype on 140 lb. watercolor paper
22½ × 30 in.

Untitled, 2016
Cyanotype on 140 lb. watercolor paper
22⅝ × 60 in.

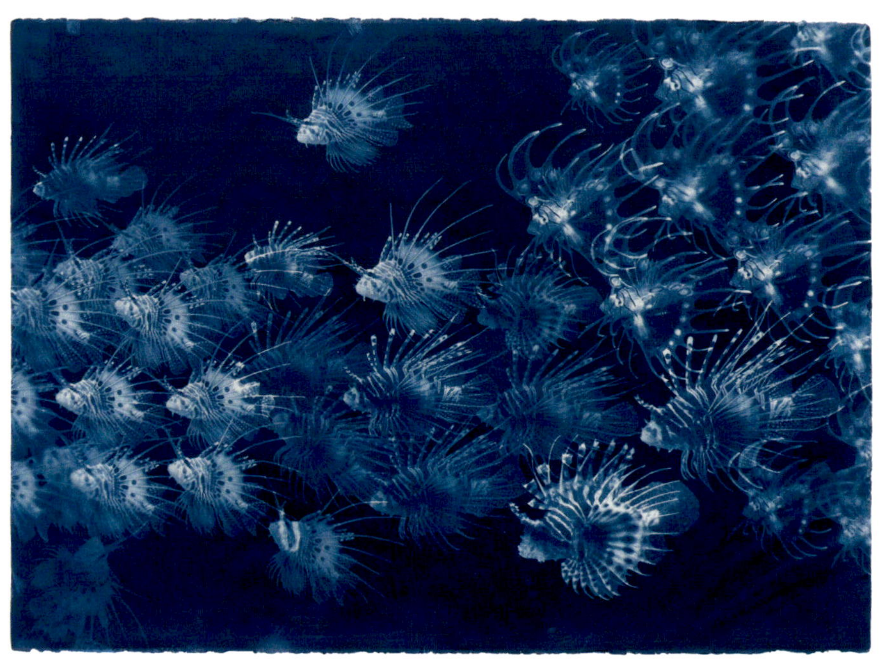

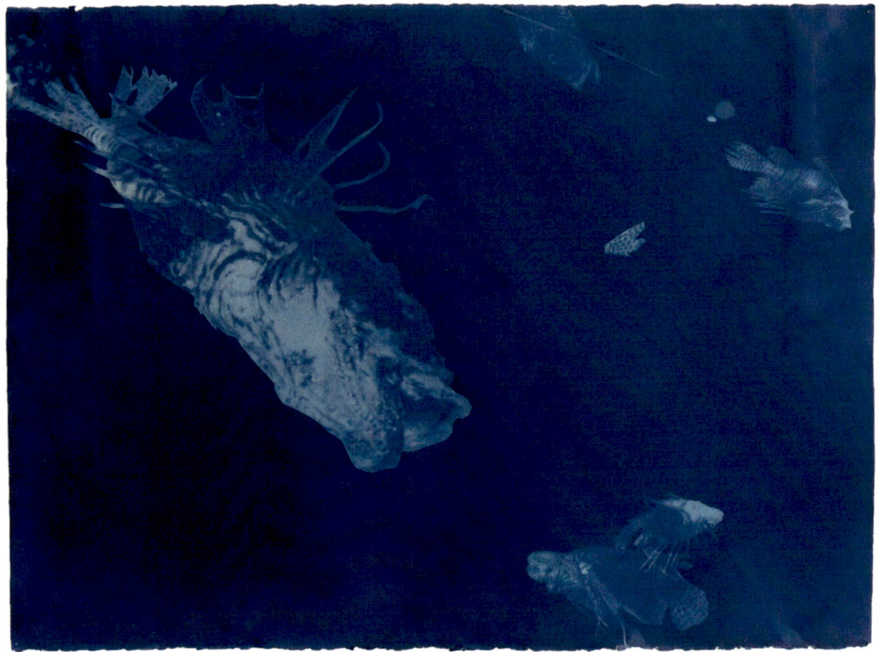

Untitled, 2016
Cyanotype on 140 lb. watercolor paper
22½ × 30 in.

Untitled, 2016
Cyanotype on 140 lb. watercolor paper
22½ × 30 in.

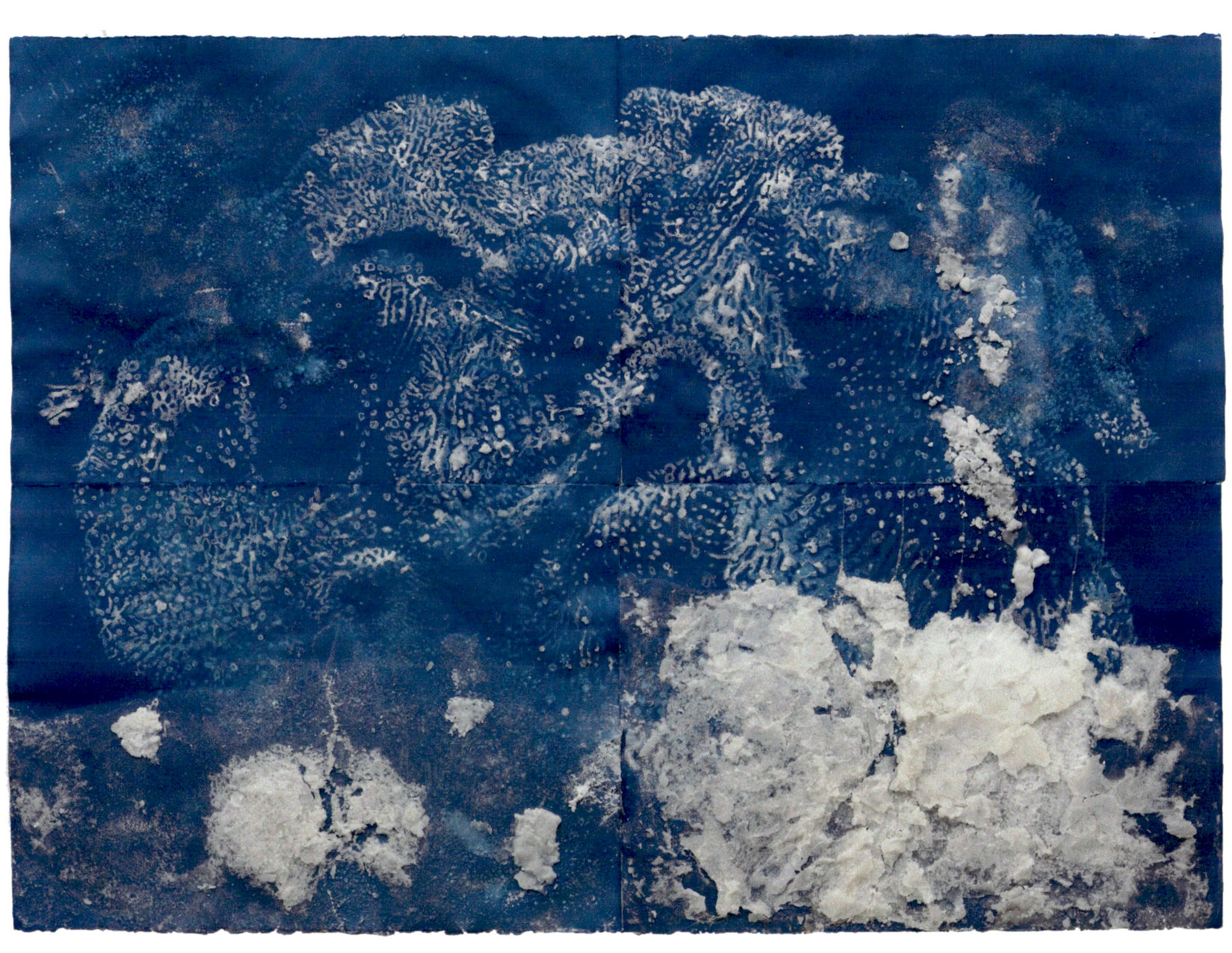

Toadstool Leather, 2019
Cyanotype and sugar
45 × 60 in.

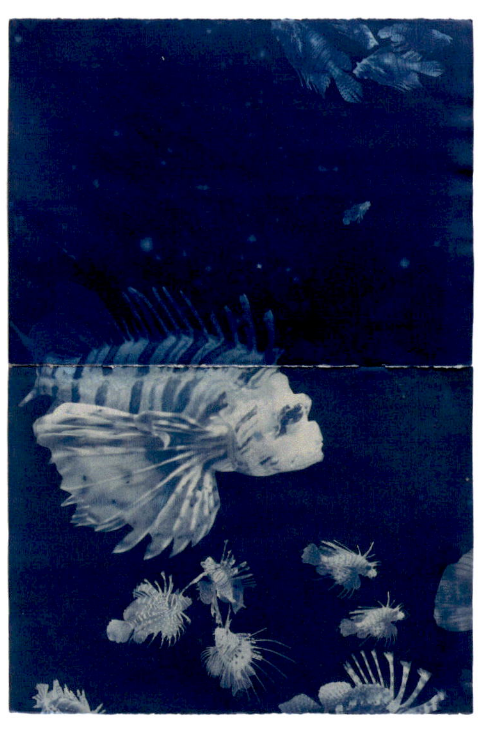
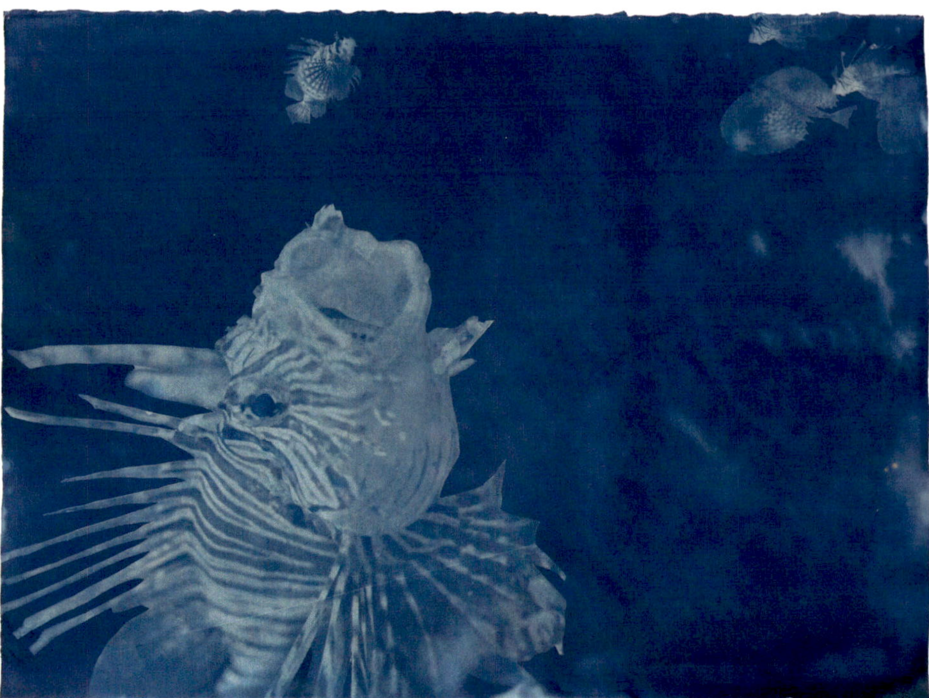
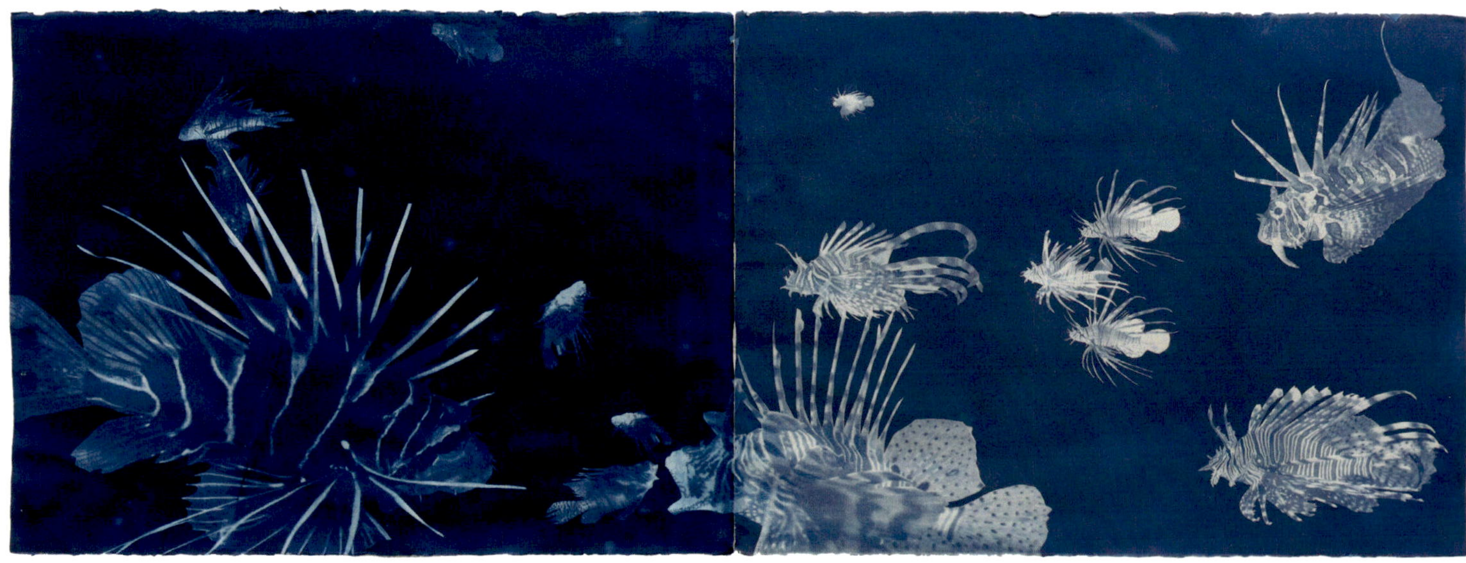

Untitled, 2016
Cyanotype on 140 lb. watercolor paper
45 × 30 in.

Untitled, 2016
Cyanotype on 140 lb. watercolor paper
22½ × 30 in.

Untitled, 2016
Cyanotype on 140 lb. watercolor paper
22⅝ × 60 in.

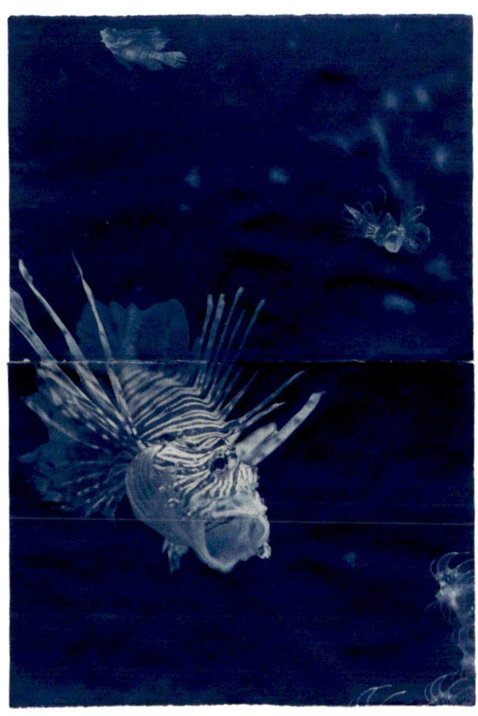

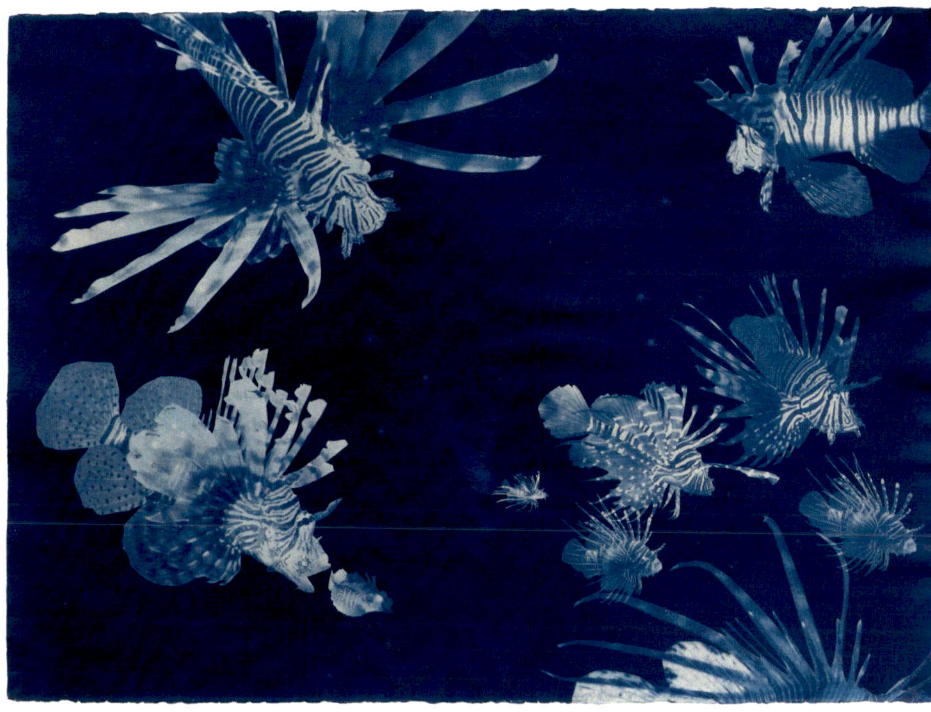

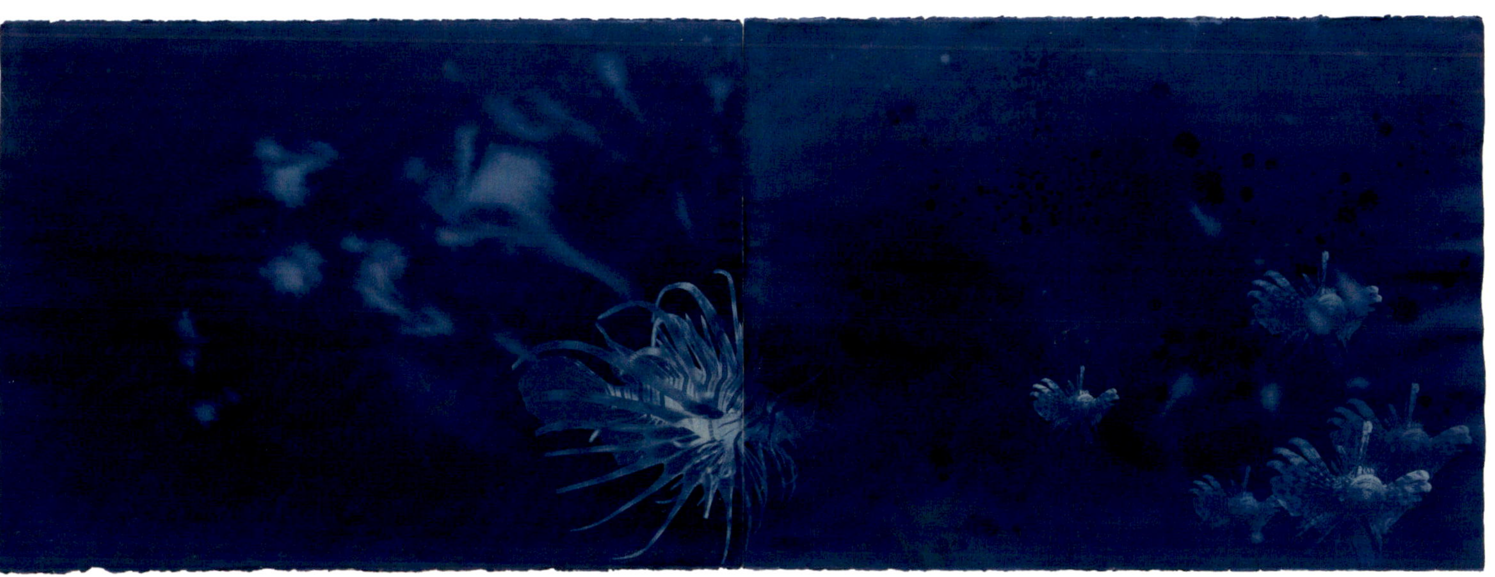

clockwise from top left

Untitled, 2016
Cyanotype on 140 lb. watercolor paper
45 × 30 in.

Untitled, 2016
Cyanotype on 140 lb. watercolor paper
22½ × 30 in.

Untitled, 2016
Cyanotype on 140 lb. watercolor paper
22⅝ × 60 in.

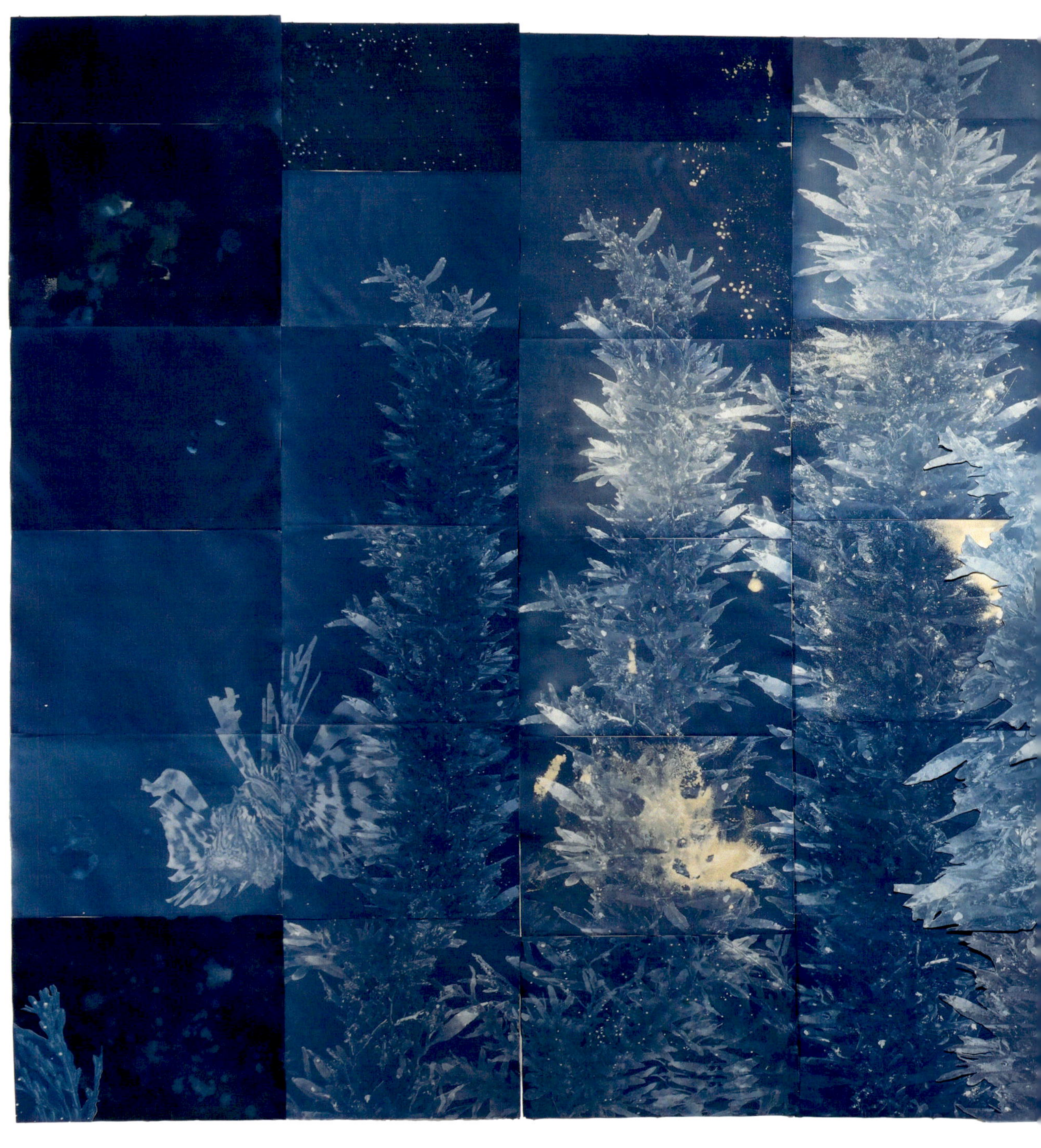

Spectre, 2017
Cyanotype on watercolor paper
Site-specific installation
Variable dimensions

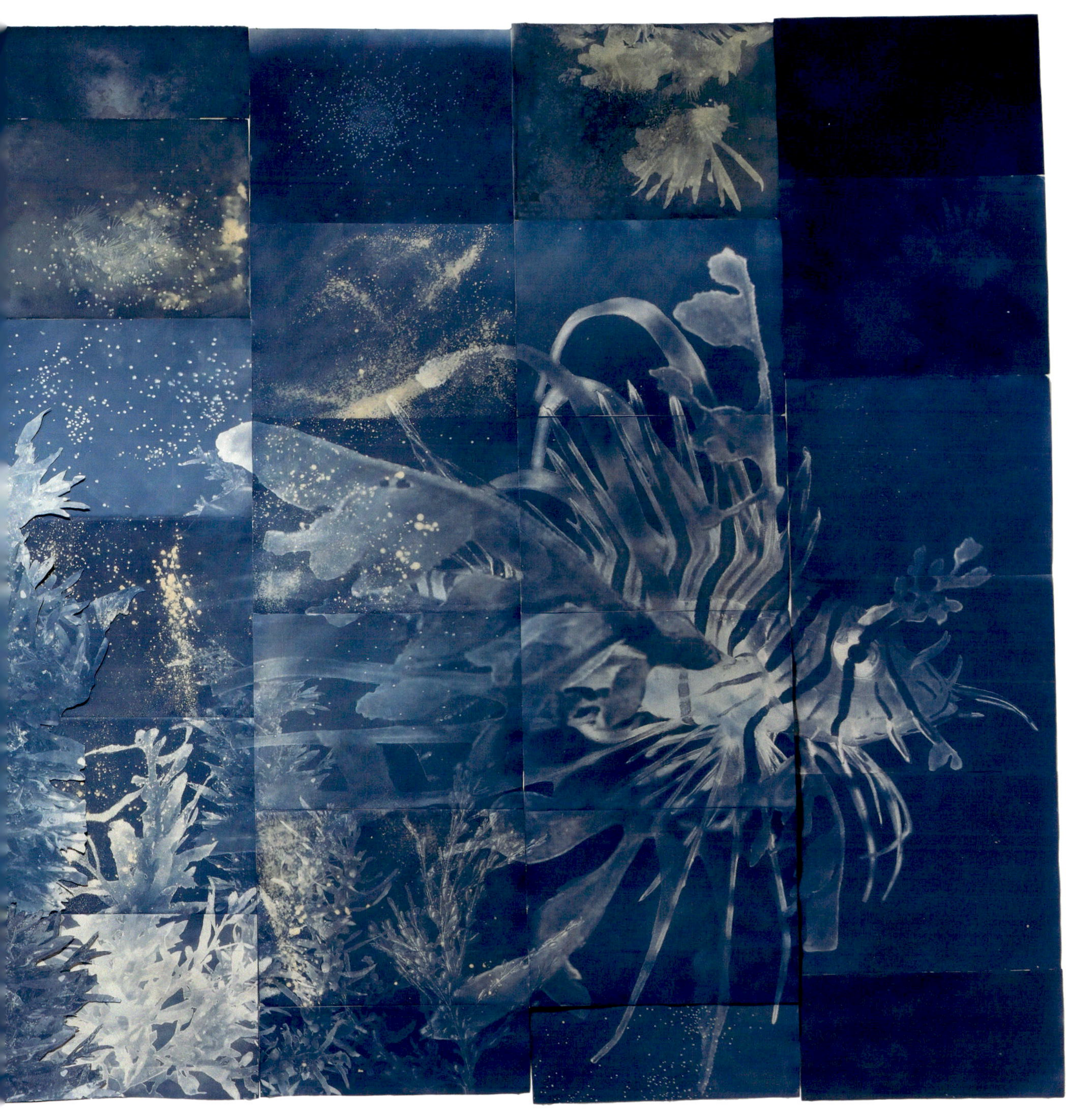

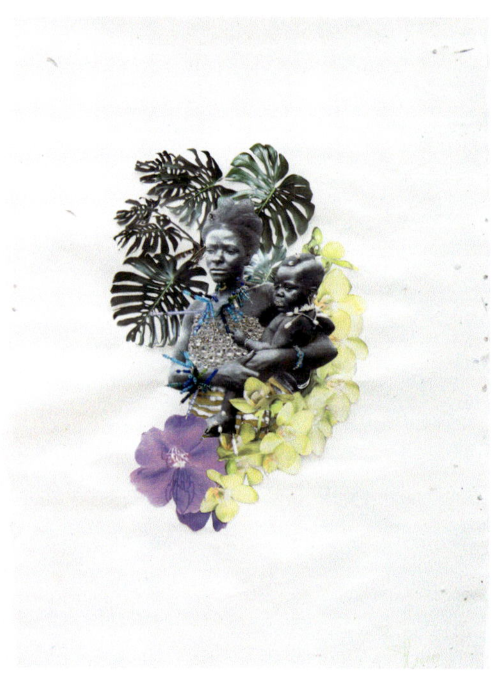 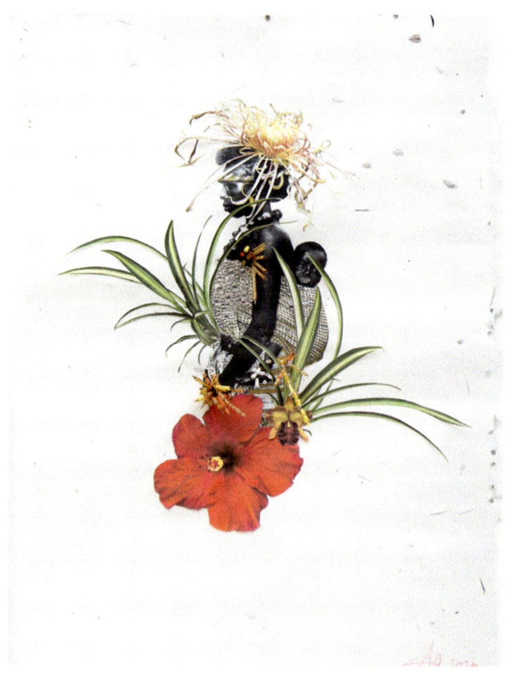

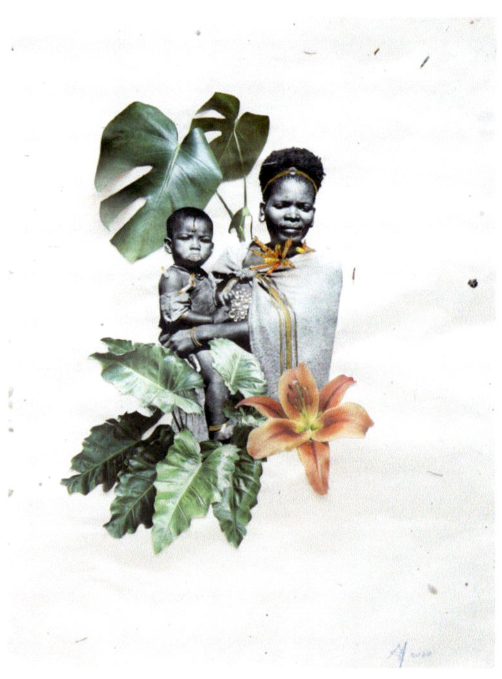 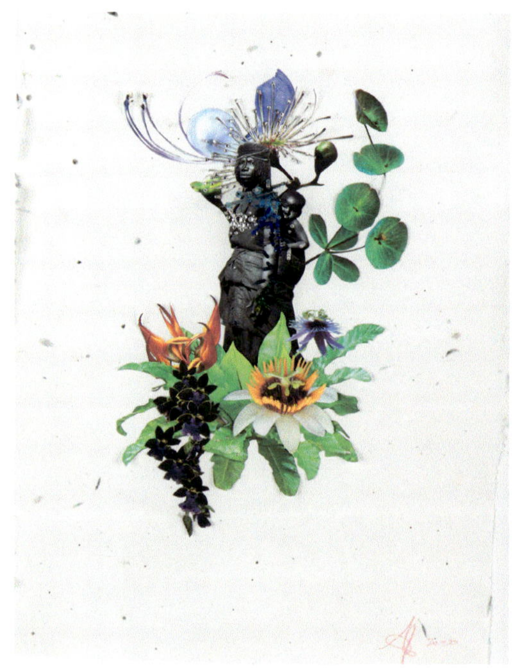

clockwise from top left

Colostrum I, 2020
Collage, ink, rhinestones, pins,
and beads on paper handmade
from traditional birthing cloth
Framed: 22 × 17 × 2 in.

Colostrum II, 2020
Collage, ink, rhinestones, pins,
and beads on paper handmade
from traditional birthing cloth
Framed: 22 × 17 × 2 in.

Colostrum IV, 2020
Collage, ink, rhinestones, pins,
and beads on paper handmade
from traditional birthing cloth
Framed: 22 × 17 × 2 in.

Colostrum VII, 2020
Collage, ink, rhinestones, pins,
and beads on paper handmade
from traditional birthing cloth
17 × 13 in.

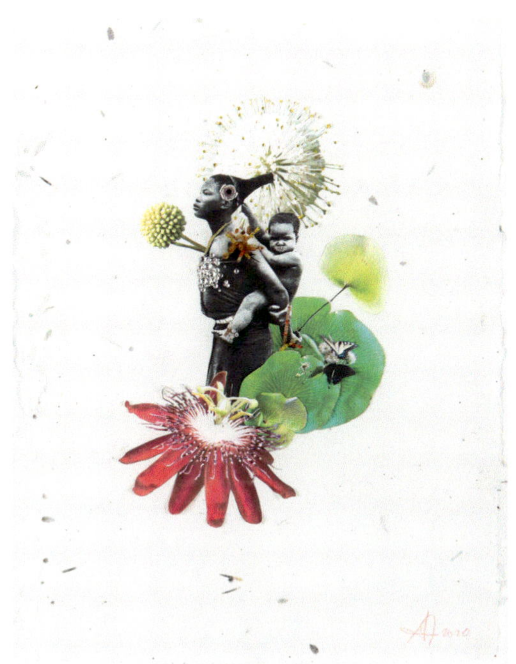

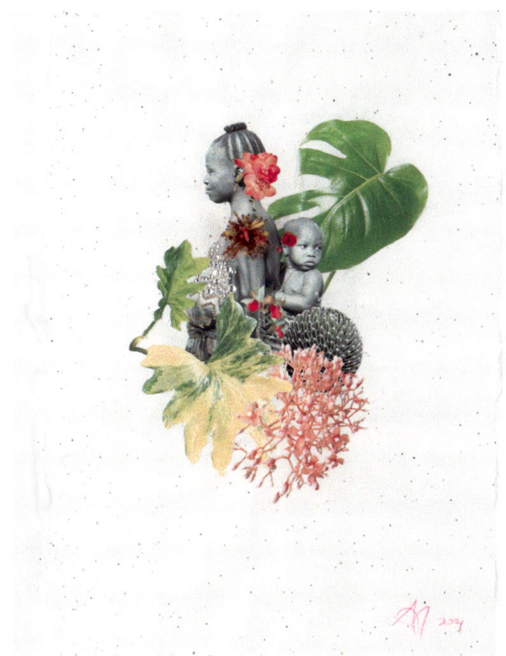

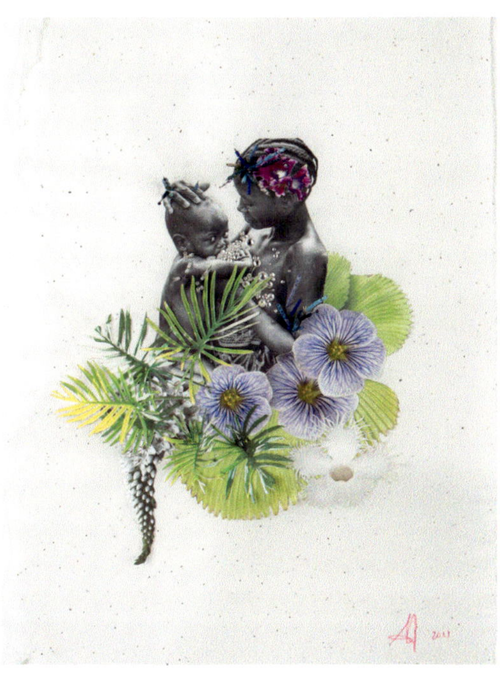

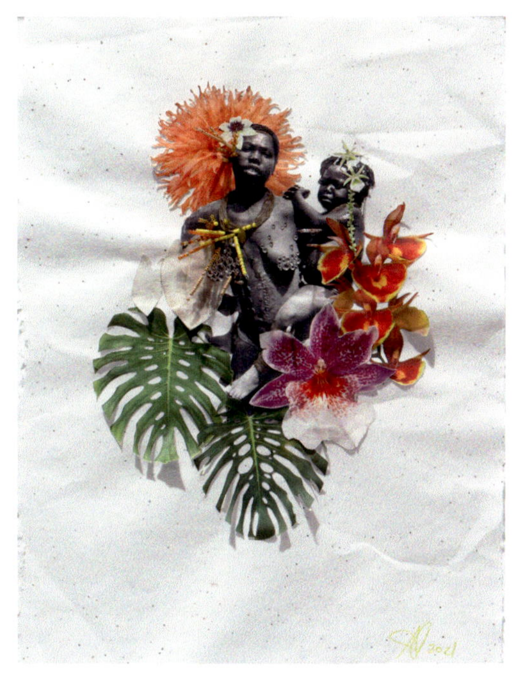

clockwise from top left

Colostrum VIII, 2020
Collage, ink, rhinestones, pins,
and beads on paper handmade
from traditional birthing cloth
17¾ × 12¼ in.

Colostrum XIII, 2021
Collage, ink, and beads
on paper handmade from
traditional birthing cloth
20 × 16 in.

Colostrum IX, 2021
Collage, ink, and beads
on paper handmade from
traditional birthing cloth
20 × 16 in.

Colostrum XIV, 2021
Collage, ink, rhinestones, pins,
and beads on paper handmade
from traditional birthing cloth
17 × 12 in.

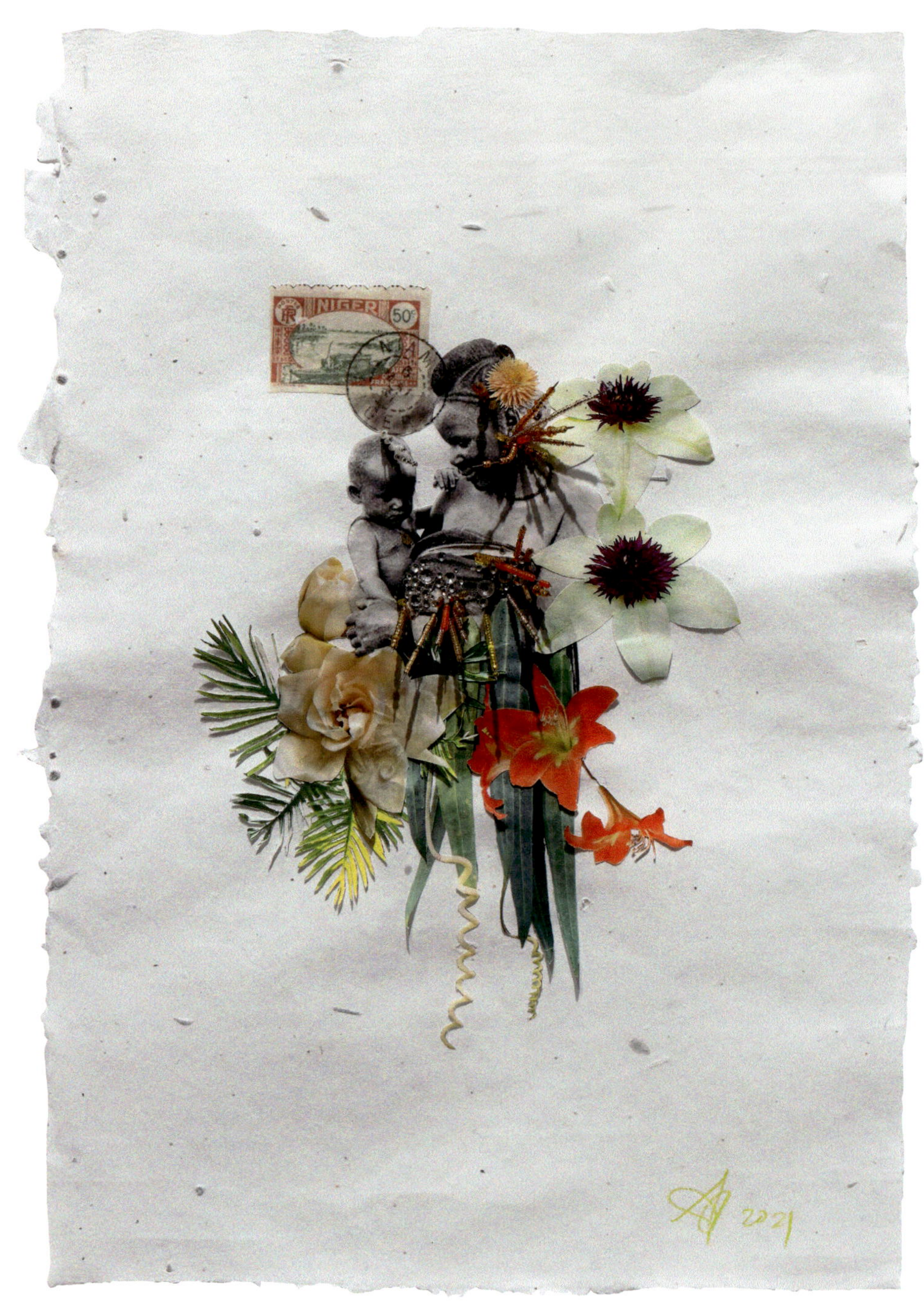

Colostrum XVII, 2021
Collage, ink, rhinestones, pins, and
beads on paper handmade from
traditional birthing cloth
17 × 12 in.

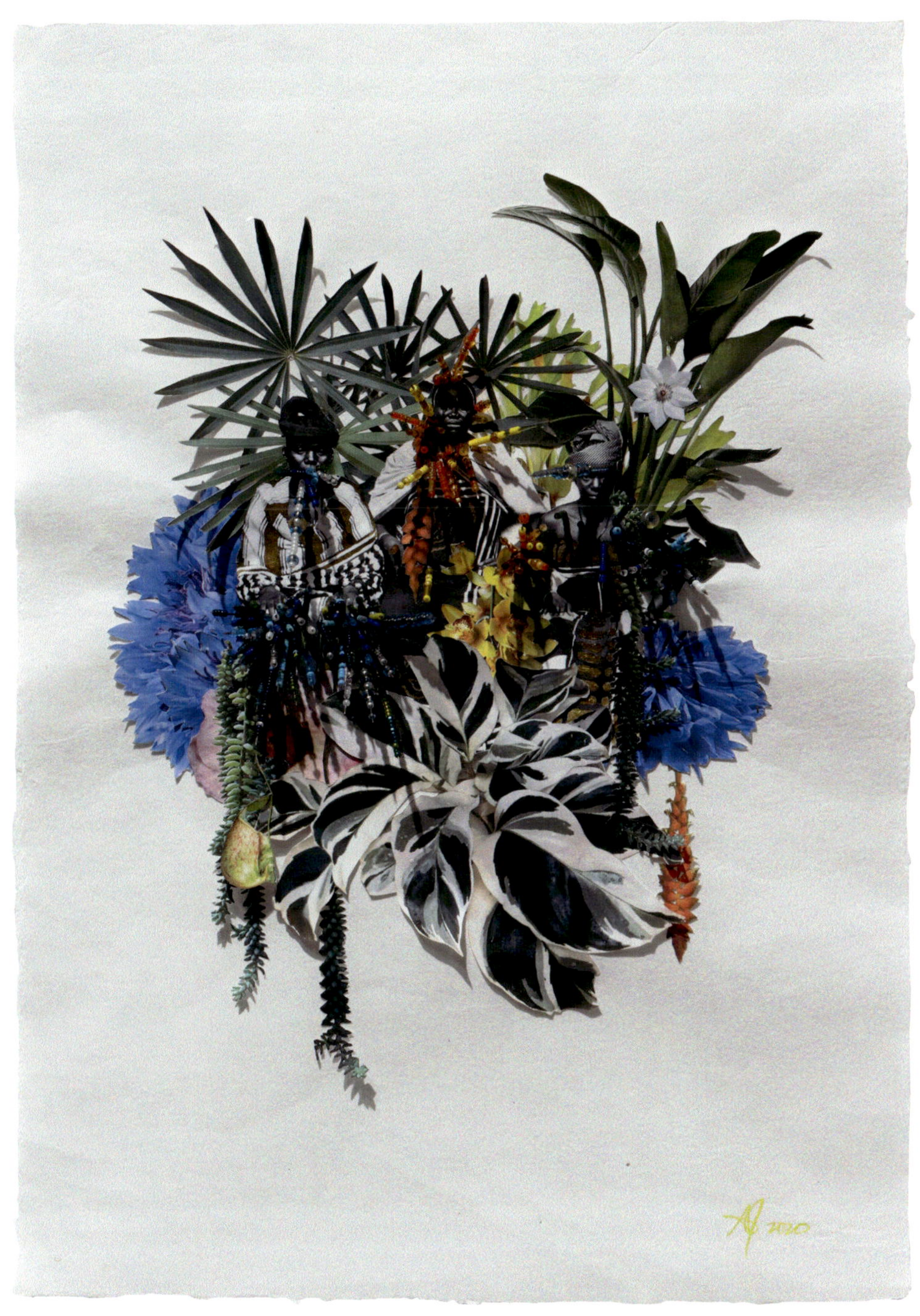

Vex XX, 2020
Collage, ink, and beads
on paper handmade from
traditional birthing cloth
17 × 13 in.

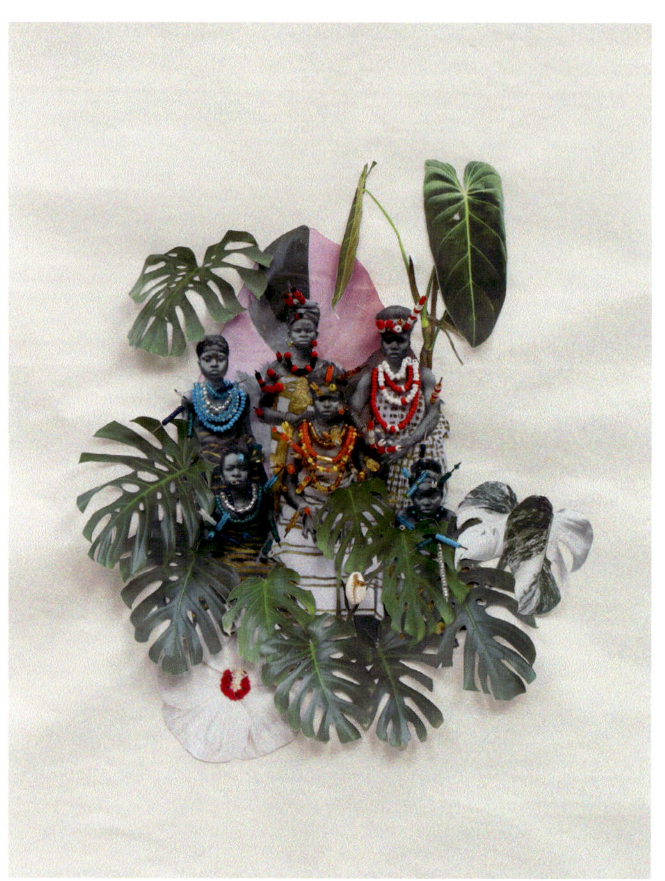

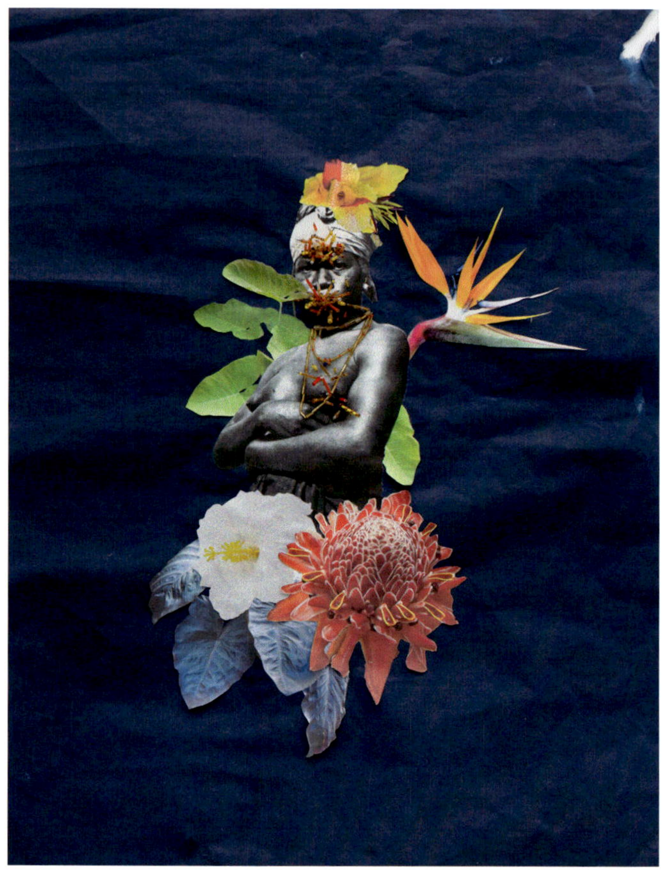

opposite

Vex VII, 2020
Collage, ink, and beads
on paper handmade from
traditional birthing cloth
22 × 16½ in.

Vex XI, 2020
Collage, ink, and beads on
handmade paper
29 × 21¾ in.

Vex VIII, 2020
Collage, ink and beads on paper
handmade from traditional
birthing cloth
22 × 16½ in.

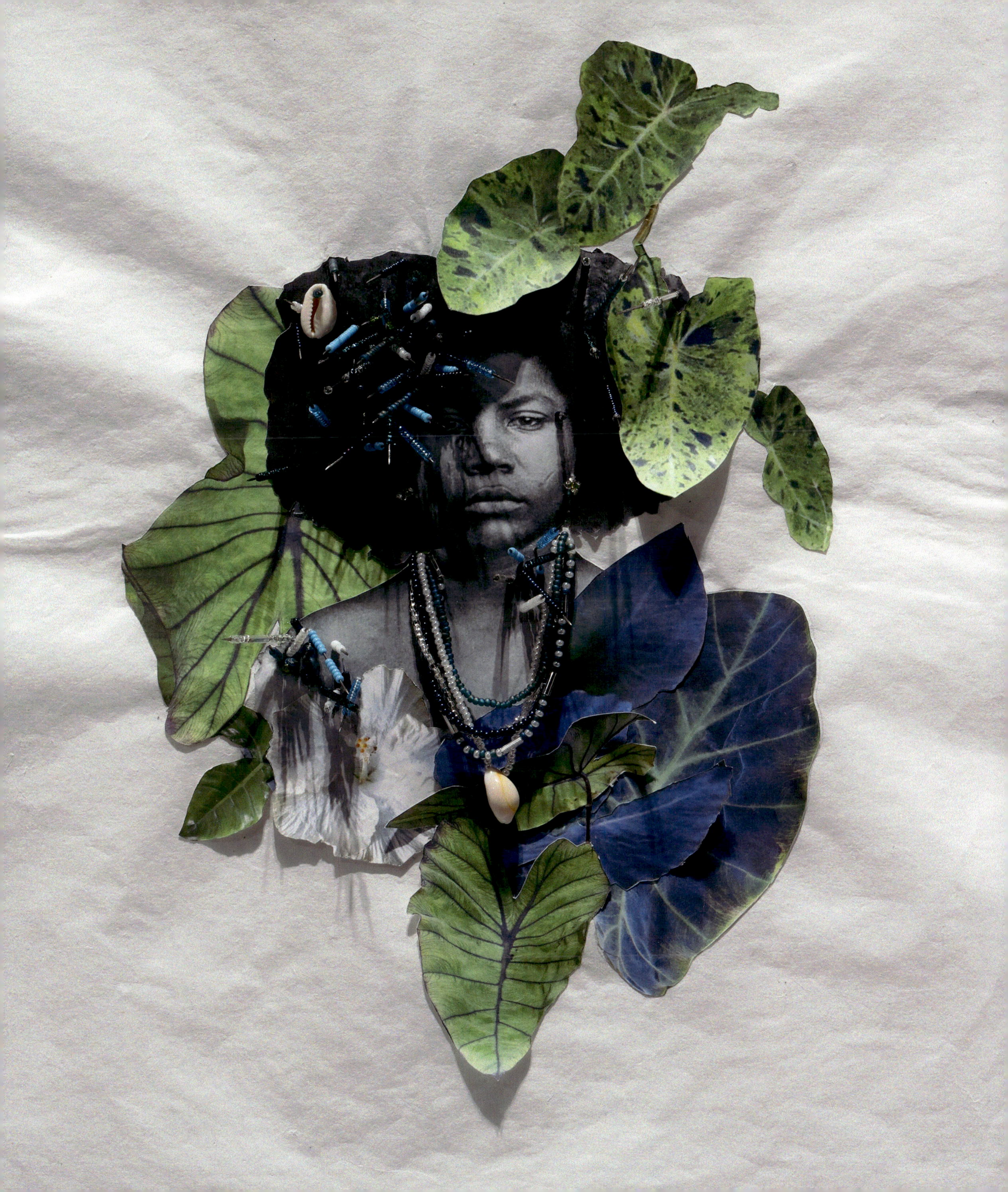

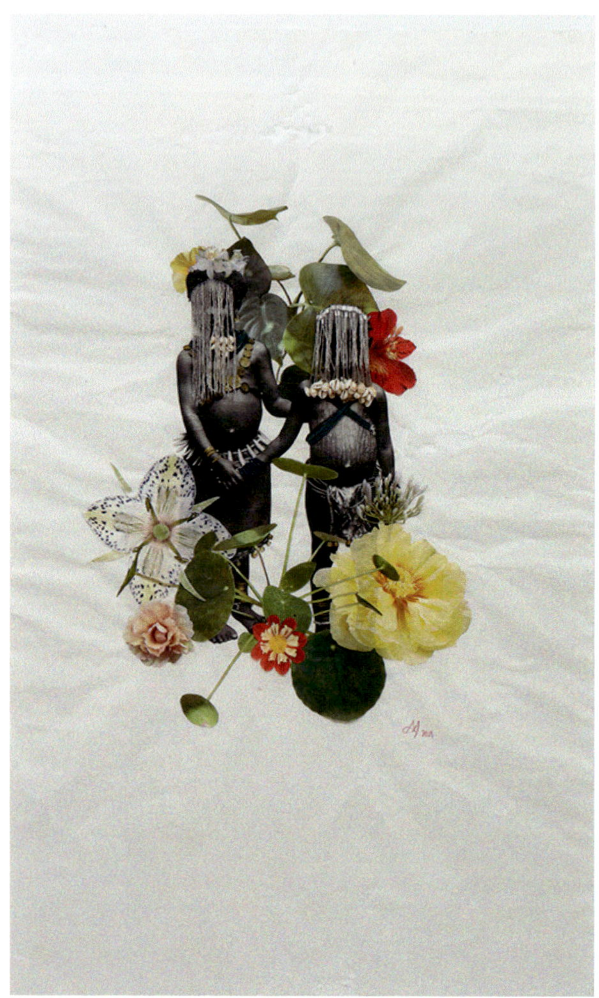

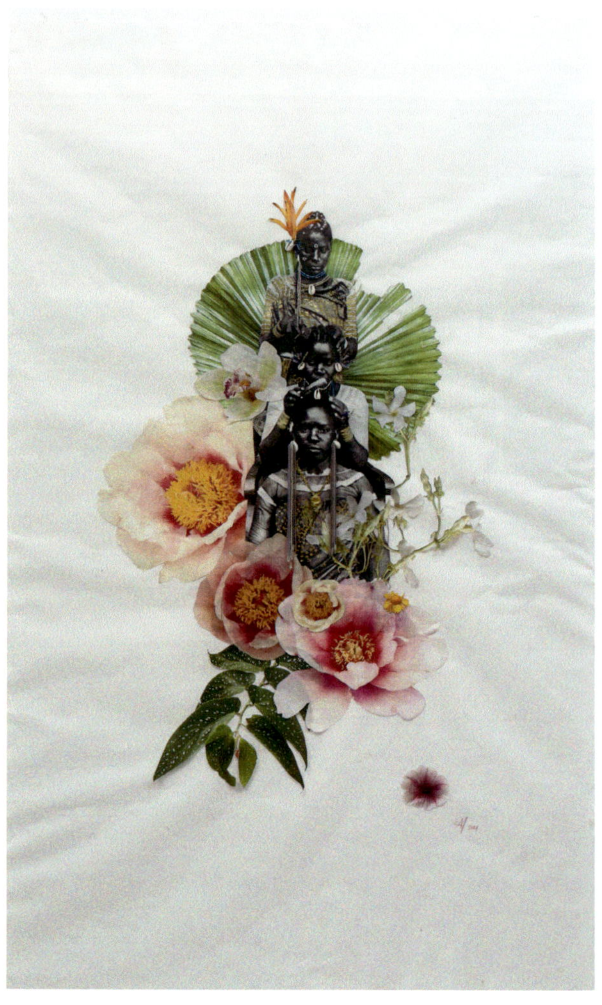

Sula Never Competed; She Simply Helped
Other Define Themselves, III, 2021
Collage, gold ink, shells, and beads on
paper handmade from traditional birthing
cloth
Framed: 55¼ × 35¼ × 2¾ in.

Sula Never Competed; She Simply Helped
Other Define Themselves, VII, 2021
Collage, gold ink, shells, pins, and beads
on paper handmade from traditional
birthing cloth
Framed: 55¼ × 35¼ × 2¾ in.

opposite

Sula Never Competed; She Simply Helped
Others Define Themselves, II, 2021
Collage, gold ink, shells, pins, and beads
on paper handmade from traditional
birthing cloth
Framed: 55¼ × 70½ × 2¾ in.

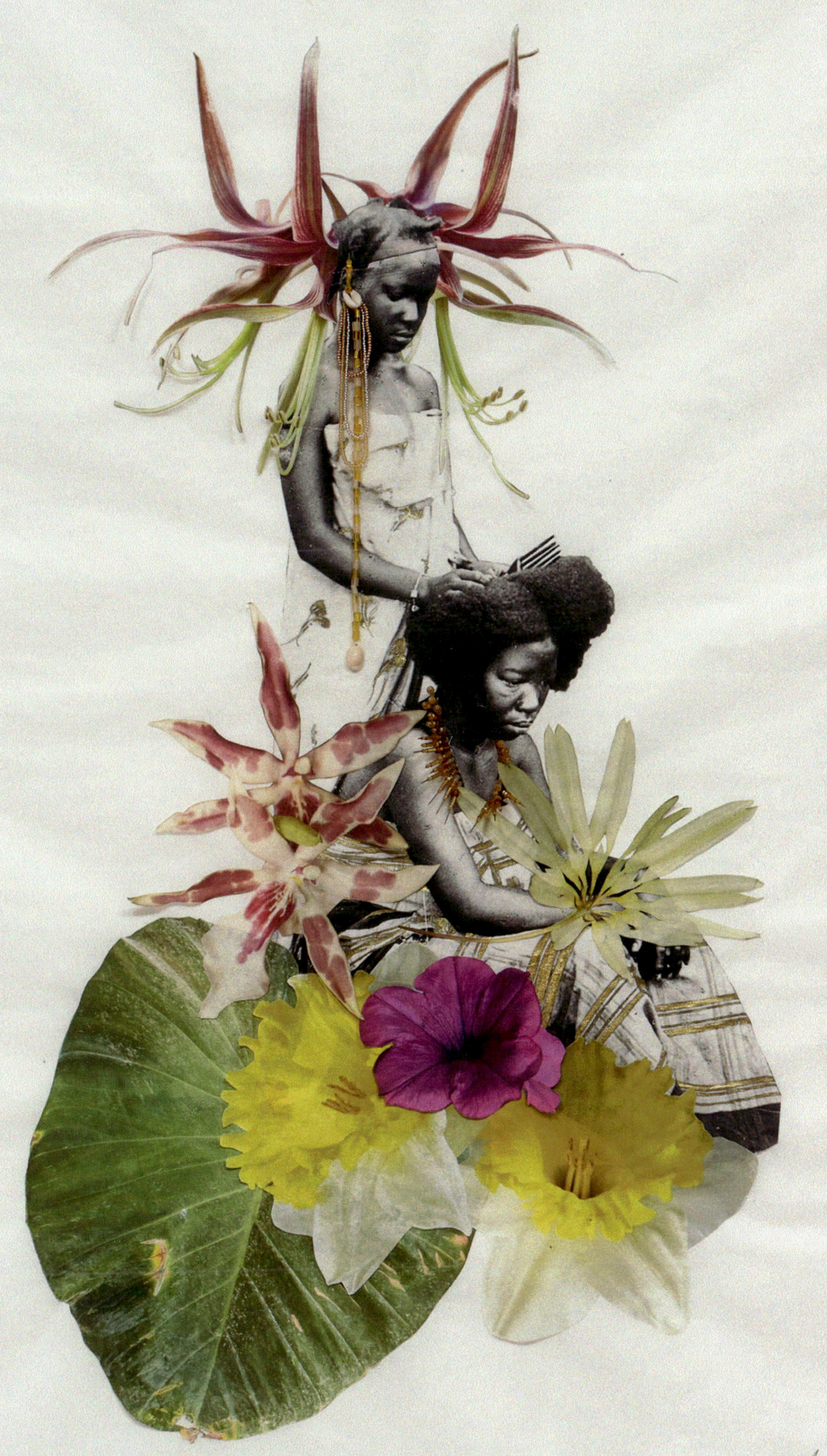

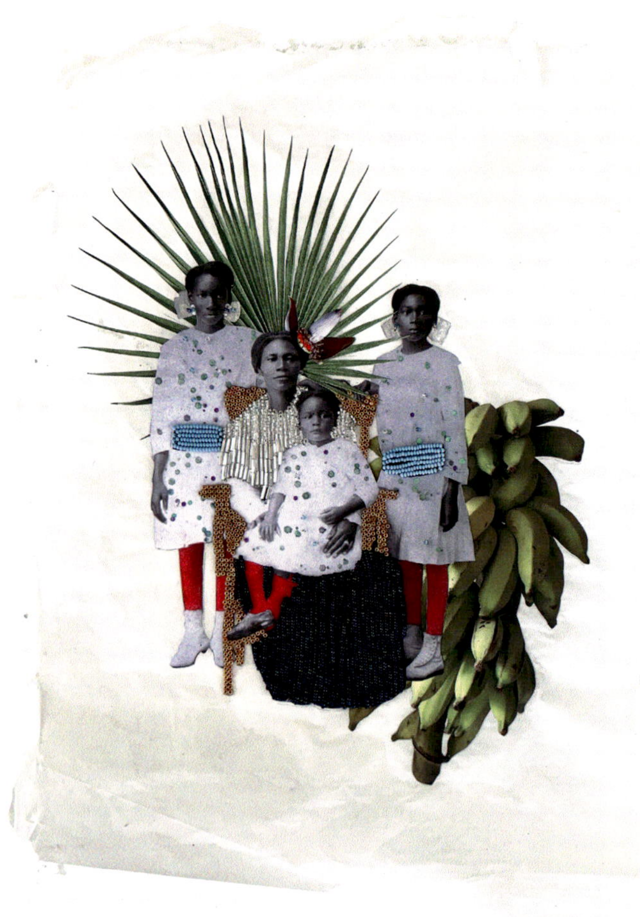

Sisters of Two Waters I, 2019
Collage, glitter, and beads on handmade
paper
18 × 12 in.

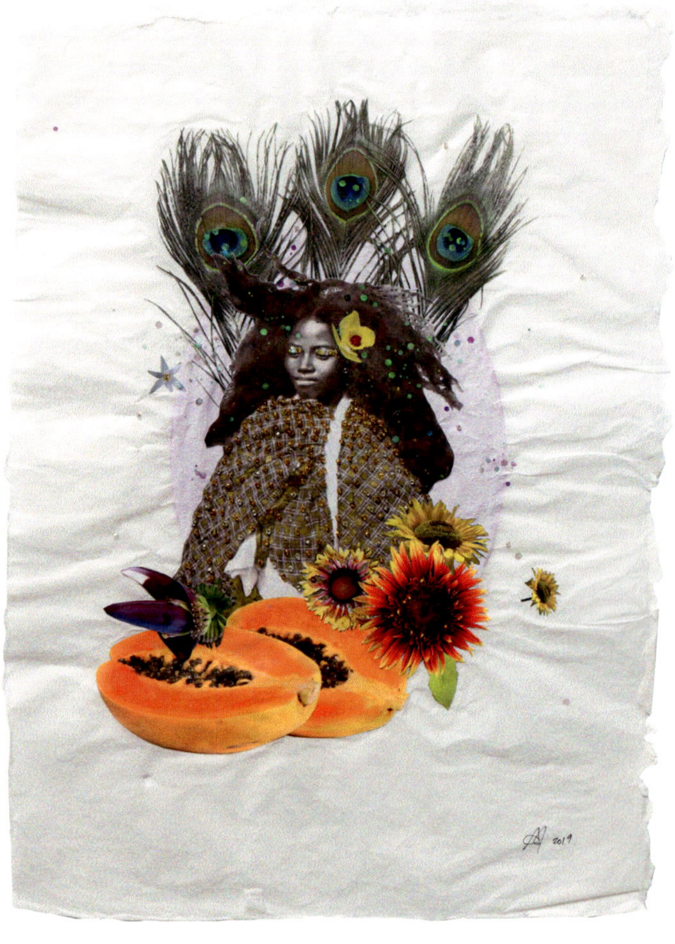

Sisters of Two Waters II, 2019
Collage, glitter, and beads on handmade
birthing cloth paper
17½ × 11½ in.

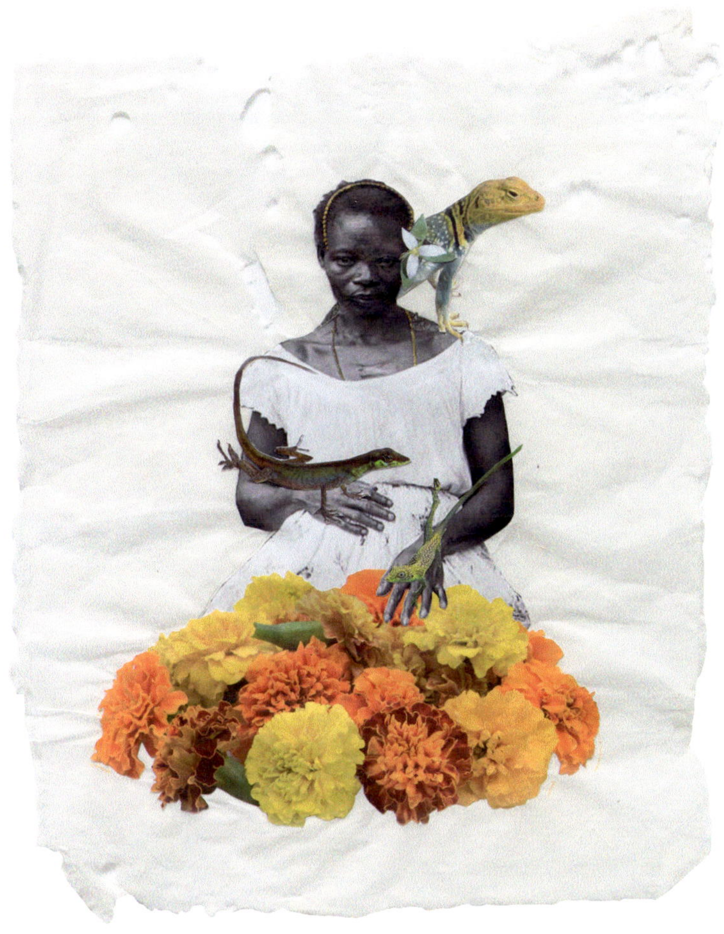

Untitled XII, 2018
Collage and watercolor on handmade
paper from birthing clothes and red
raspberry tea
12 × 9 in.

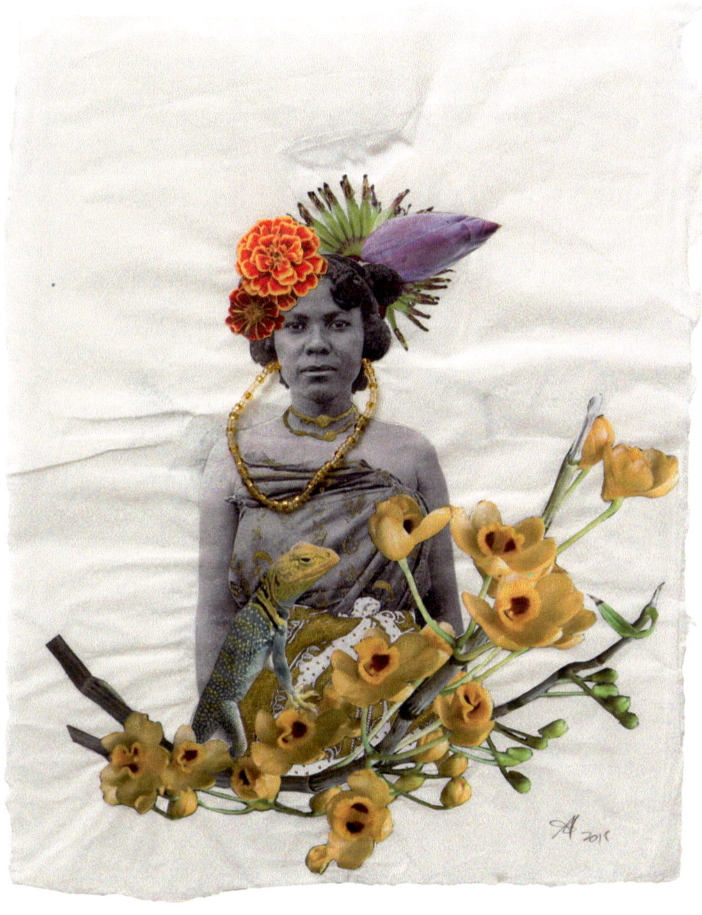

Untitled, 2018
Collage, glitter, and beads on handmade
birthing cloth paper
12 × 9 in.

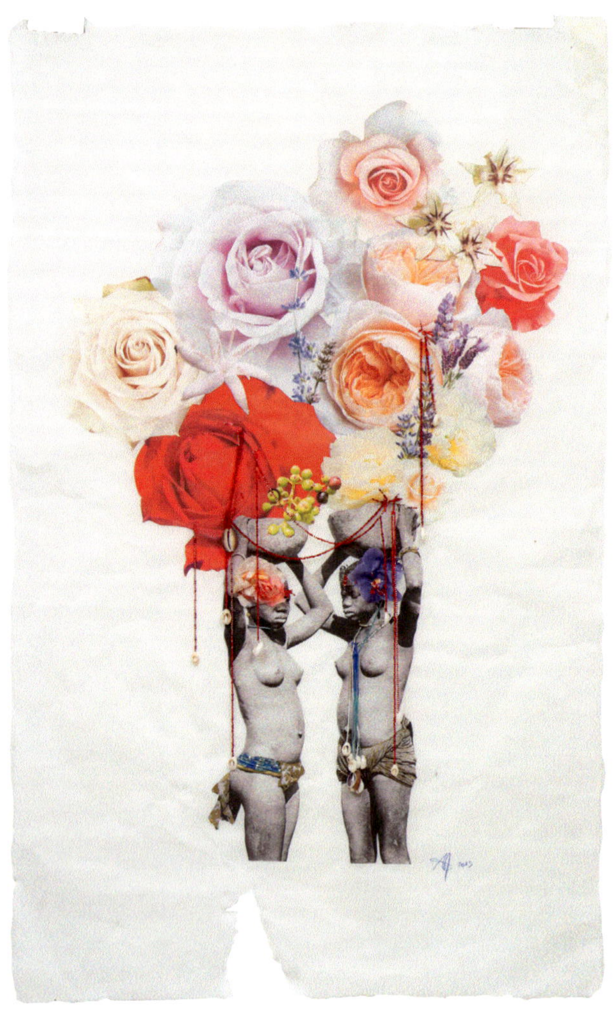

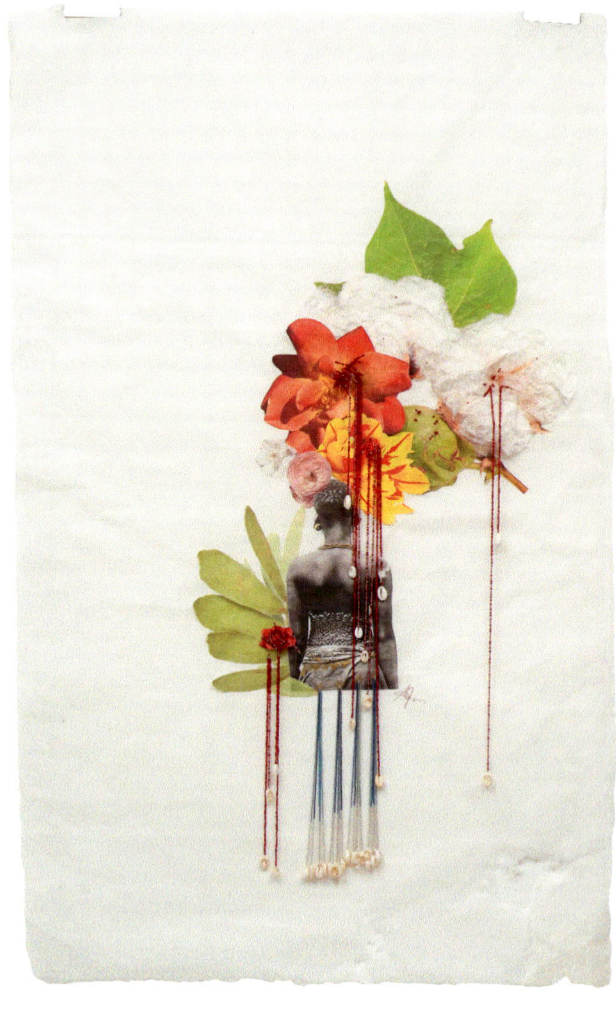

The Load is Heavy, and My Back is
Tired II, 2023
Collage, gold ink, pins, and beads
on paper handmade from traditional
birthing cloth
50 × 30 × 2 in.

The Load is Heavy, and My Back is
Tired I, 2023
Collage, gold ink, pins, and beads
on paper handmade from traditional
birthing cloth
50 × 30 × 2 in.

The Load is Heavy, and My Back is
Tired IV, 2023
Collage, gold ink, pins, and beads
on paper handmade from traditional
birthing cloth
50 × 30 × 2 in.

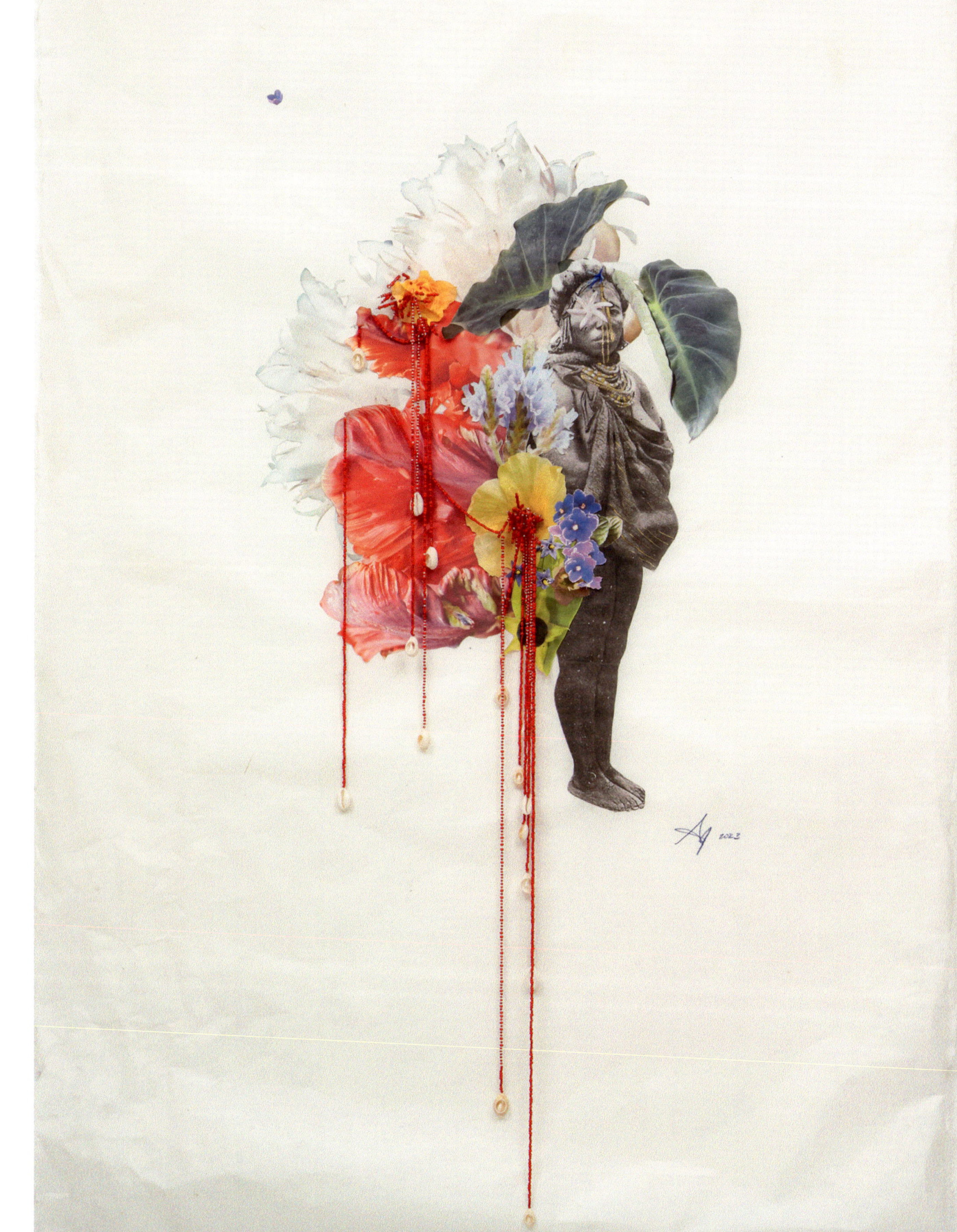

Blueprint, I, 2016
Embossed watercolor paper
22 × 15½ in.

Blueprint, II, 2016
Embossed watercolor paper
22 × 15½ in.

opposite

Blueprint, III, 2016
Embossed watercolor paper
22 × 15½ in.

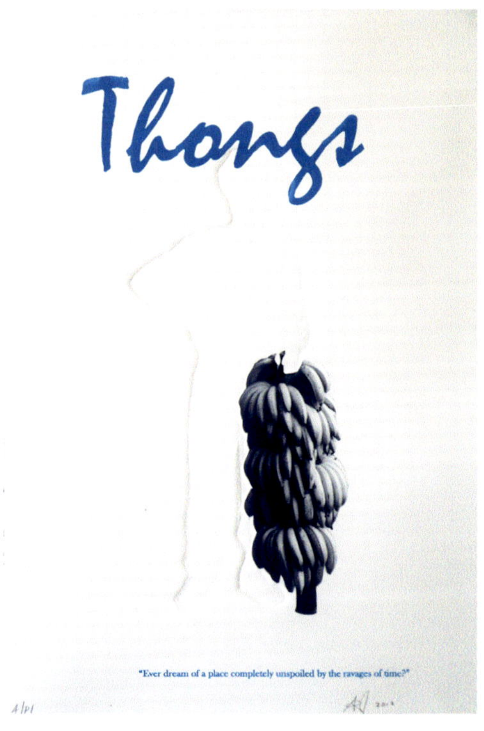

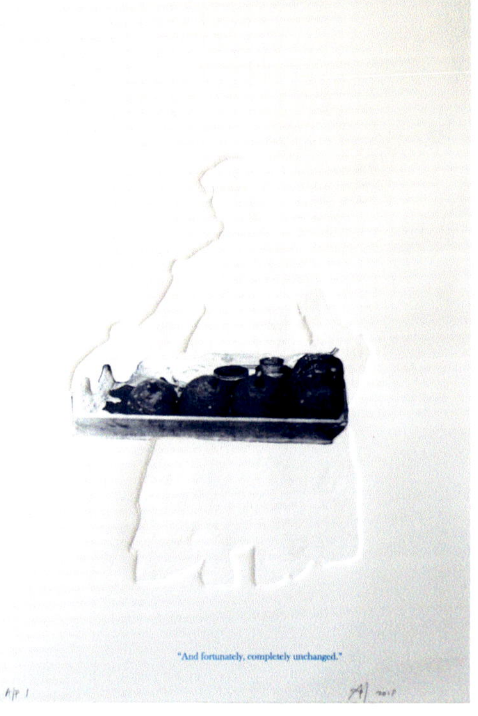

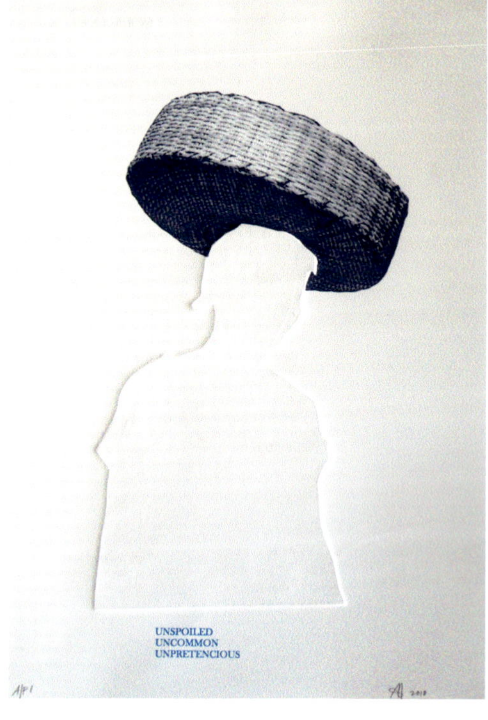

"Ever dream of a place completely unspoiled by the ravages of time?", from the portfolio **Thongs: Experience the Luxury Included**, 2010
Color offset lithograph with embossing on paper
22⅛ × 15 in.

"And fortunately, completely unchanged.", from the portfolio **Thongs: Experience the Luxury Included**, 2010
Color offset lithograph with embossing on paper
22⅛ × 15 in.

Unspoiled, Uncommon, Unpretentious, from the portfolio **Thongs: Experience the Luxury Included**, 2010
Color offset lithograph with embossing on paper
22⅛ × 15 in.

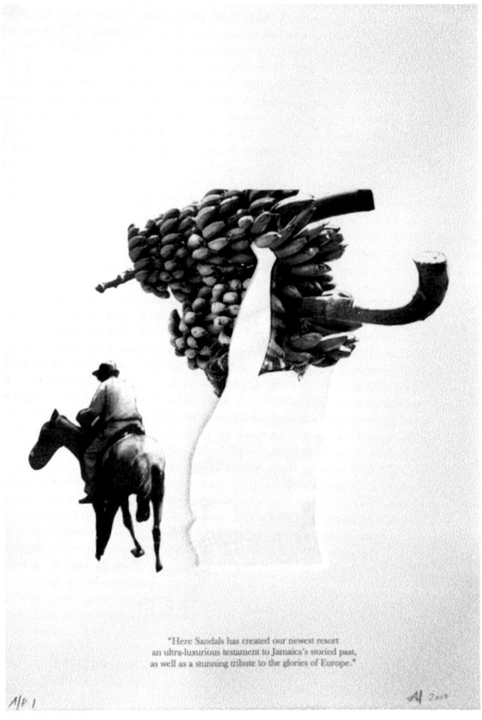

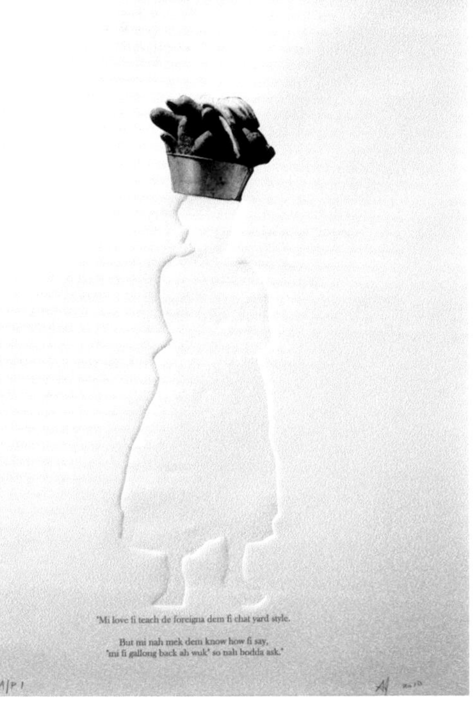

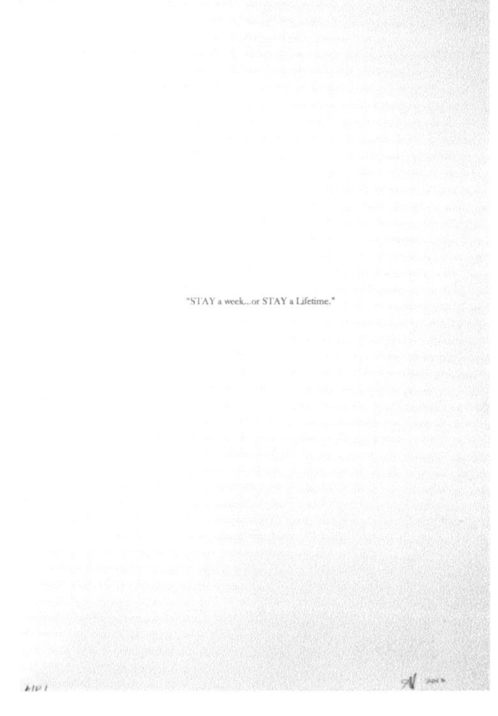

"Here Sandals has created our newest resort and ultra-luxurious testament to Jamaica's storied past, as well as a stunning tribute to the glories of Europe", from the portfolio Thongs: Experience the Luxury Included, 2010
Color offset lithograph with embossing on paper
22⅛ × 15 in.

Mi Love Fi Teach de foreigna dem fi chat yard style, but mi nah mek dem know how fi say "mi fi gallong back ah wuk" so nah bodda, from the portfolio Thongs: Experience the Luxury Included, 2010
Color offset lithograph with embossing on paper
22⅛ × 15 in.

"Stay a week… or stay a lifetime.", from the portfolio Thongs: Experience the Luxury Included, 2010
Color offset lithograph with embossing on paper
22⅛ × 15 in.

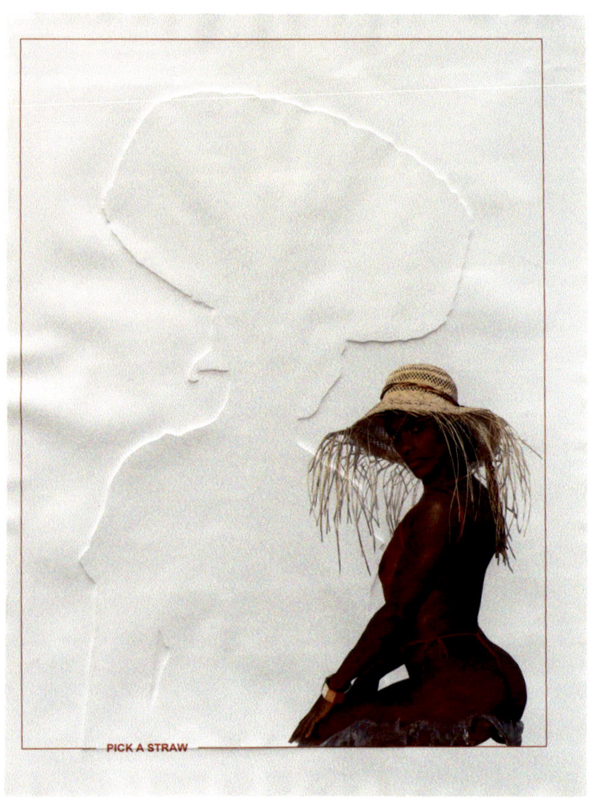

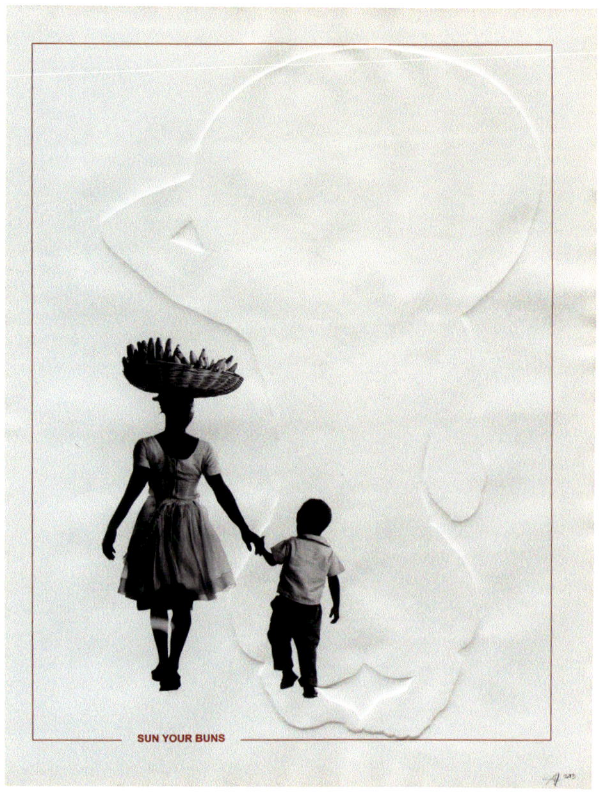

Pick a straw, 2013
From the series I wanna Be Loved
C-print, embossing, and archetypes
22 × 30 in.

Sun Your Buns, 2013
From the series I wanna Be Loved
C-print, embossing, and archetypes
22 × 30 in.

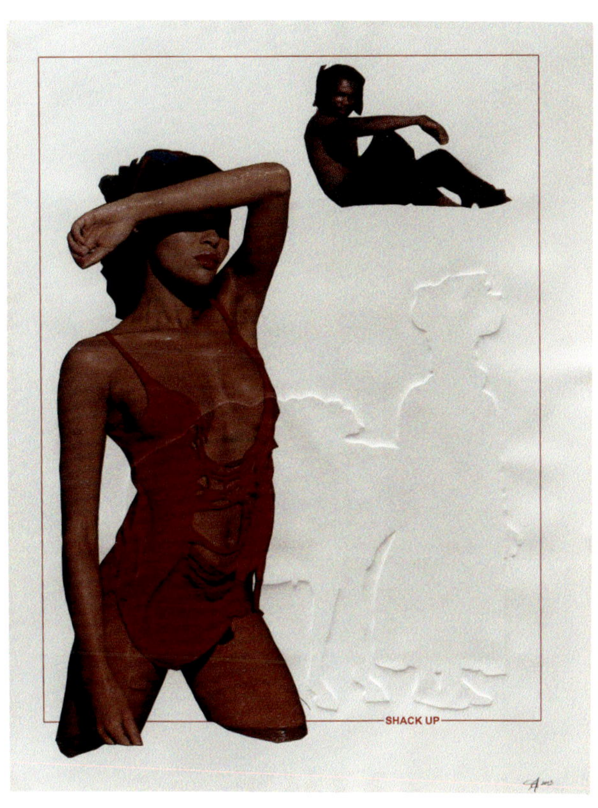

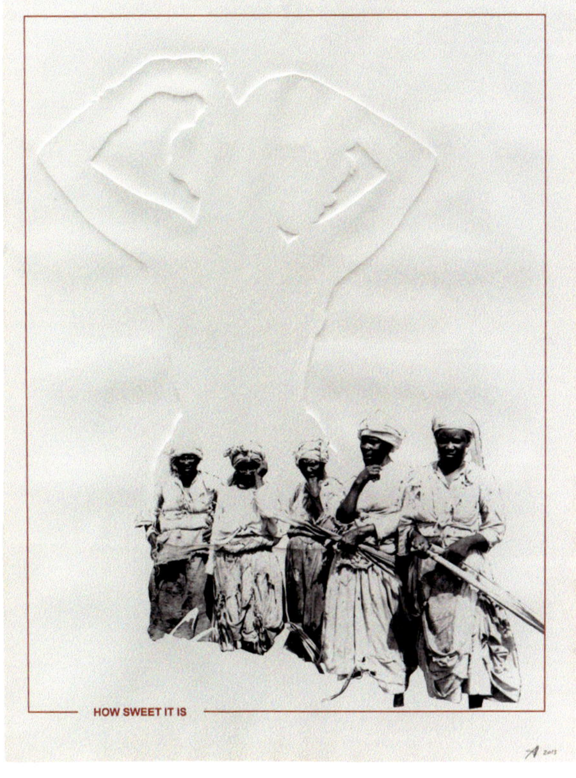

Shacking up, 2013
From the series I wanna Be Loved
C-print, embossing, and archetypes
22 × 30 in.

How Sweet it is, 2013
From the series I wanna Be Loved
C-print, embossing, and archetypes
22 × 30 in.

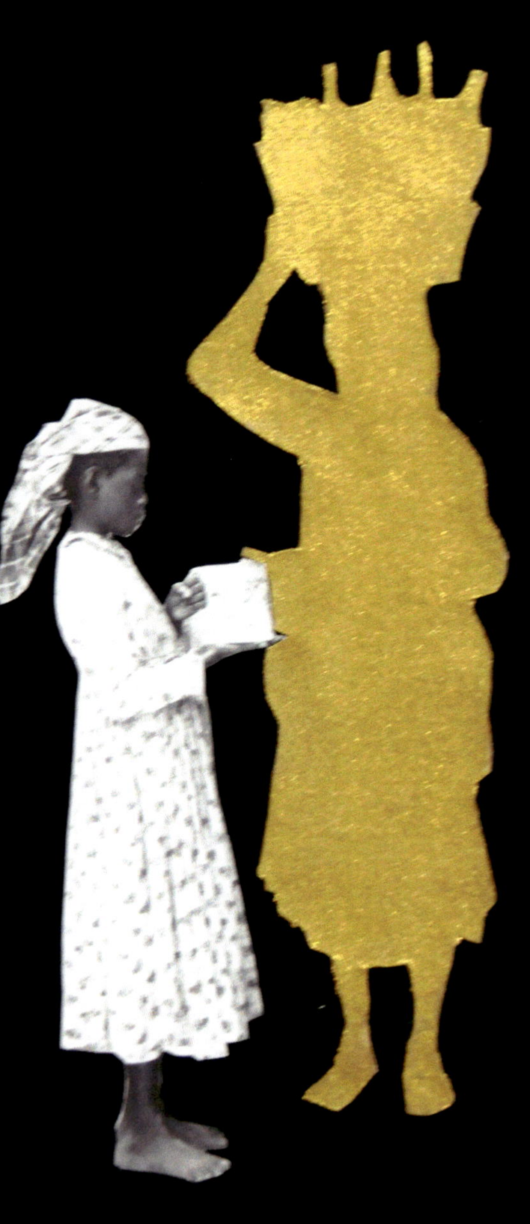

left

Crowning IV, 2014
Collage and ink
14 × 11 in.

opposite

Crowning V, 2014
Collage, ink, and color pencil
14 × 11 in.

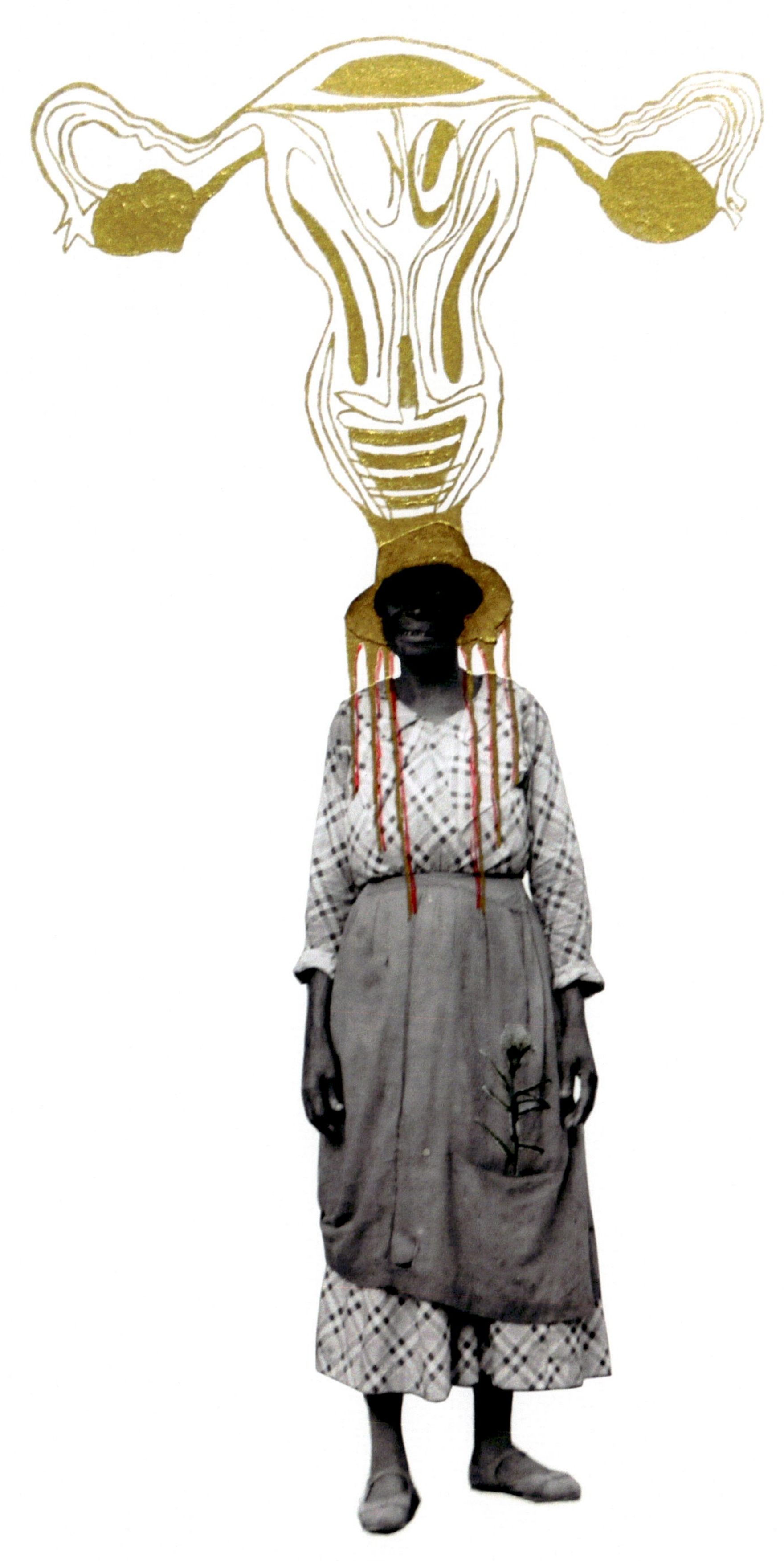

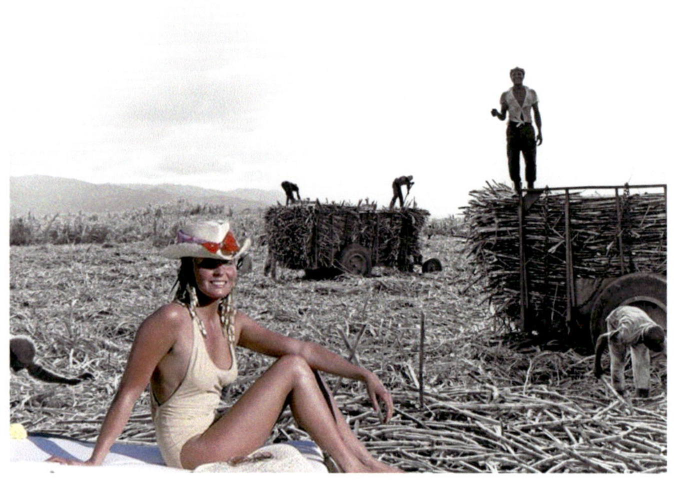

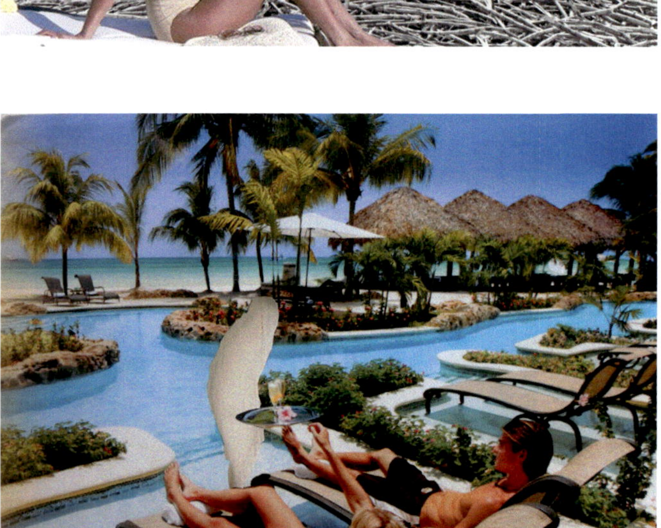

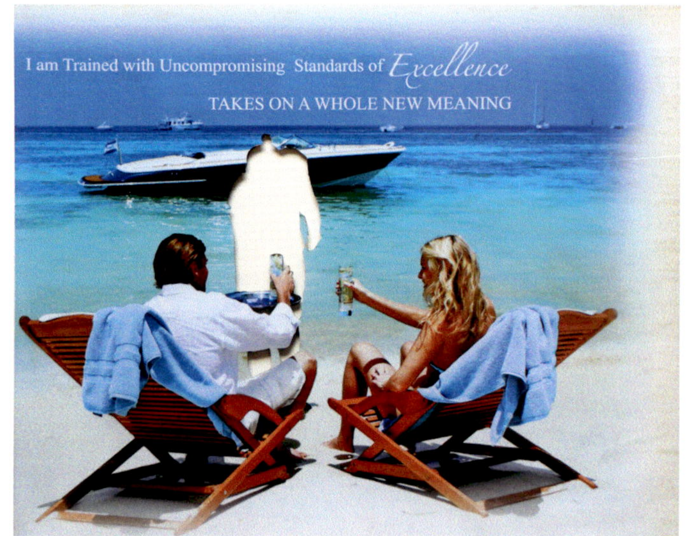

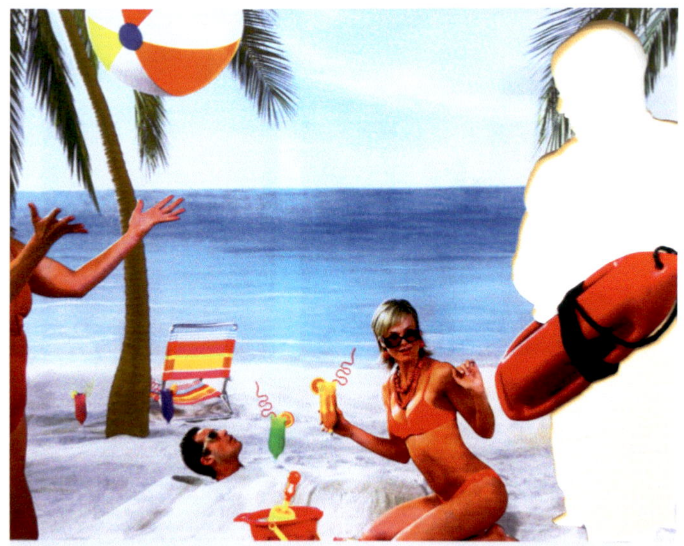

clockwise from top left

Boopsie, 2008
Digital collage
12 × 10 in.

Dexter is Trained With
Uncompromising Standard of
Excellence, 2008
Photo cutout
15¾ × 13 in.

Your Tropical Indulgence
Awaits, 2008
Photo cutout
15 × 13 in.

Dexter offers a Whole New
Definition of Sublime, 2008
Photo cutout
15¾ × 13 in.

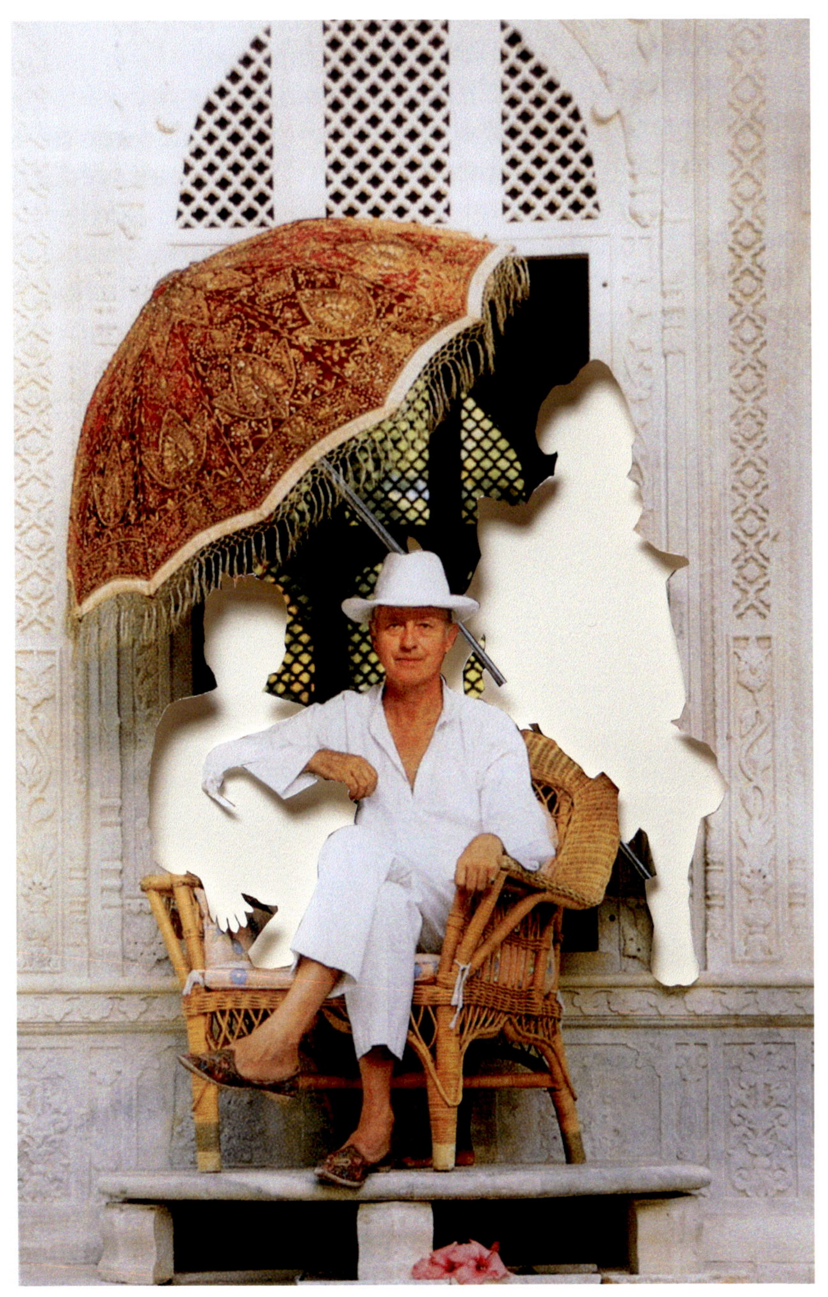

Royal Cut, 2008
Photo cutout
20 × 15 in.

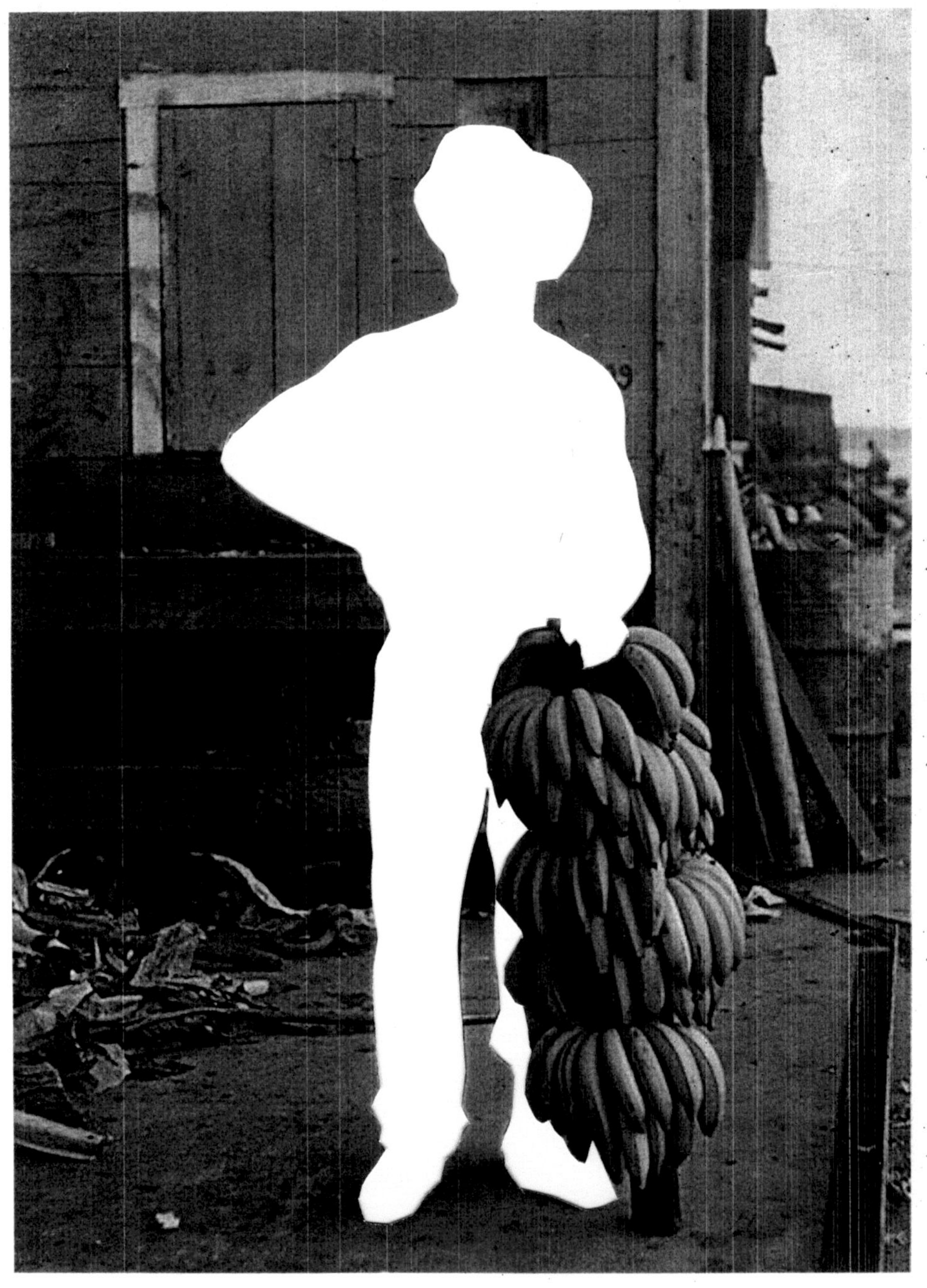

above

Daylight Cum An' Mi Waan Guh Home, 2007
Photo cutout
15 × 13½ in.

opposite; clockwise from top left

All Fruits Ripe, 2007
Photo cutout
15½ × 11½ in.

Untitled, 2008
Photo cutout
17¼ × 12¼ in.

'Im Hole 'Im Canher, 2007
Photo cutout with Plexi frame
24 × 17 in.

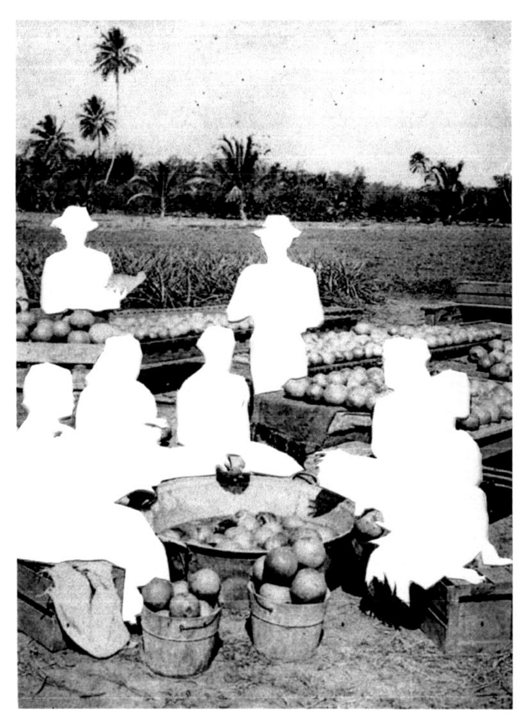

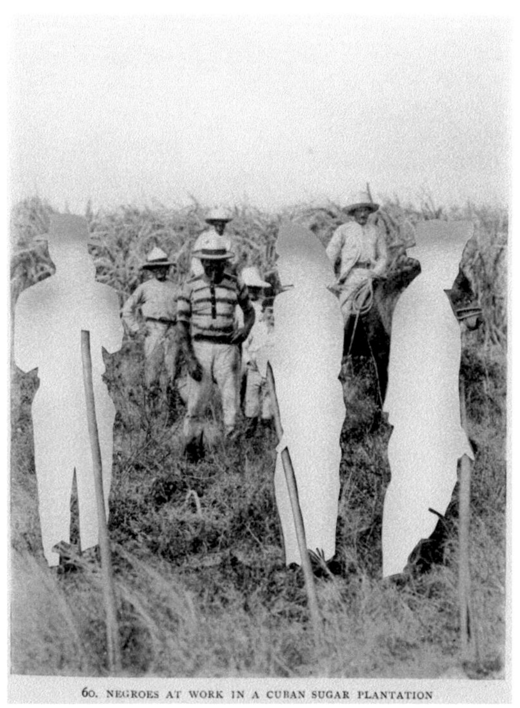

60. NEGROES AT WORK IN A CUBAN SUGAR PLANTATION

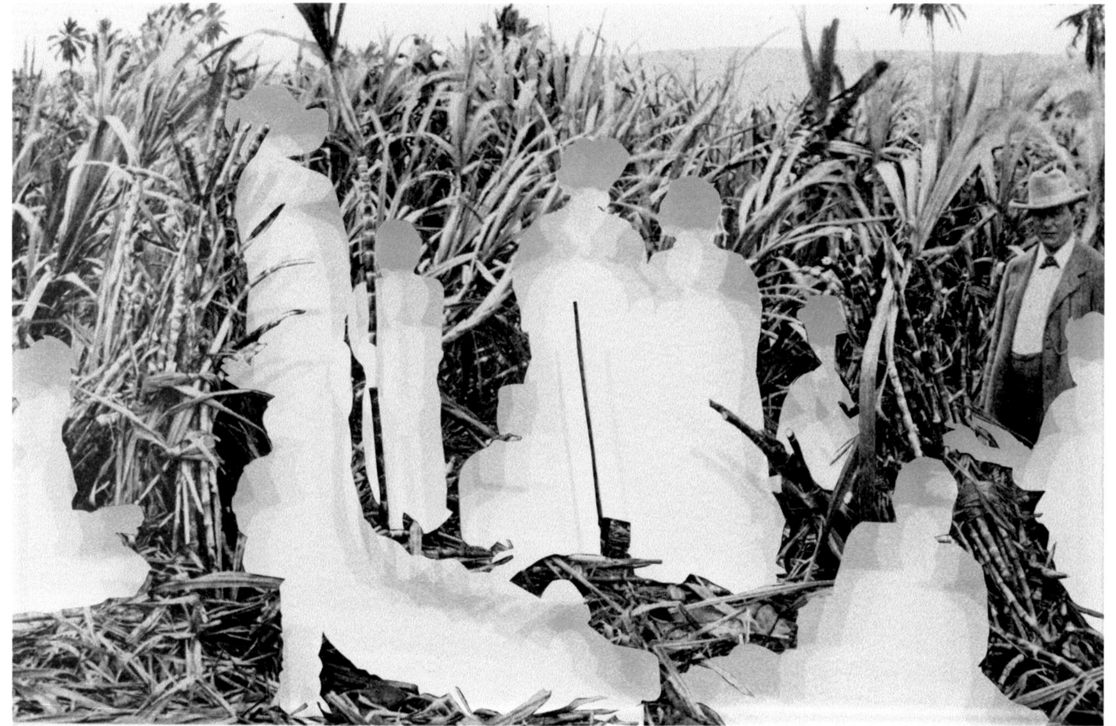

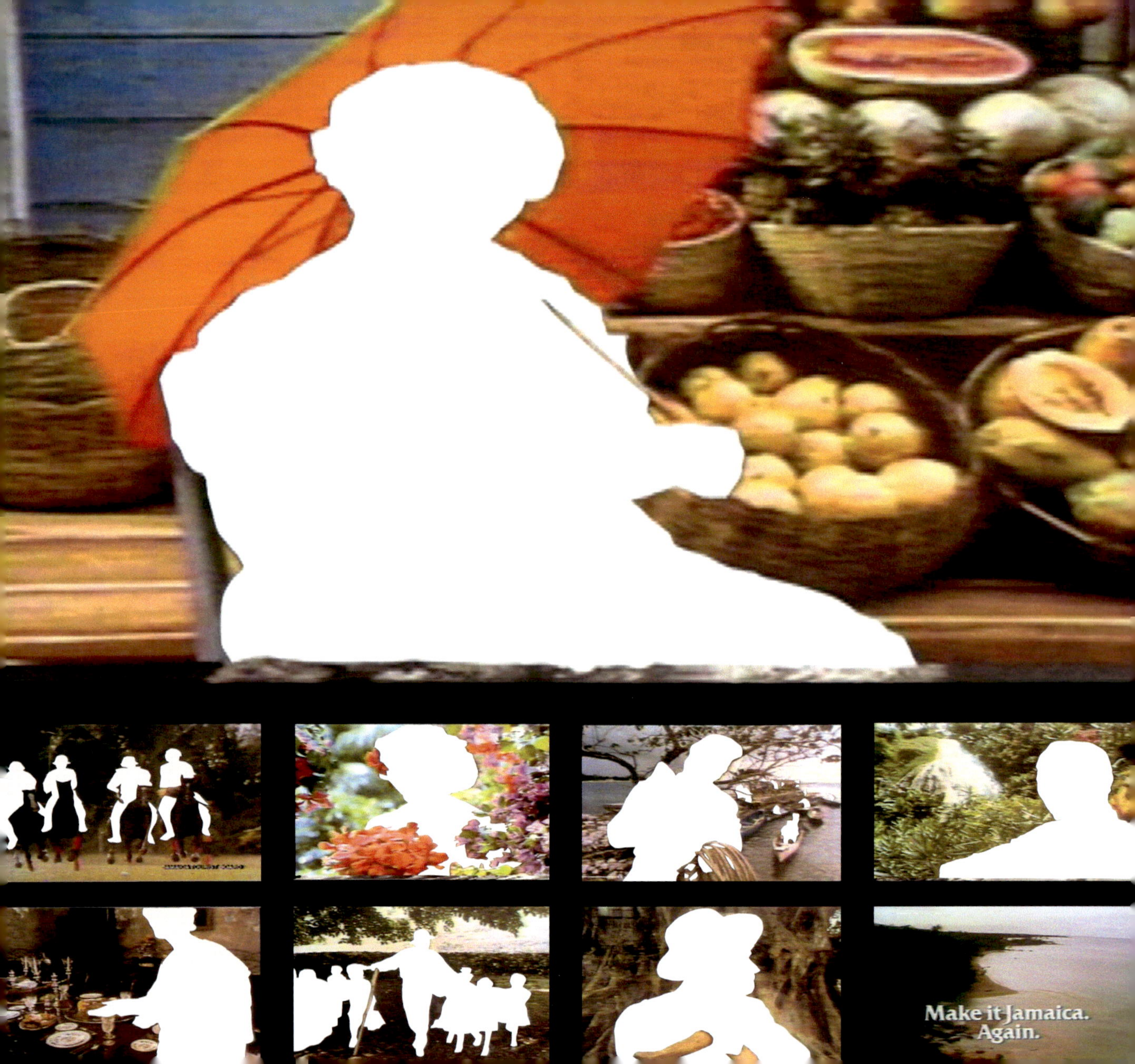

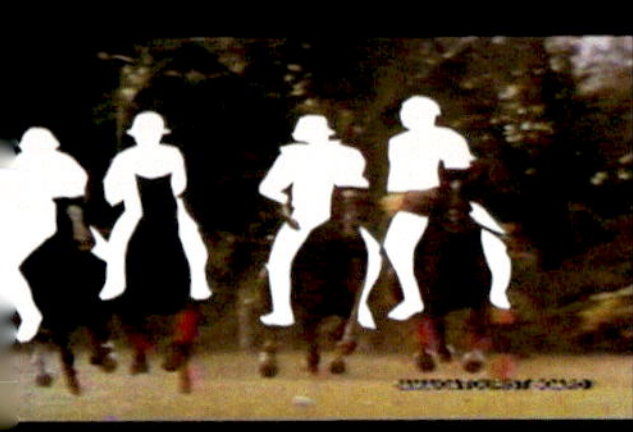
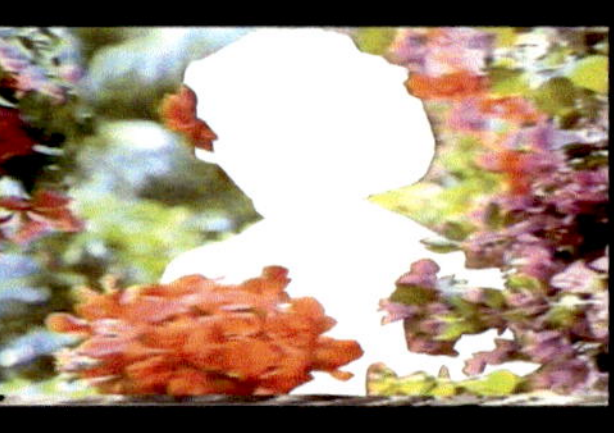
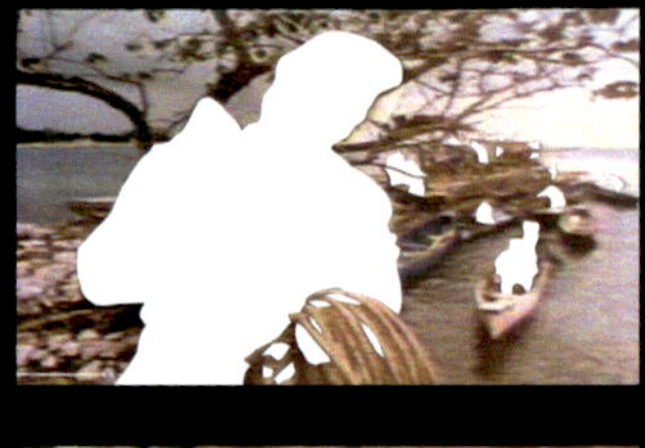
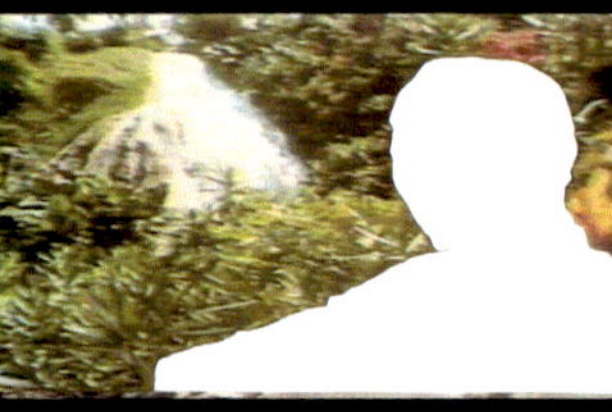
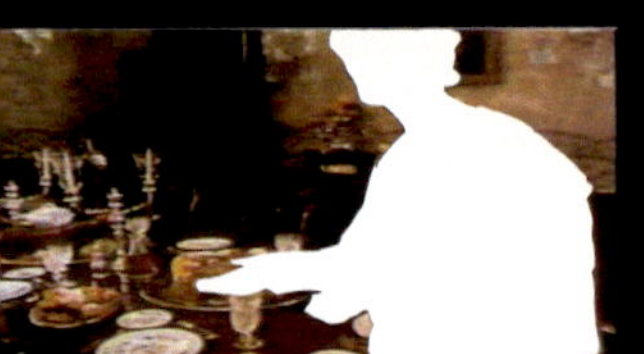
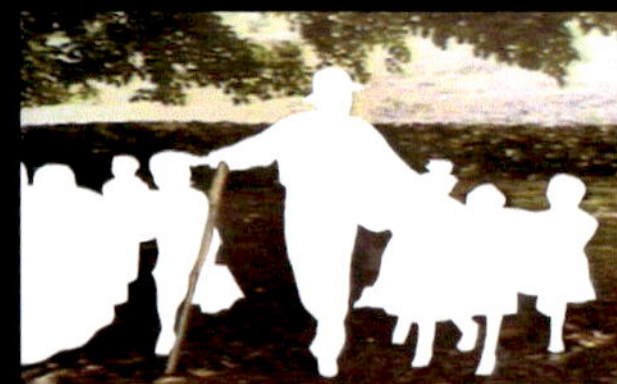
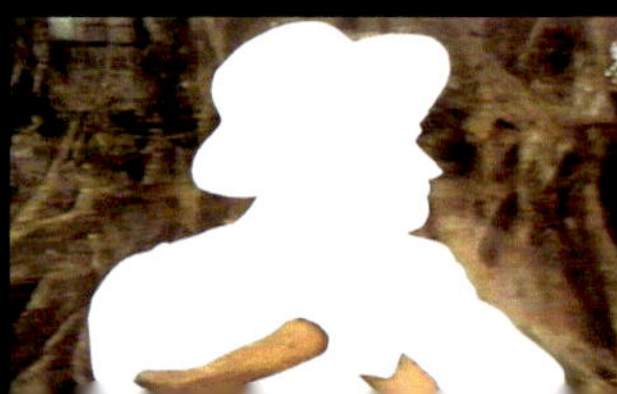
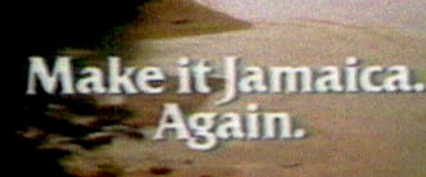
Make it Jamaica.
Again.

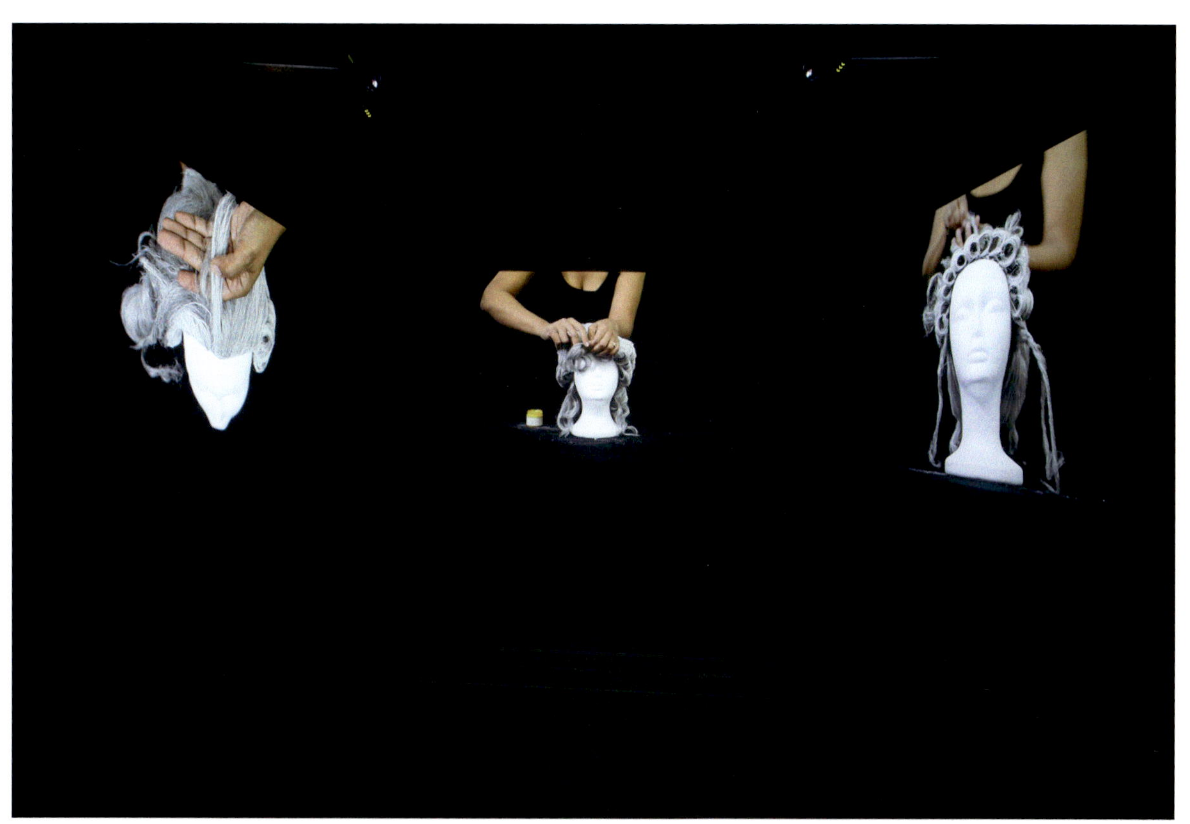

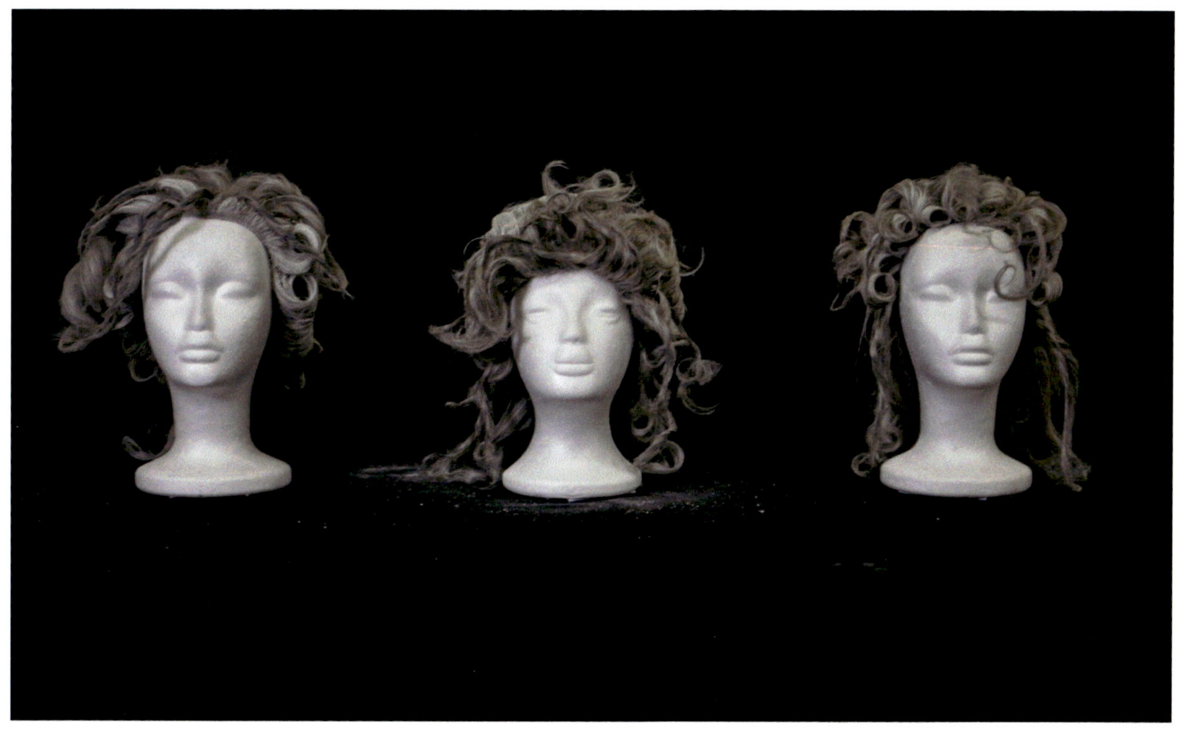

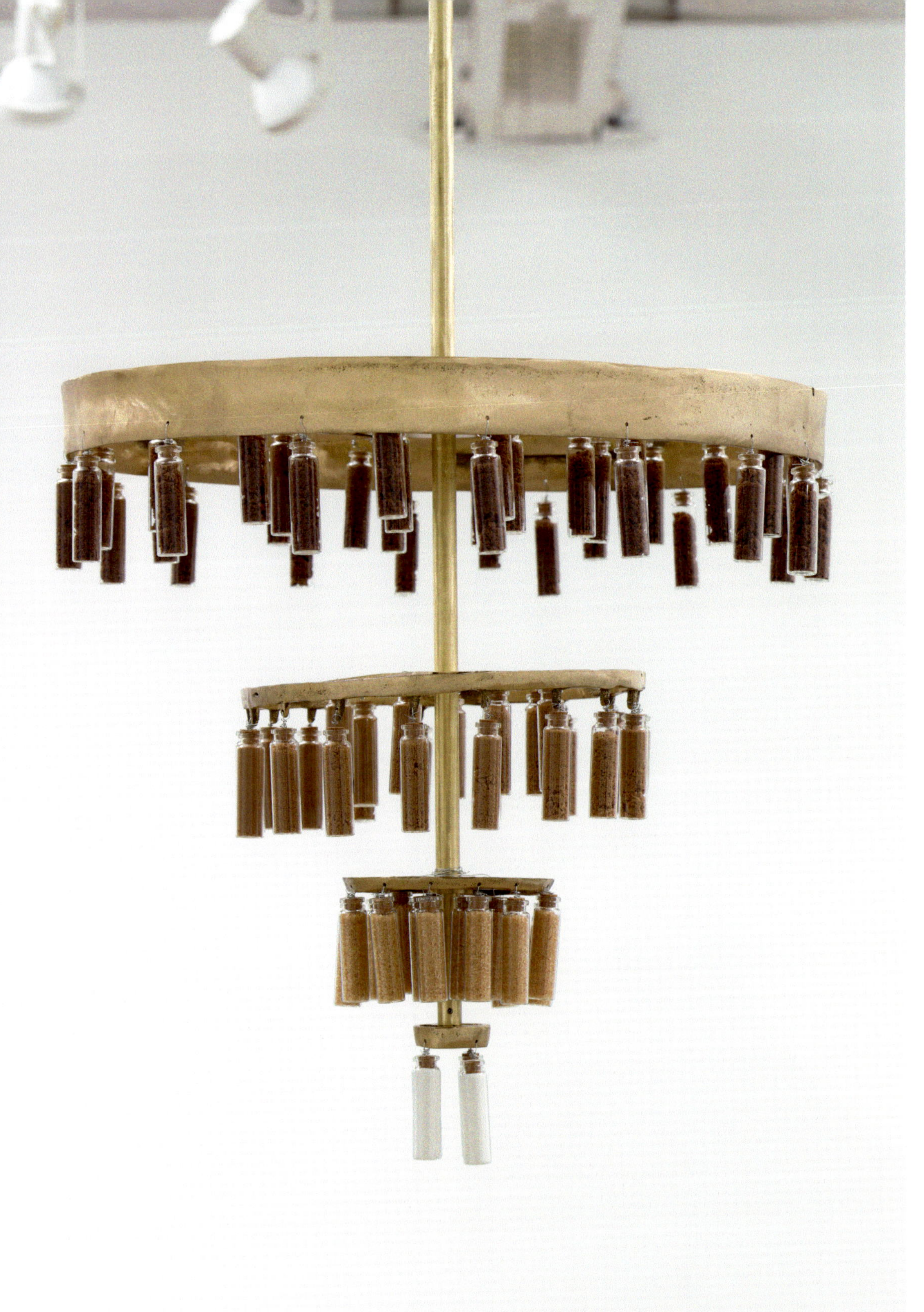

Endosymbiotic Theory, 2019
Brass, glass, and sugar
56 × 23 in.

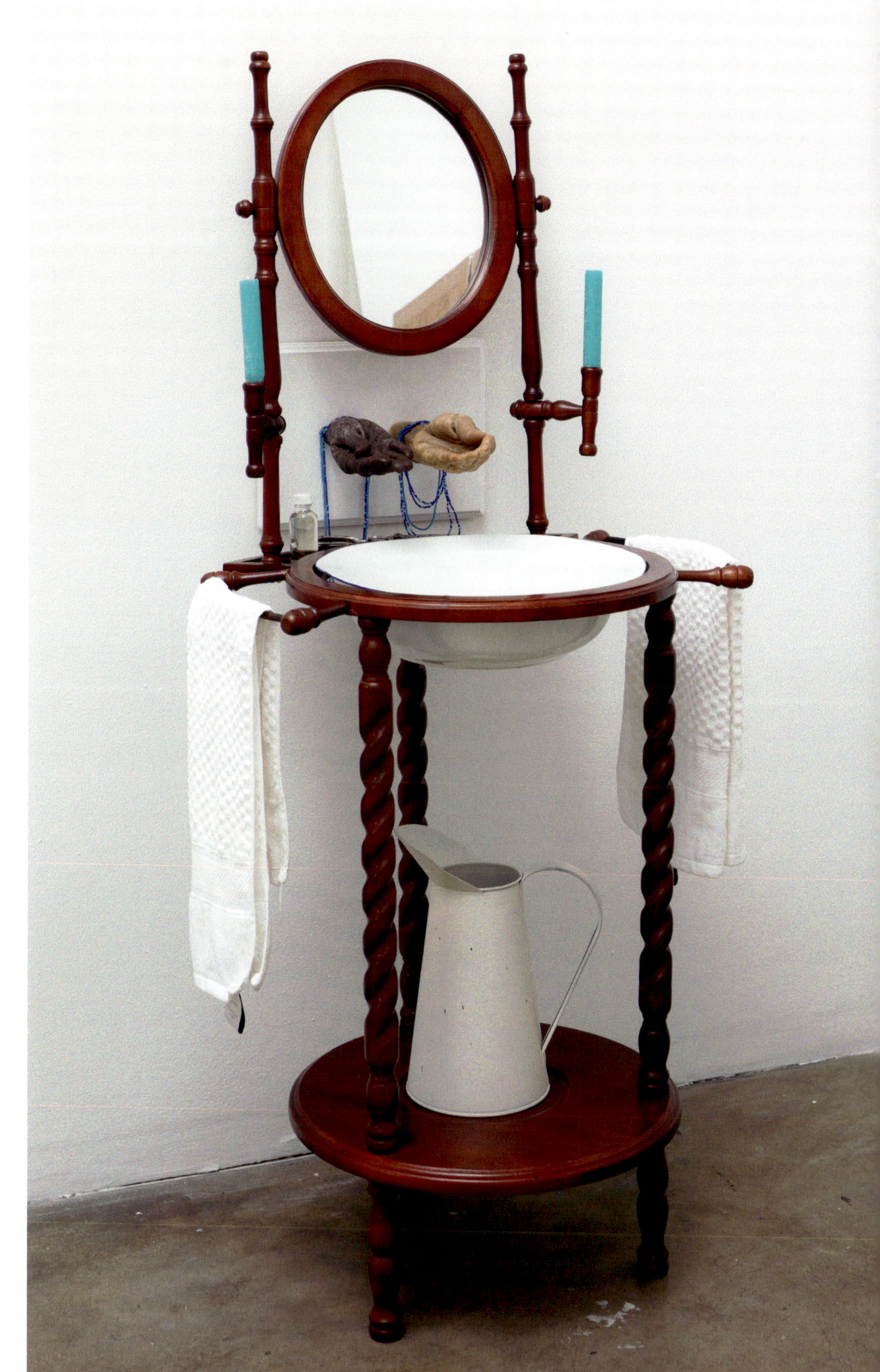

Pure, 2017
Black soap, dry sink, towels, candles,
scissors, pitcher, bottle, and jewelry
48 × 24 × 20 in.

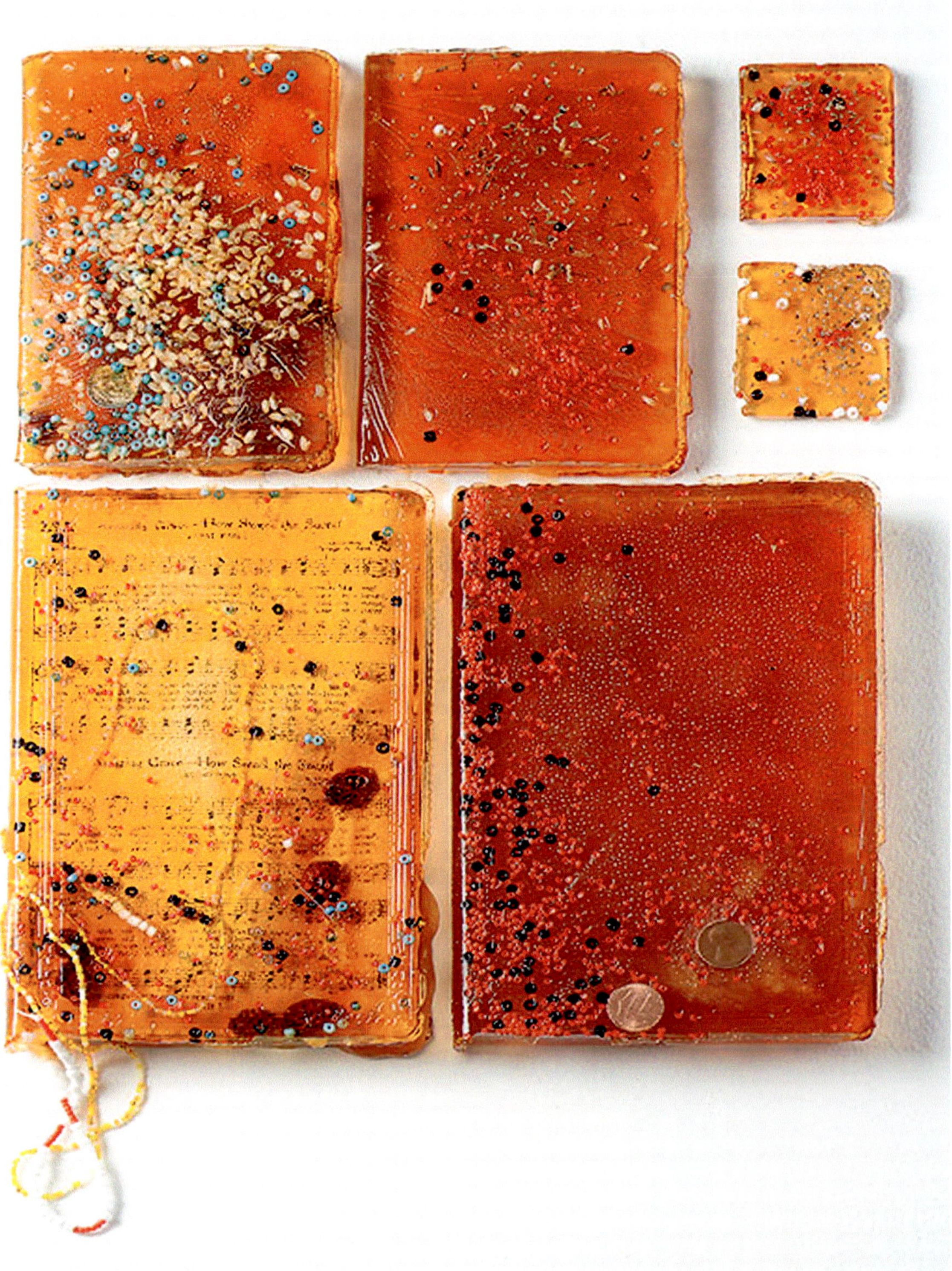

     Between Too Late & Too Early

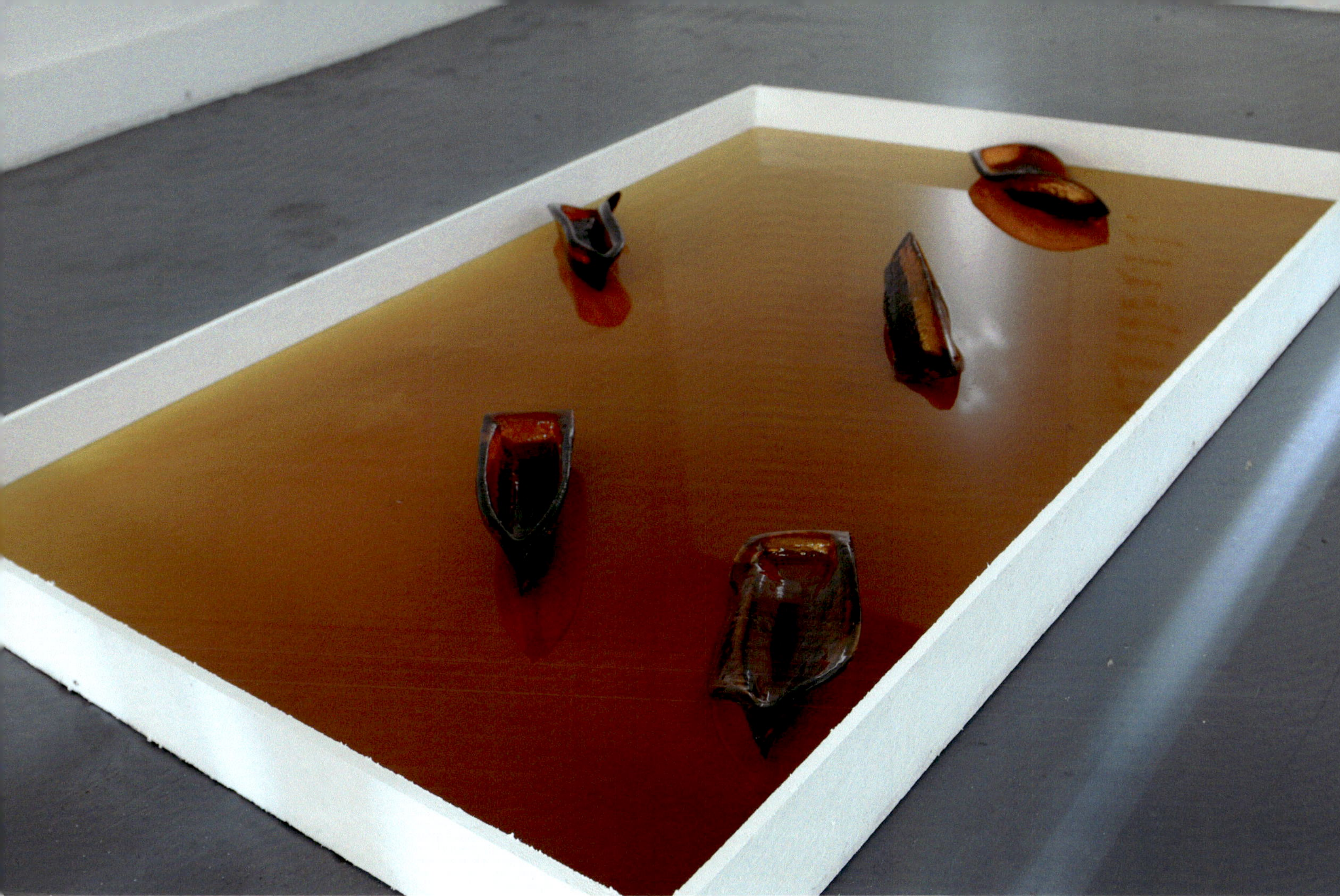

Proverbs, 12:22, 2018
Sugar, beads, rice, herbs, spices,
and paper
Site-specific installation
Variable dimensions

Bato Disik, 2013
Sugar, resin, saltwater
Site-specific installation
Variable dimensions

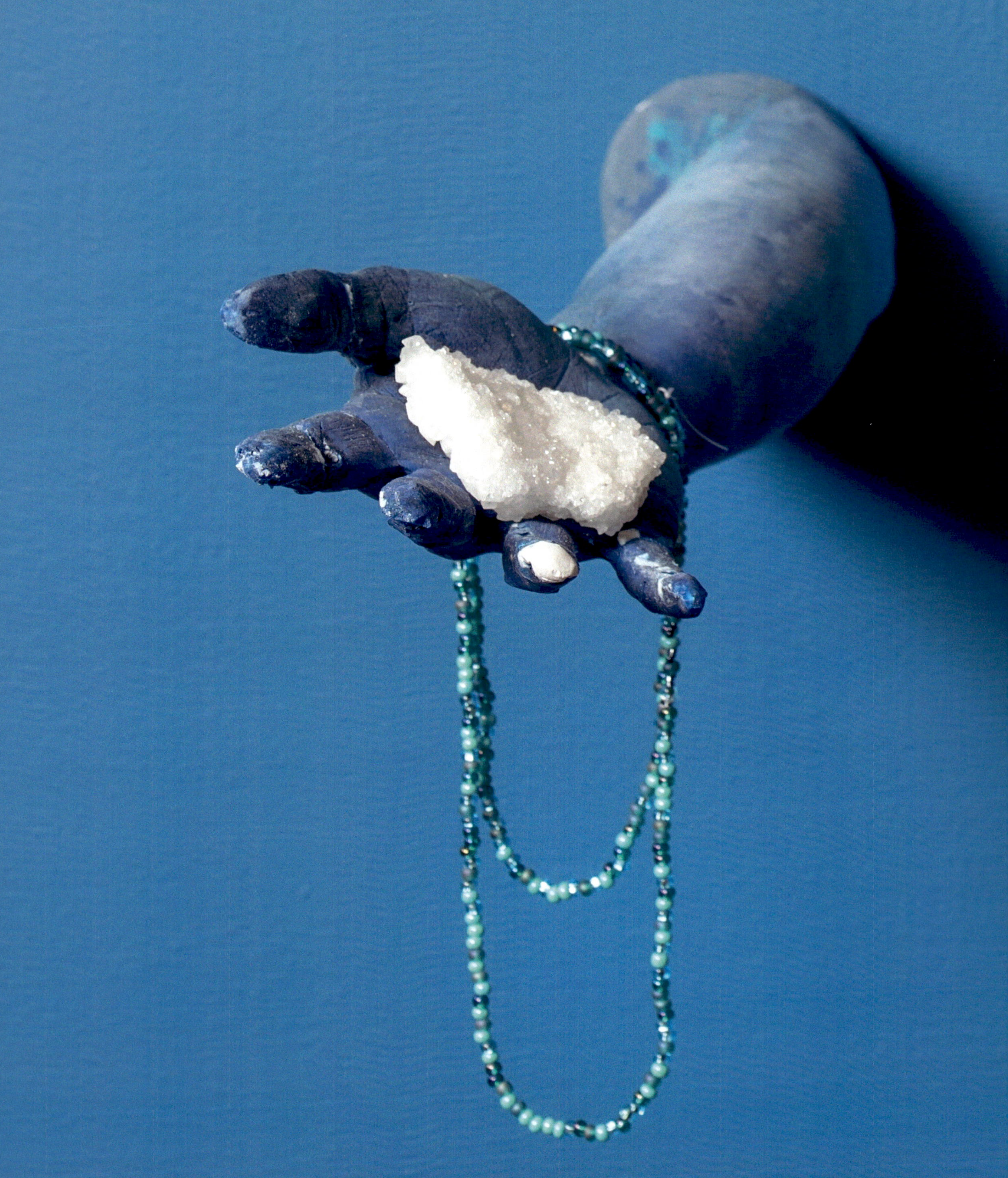

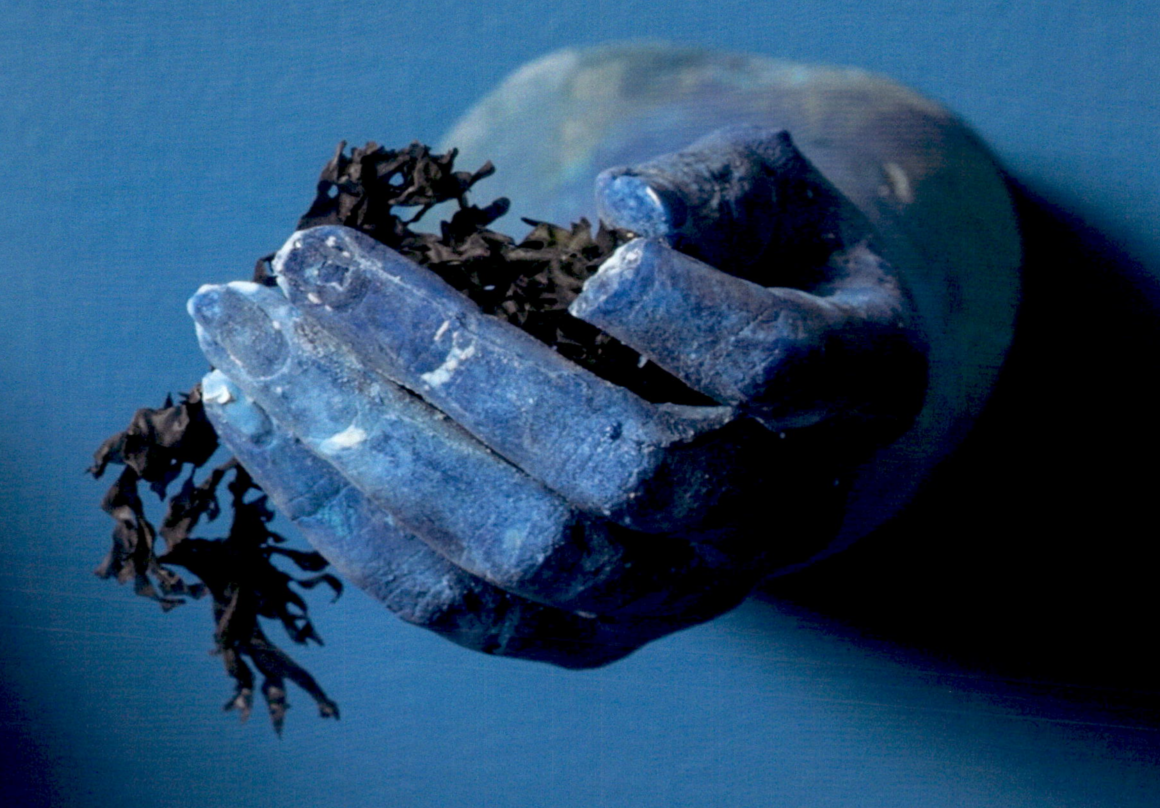

Commission & Installation Views

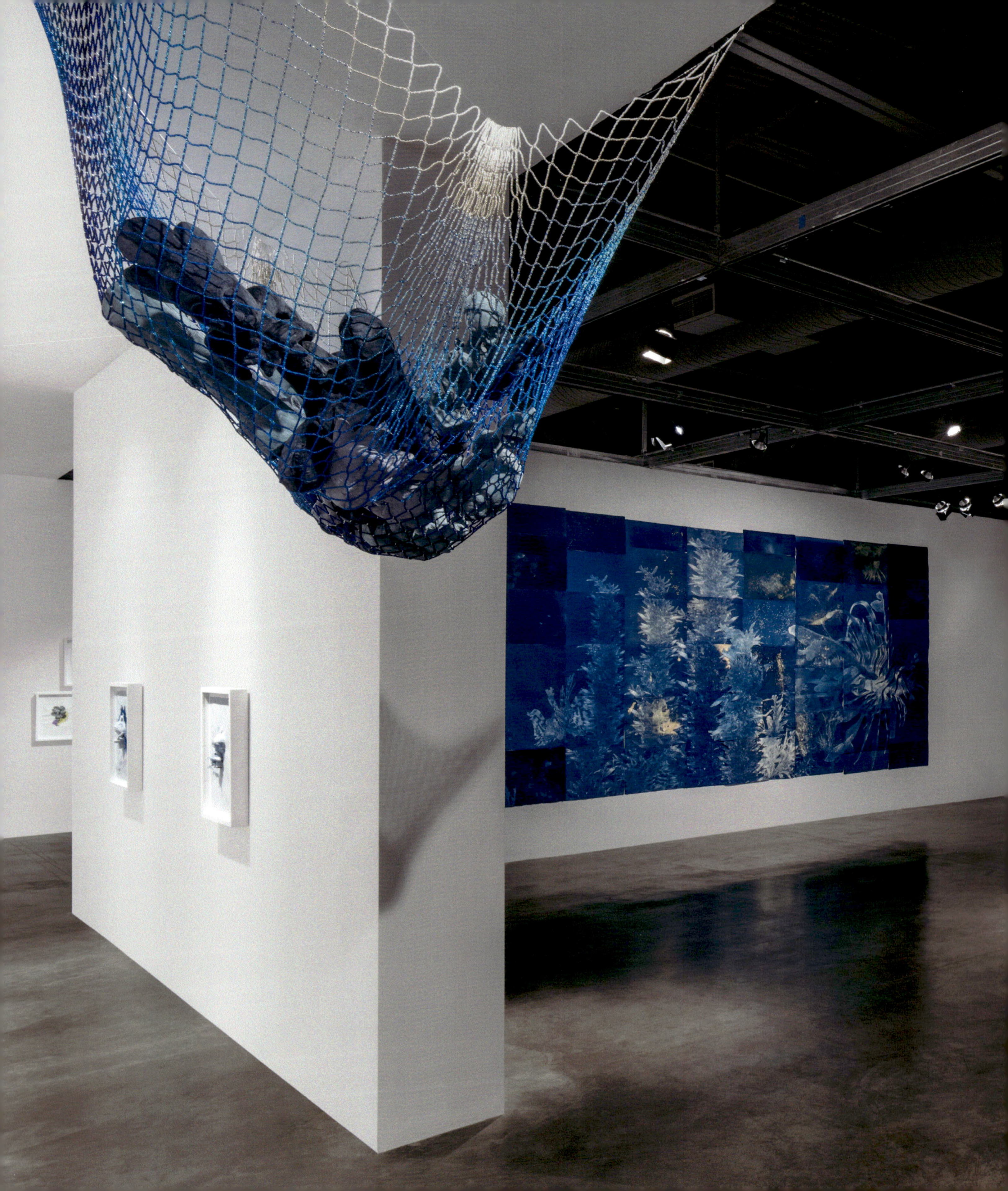

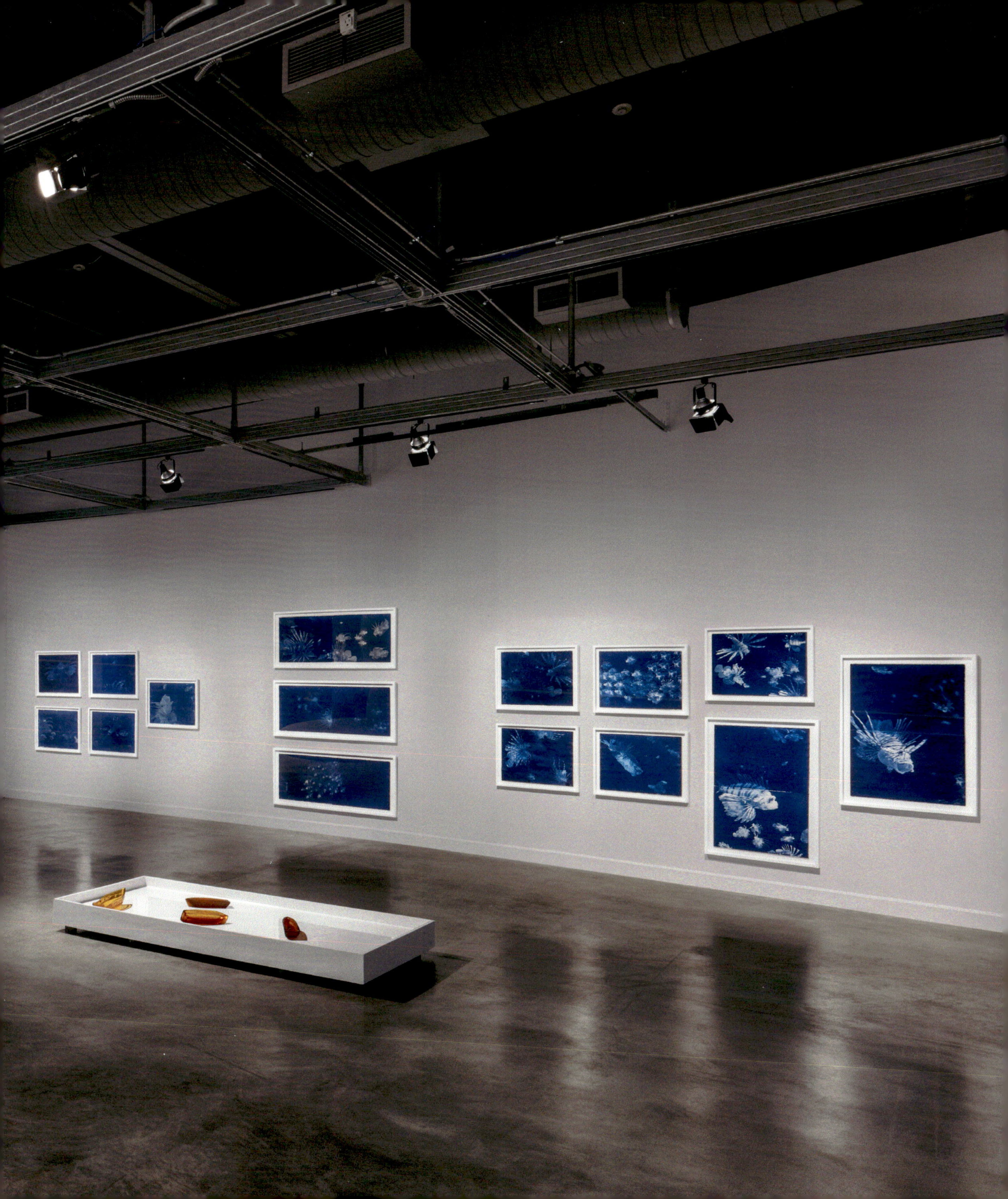

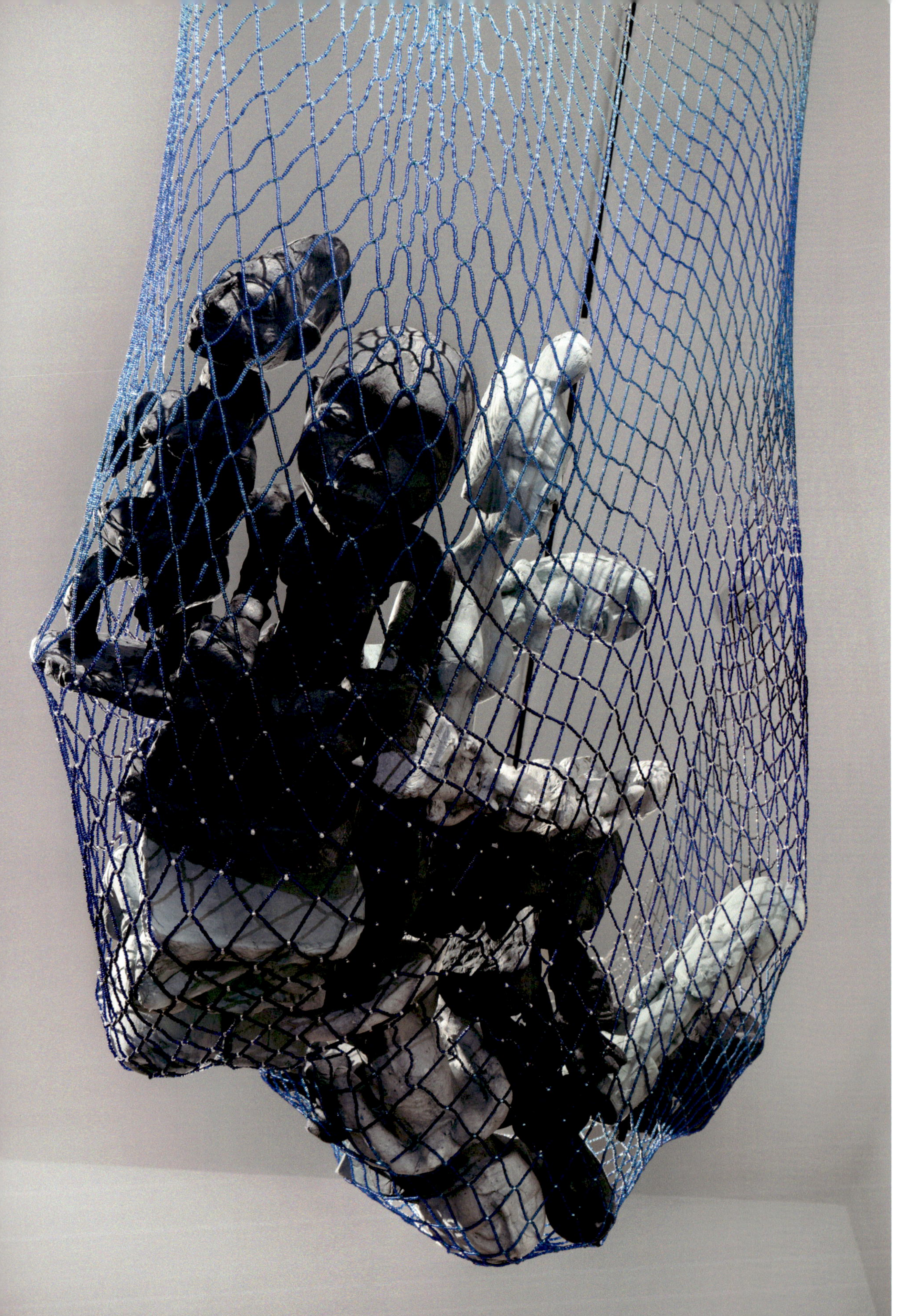

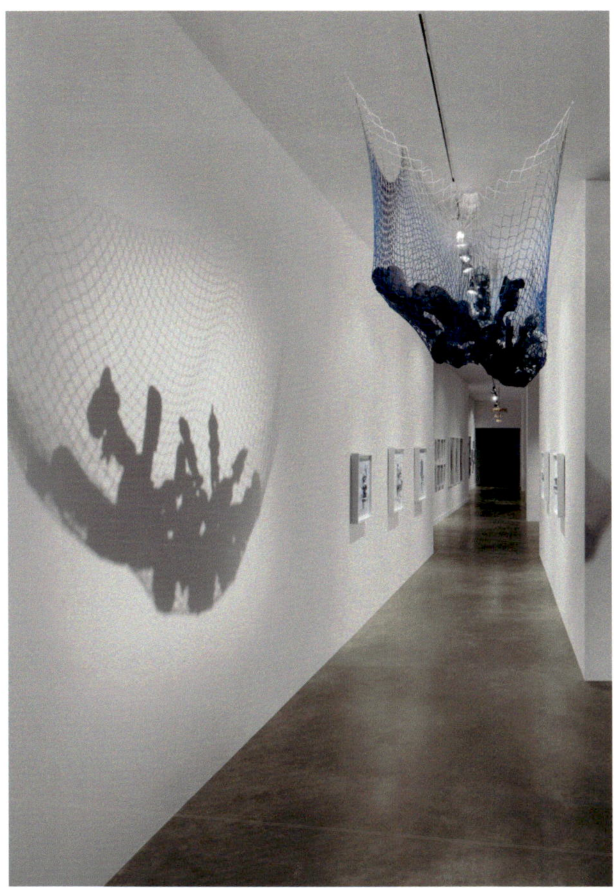

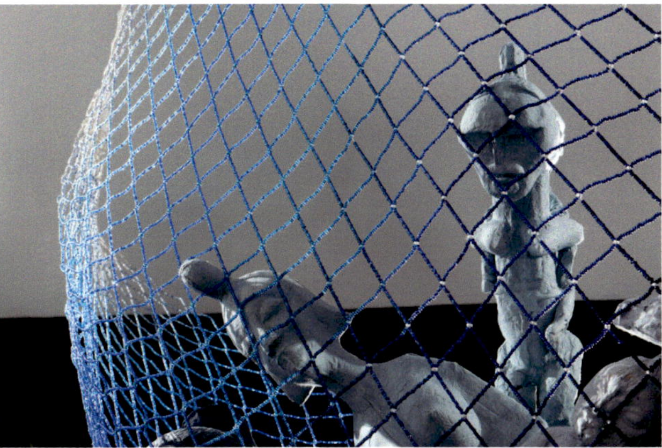

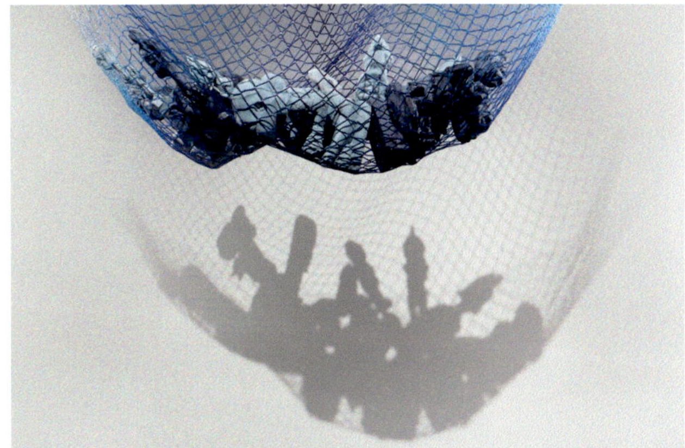

previous spread

Between Too Late & Too Early, 2024.
Installation view

this spread and previous (detail)

"...there is no me. There is I and I, which
is you too. You and I intertwined.", 2024.
17 pulped paper sculptures, 115 1/2 x 104 in.
Installation view

overleaf

The Wailing Room, 2024.
Sugar, sound. Site-specific installation.
Installation view

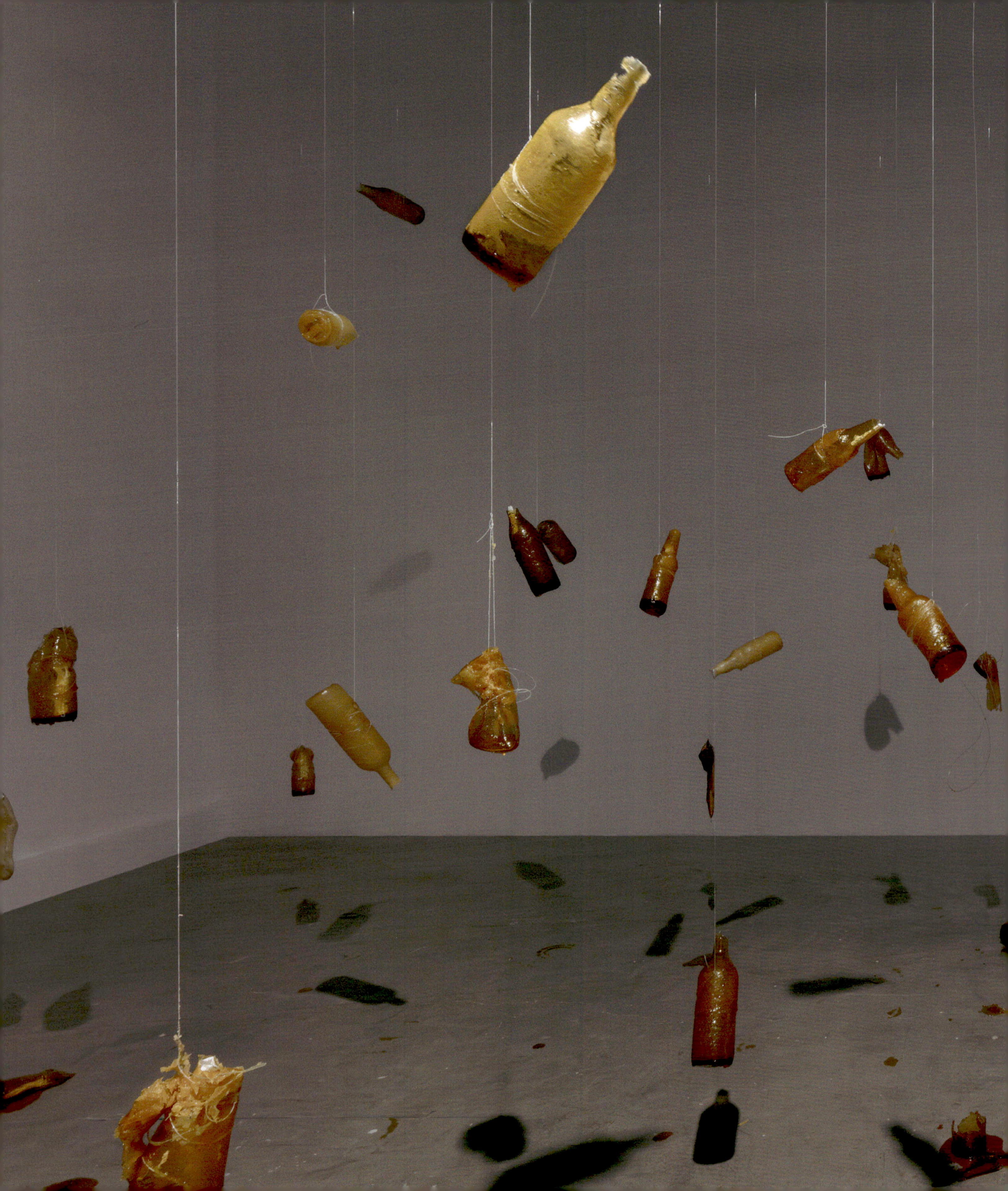

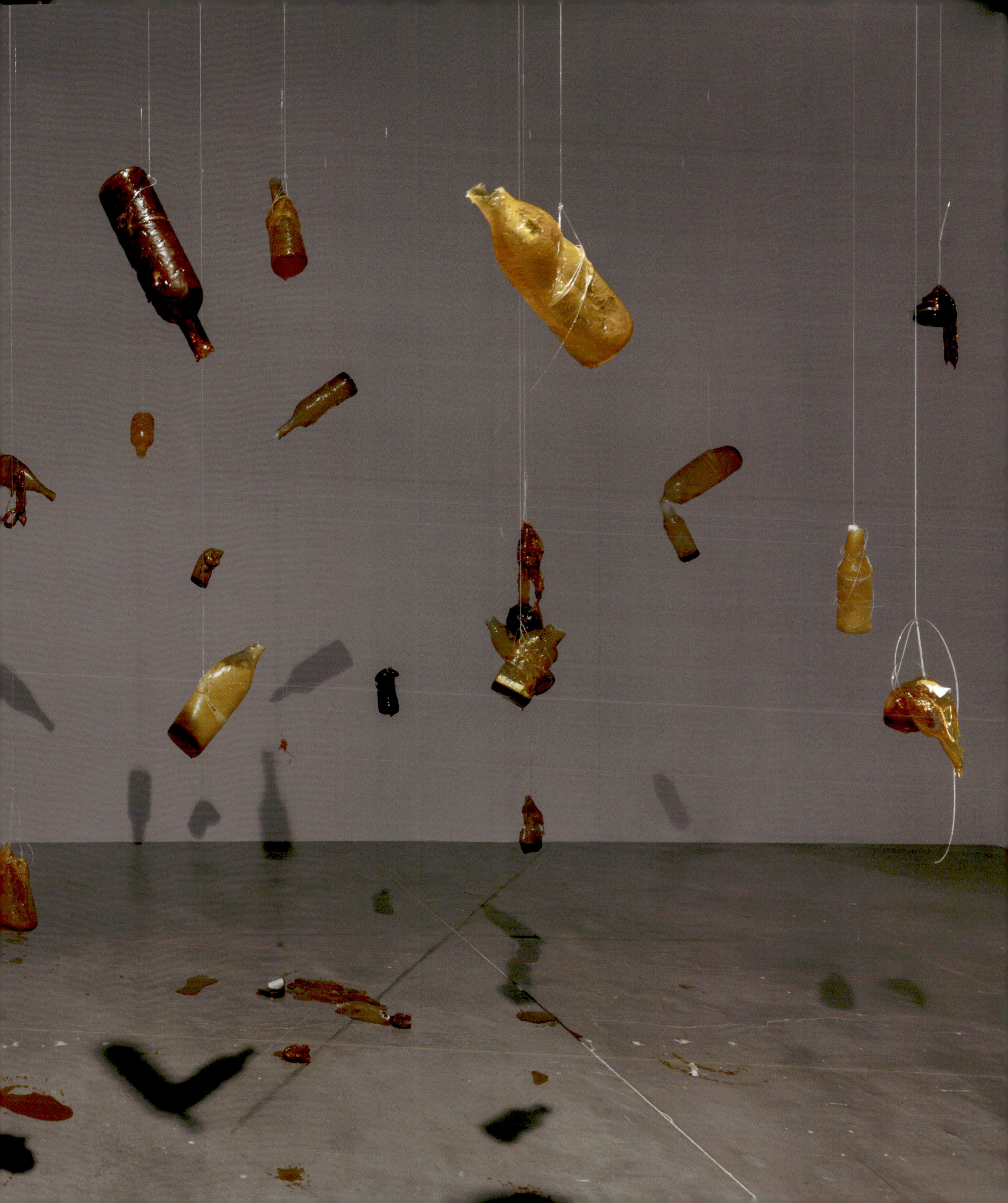

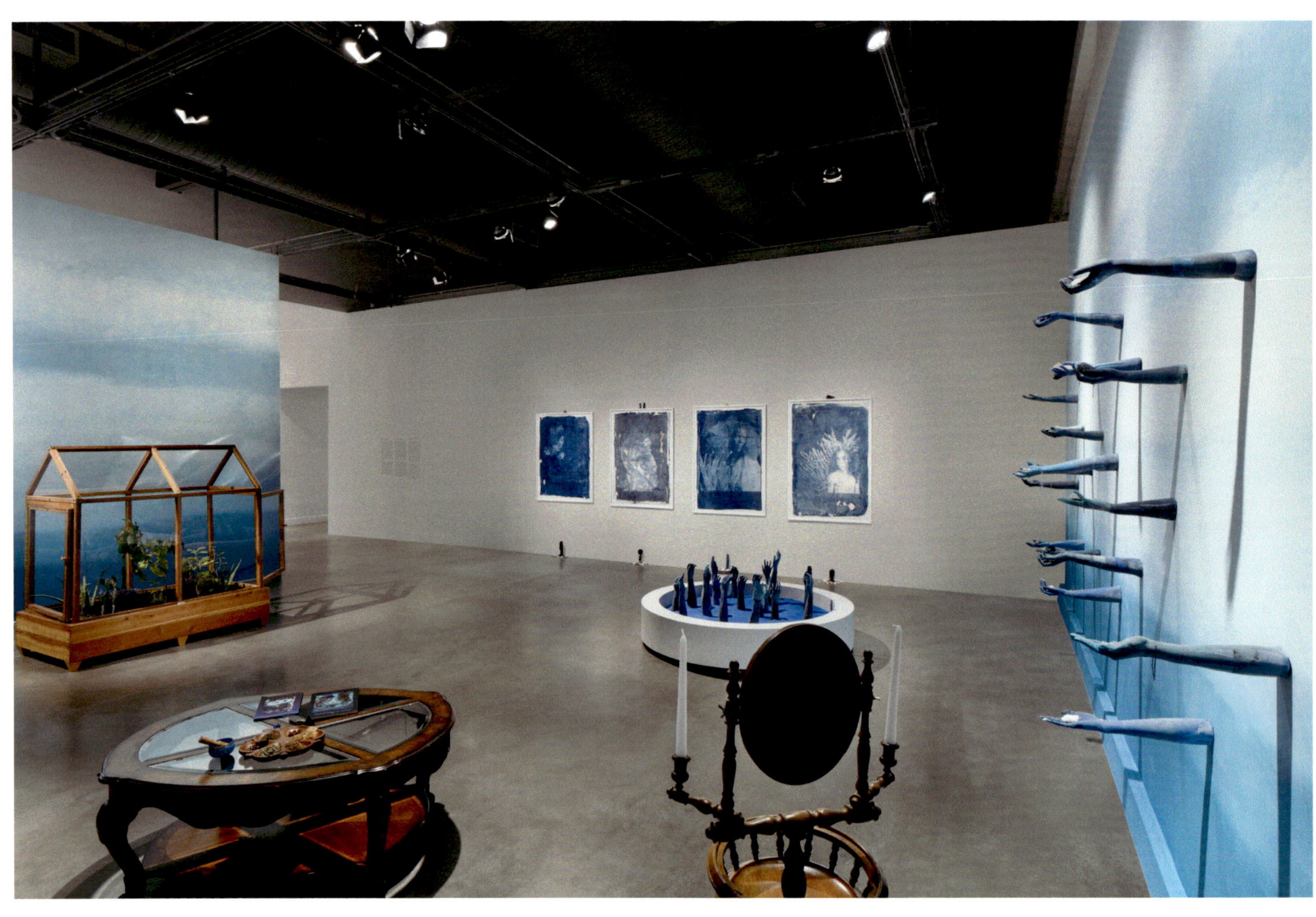

Between Too Late & Too Early, 2024.
Installation views

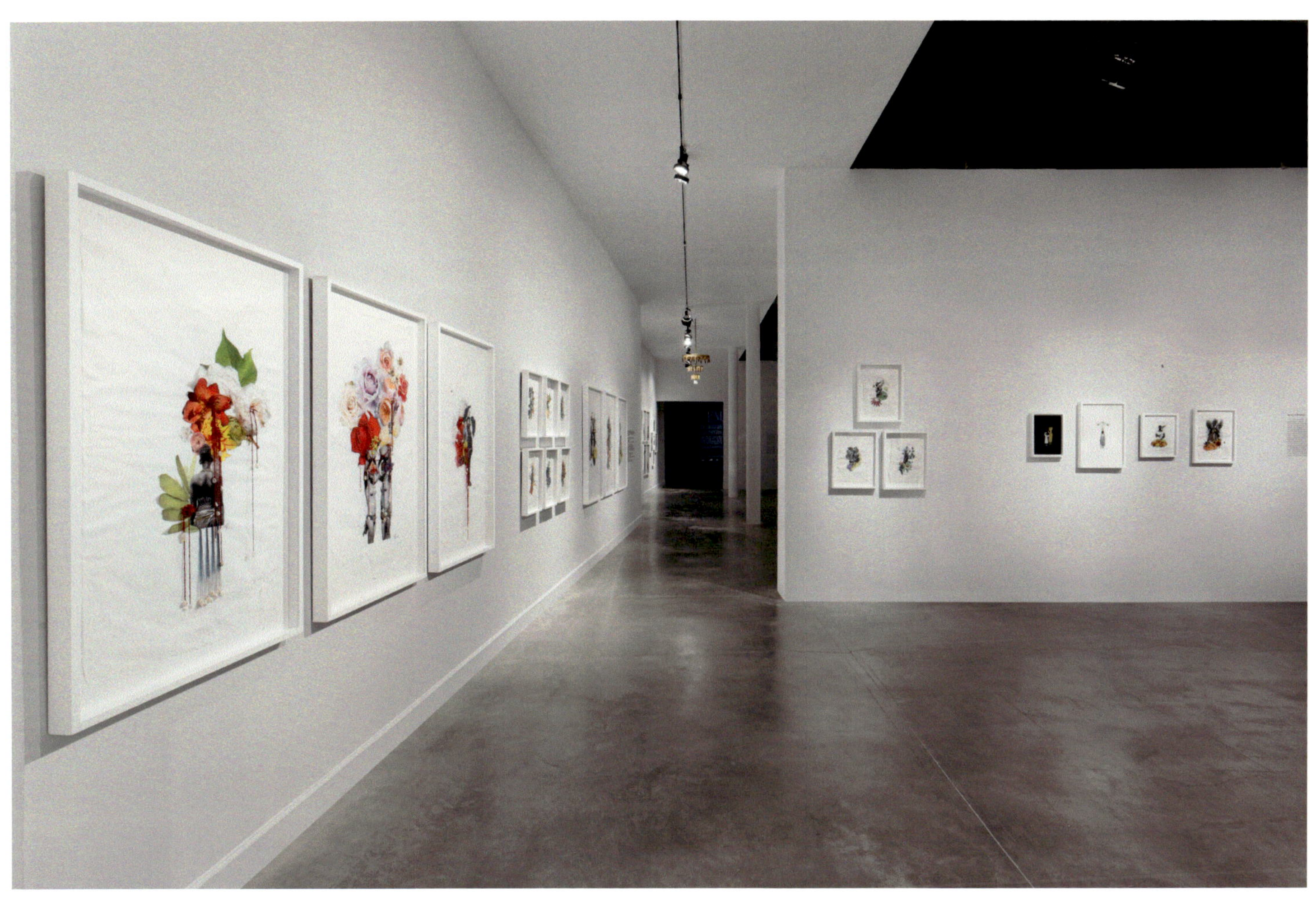

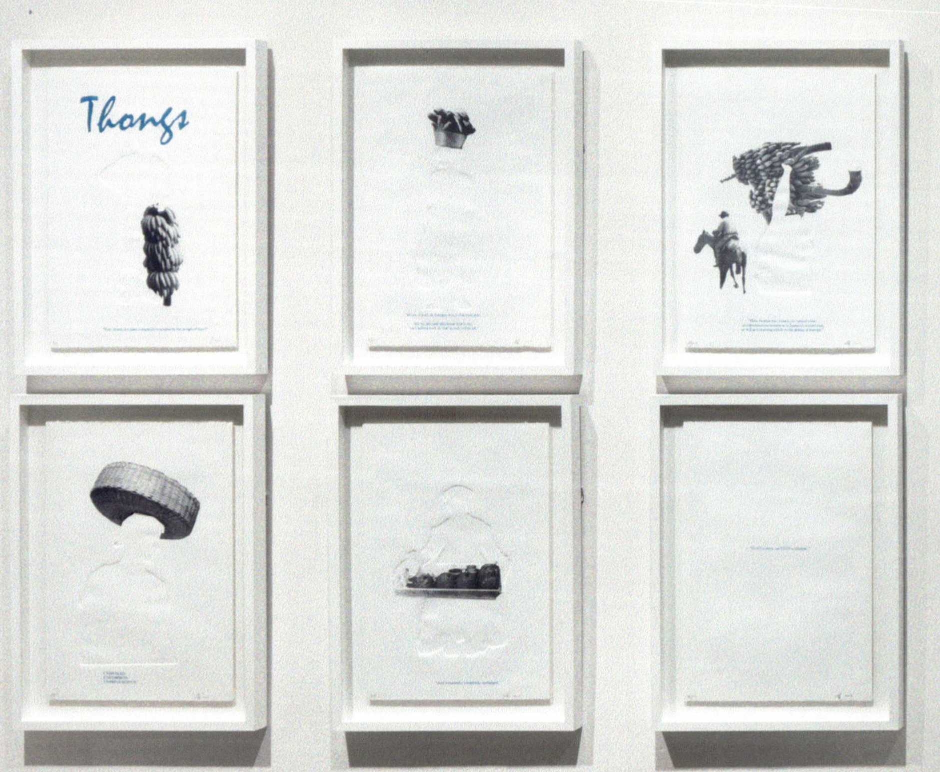
Thongs

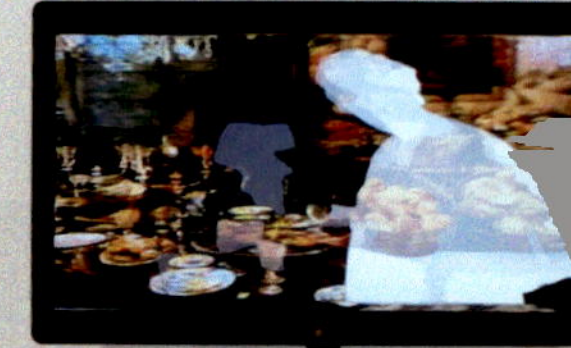

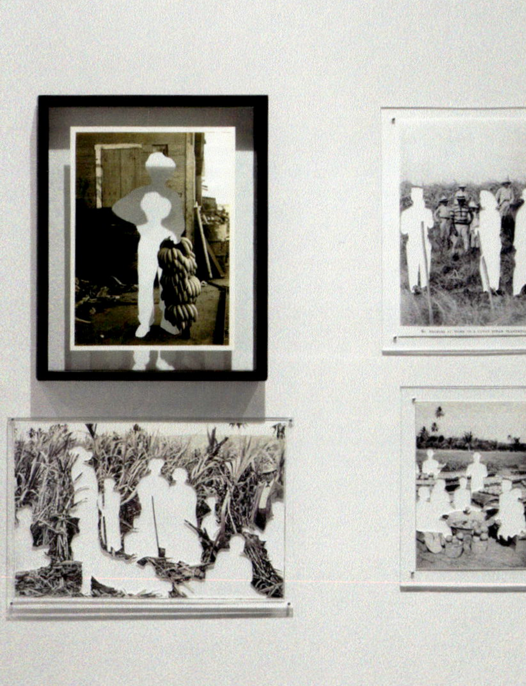
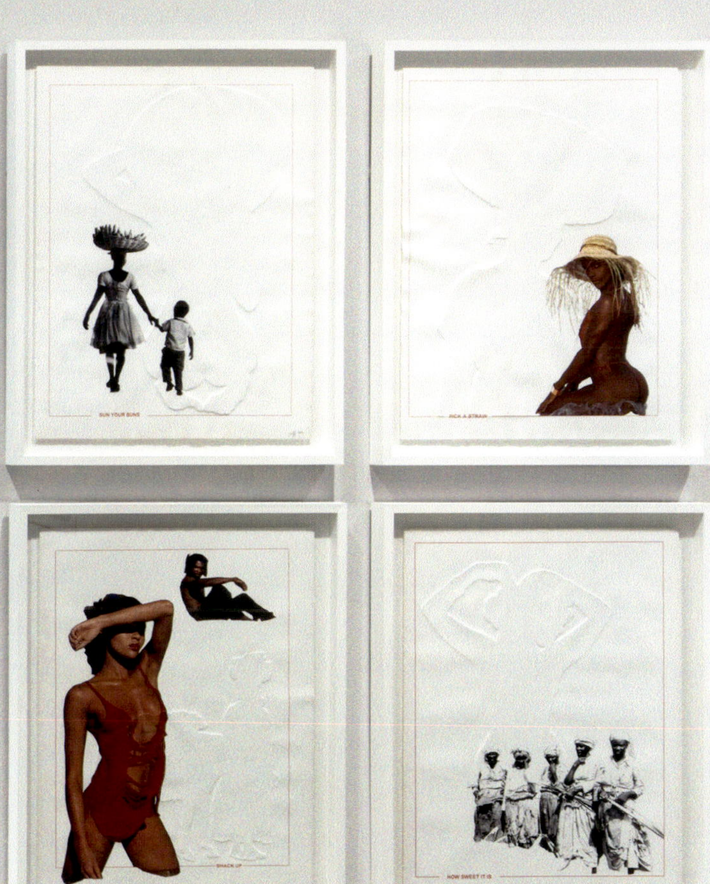

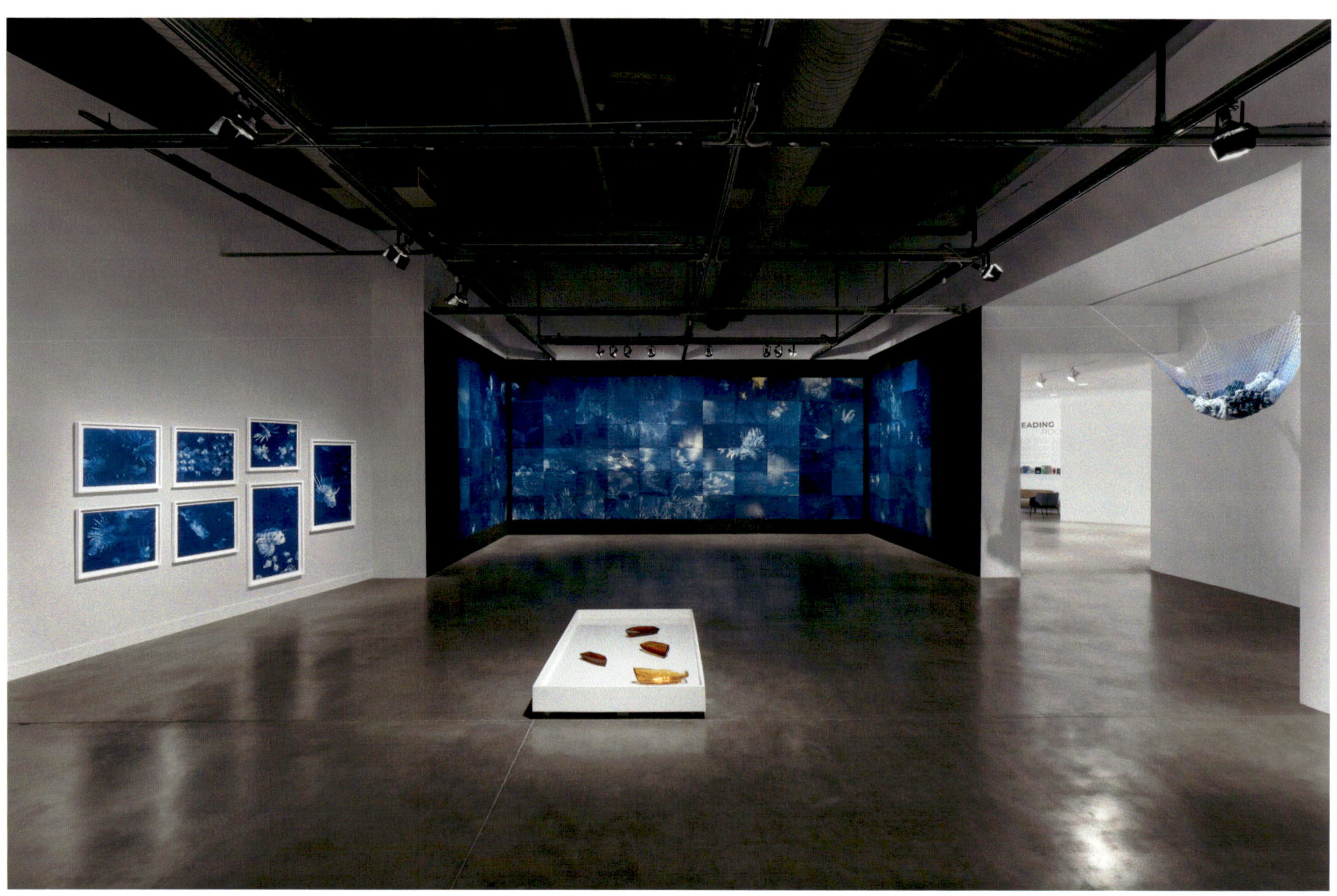

this spread and previous

Between Too Late & Too Early, 2024.
Installation views

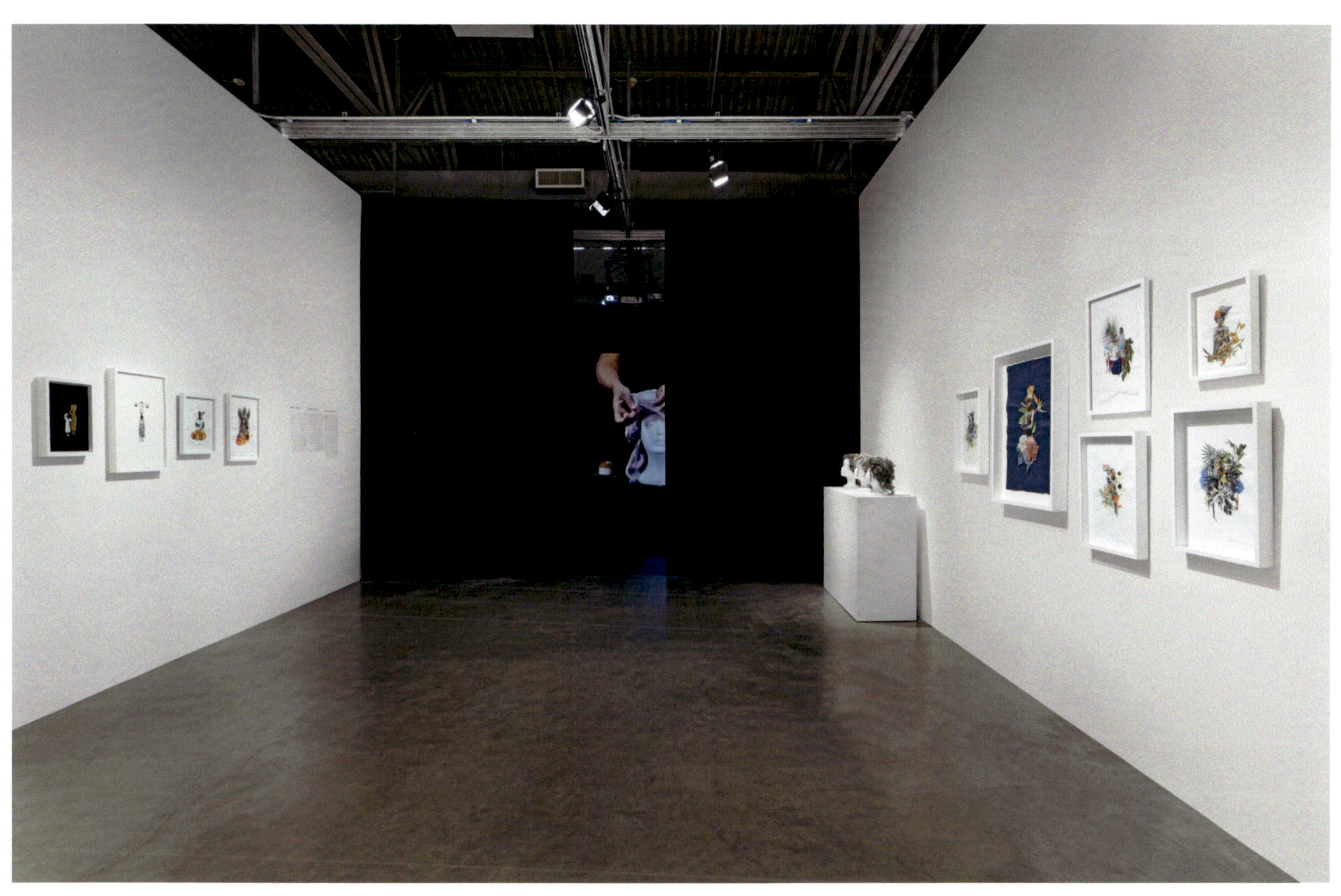

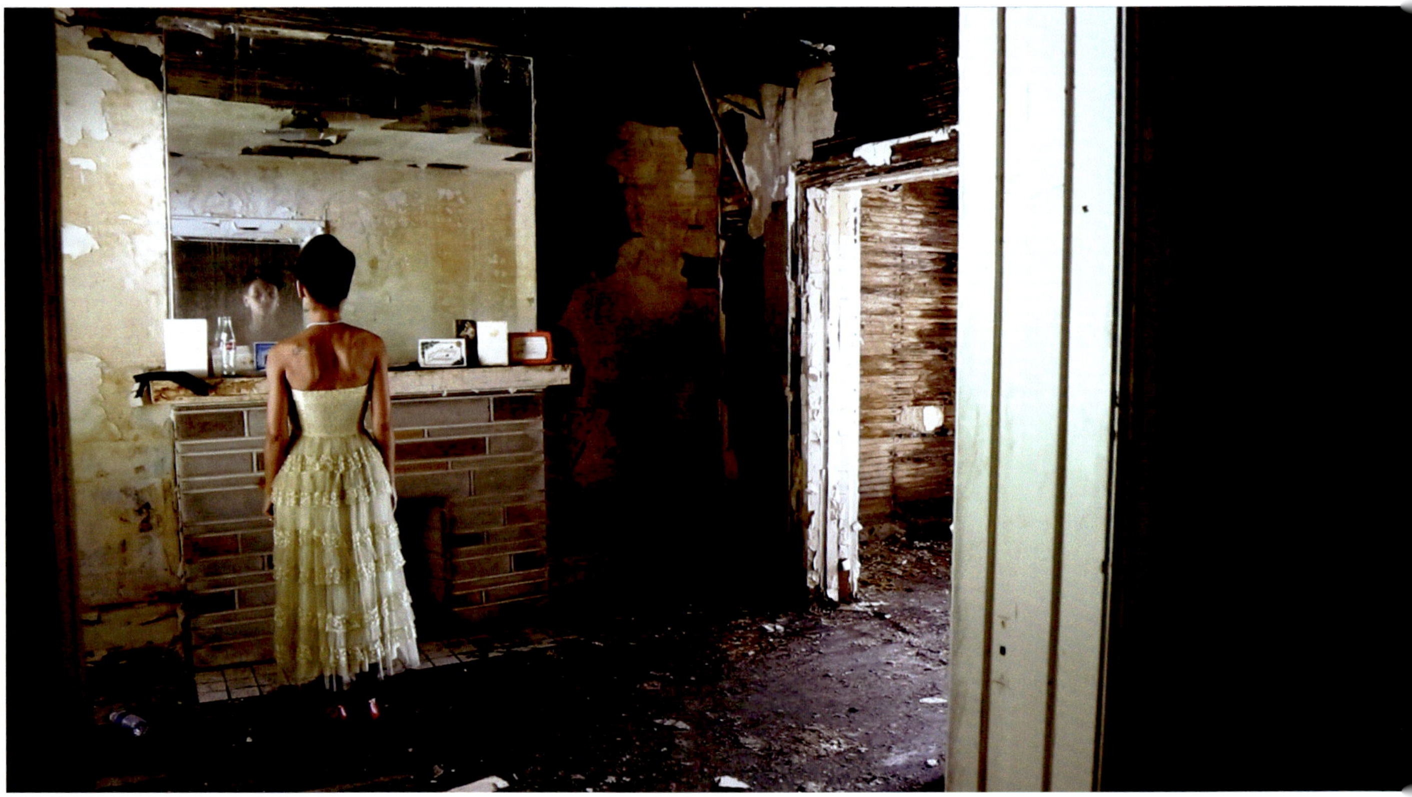

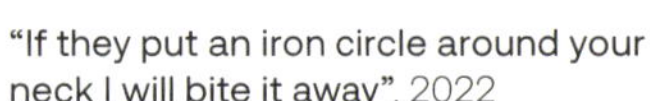

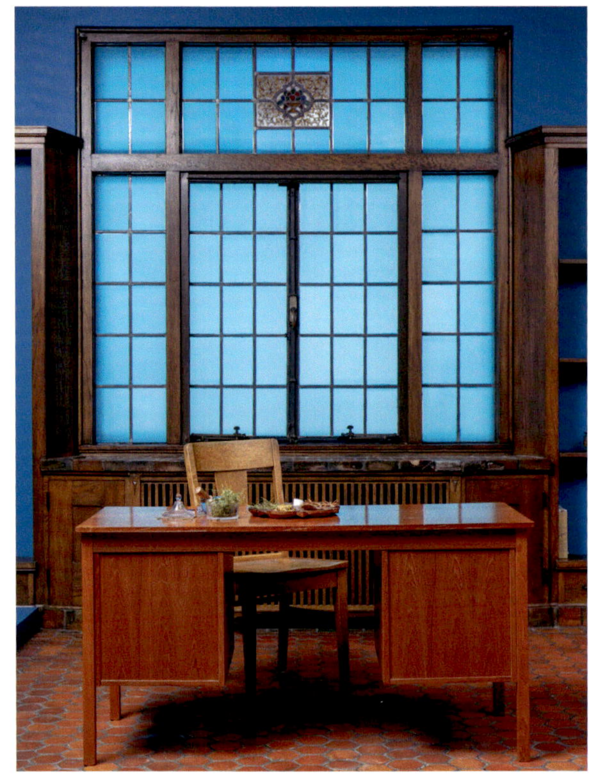

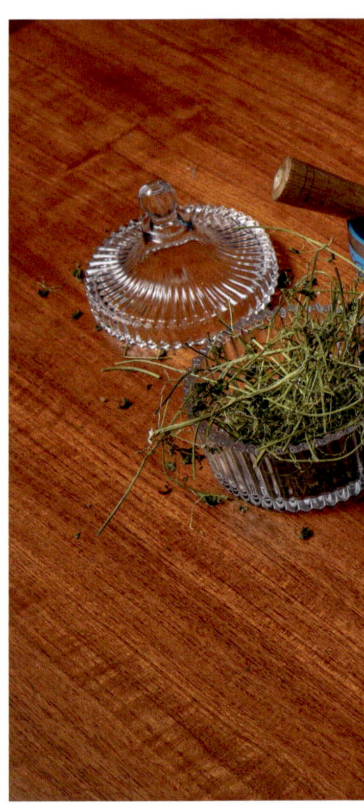

"If they put an iron circle around your neck I will bite it away", 2022
Resin, pigments, beads, shells, crystals, paper pulp, coral, beads, and stones
Site-specific installation

Alisha Wormsley
Children of NAN: Mothership, 2018
Digital film
42 minutes 2 seconds

Included in the installation, this video by Alisha Wormsley is in keeping with Chung's practice of highlighting other artist's work in her exhibitions when their work and content align.

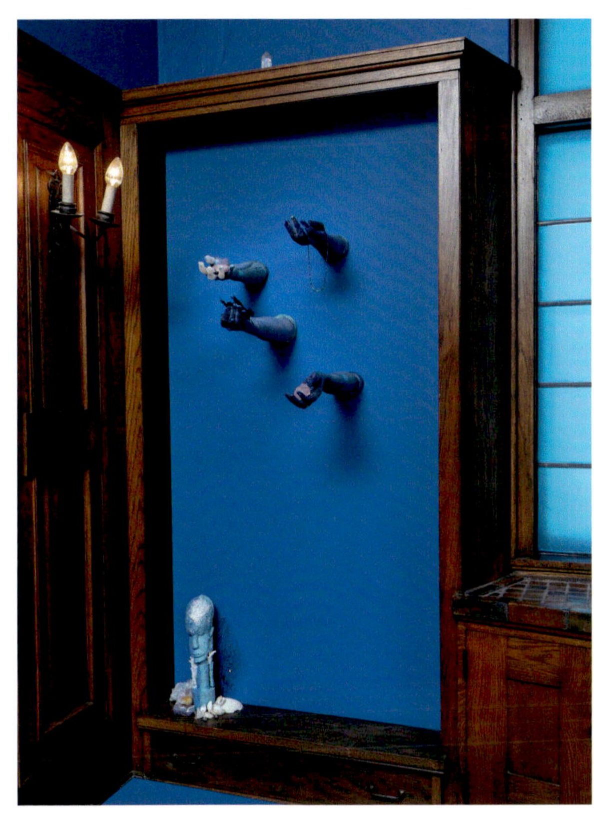

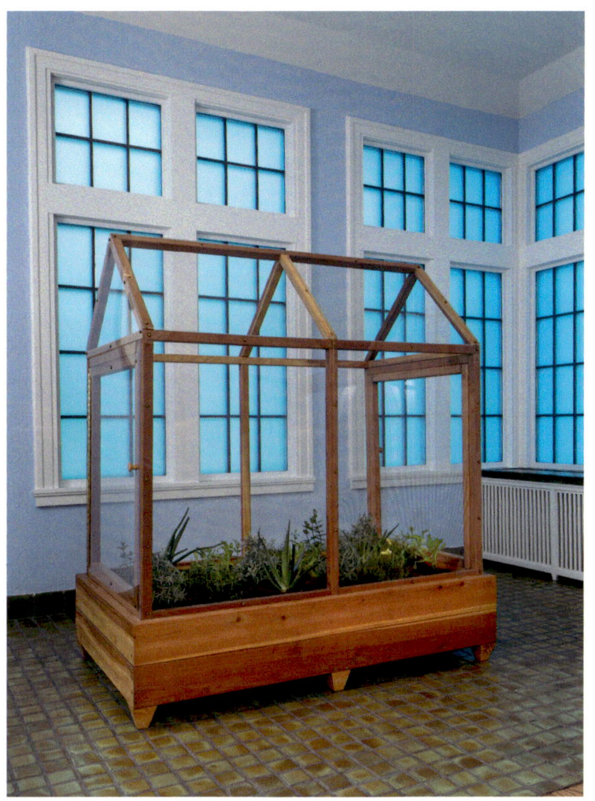

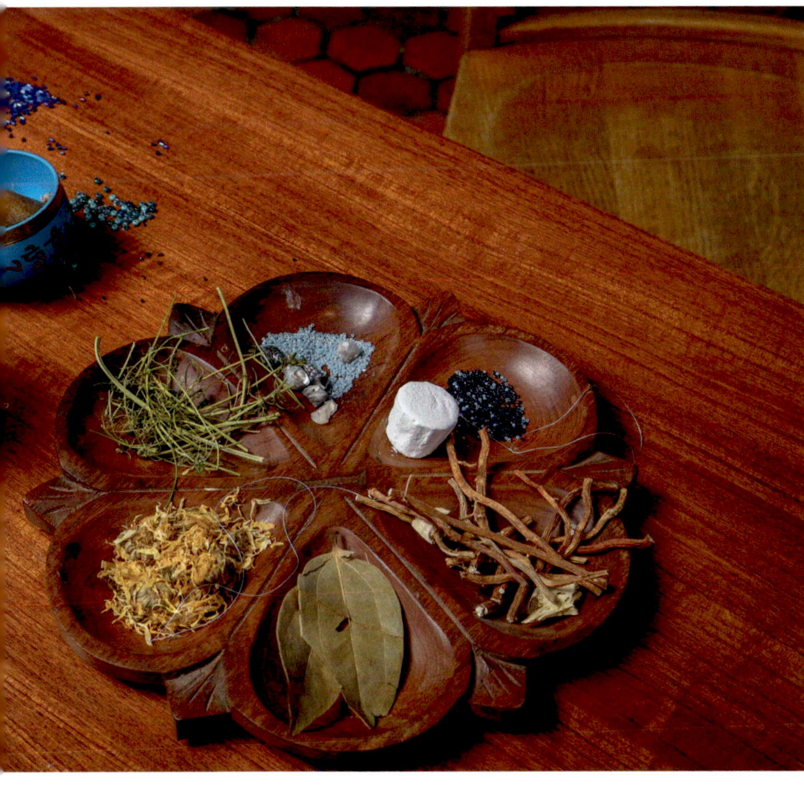

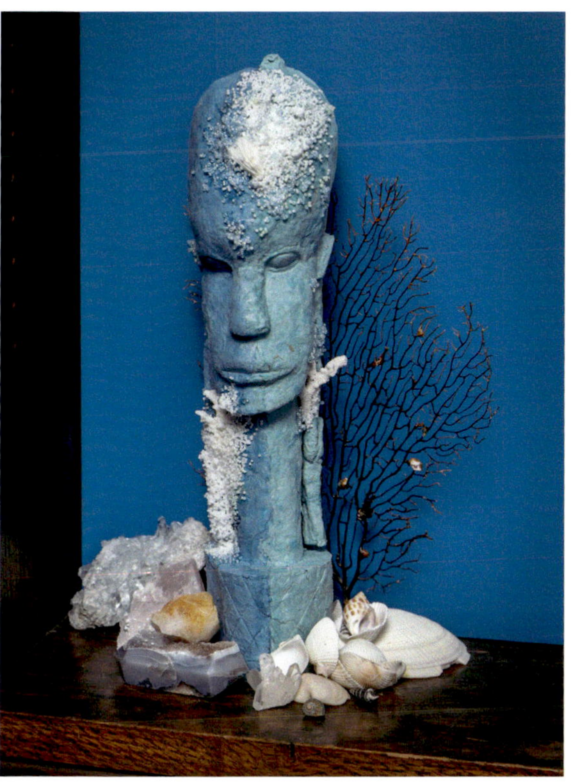

List of Exhibited Works

All Fruits Ripe, 2007
Photo cutout
15½ × 11½ in.
p. 75

Daylight Cum An' Mi Waan Guh Home, 2007
Photo cutout
15 × 13½ in.
pp. 24, 74

'Im Hole 'Im Canher, 2007
Photo cutout with Plexi frame
24 × 17 in.
p. 75

Boopsie, 2008
Digital collage
12 × 10 in.
p. 72

Dexter offers a Whole New Definition of Sublime, 2008
Photo cutout
15¾ × 13 in.
p. 72

Dexter is Trained With Uncompromising Standard of Excellence, 2008
Photo cutout
15¾ × 13 in.
pp. 23, 72

Royal Cut, 2008
Photo cutout
20 × 15 in.
p. 73

Untitled, 2008
Photo cutout
17¼ × 12¼ in.
p. 75

Your Tropical Indulgence Awaits, 2008
Photo cutout
15 × 13 in.
p. 72

Come Back to Jamaica, 2009
Stop animation
1 minute 9 seconds
p. 76

"And fortunately, completely unchanged.", from the portfolio Thongs: Experience the Luxury Included, 2010
Color offset lithograph with embossing on paper
22⅛ × 15 in.
p. 66

"Ever dream of a place completely unspoiled by the ravages of time?", from the portfolio Thongs: Experience the Luxury Included, 2010
Color offset lithograph with embossing on paper
22⅛ × 15 in.
p. 66

"Here Sandals has created our newest resort and ultra-luxurious testament to Jamaica's storied past, as well as a stunning tribute to the glories of Europe", from the portfolio Thongs: Experience the Luxury Included, 2010
Color offset lithograph with embossing on paper
22⅛ × 15 in.
pp. 4, 67

Mi Love Fi Teach de foreigna dem fi chat yard style, but mi nah mek dem know how fi say "mi fi gallong back ah wuk" so nah bodda, from the portfolio Thongs: Experience the Luxury Included, 2010
Color offset lithograph with embossing on paper
22⅛ × 15 in.
p. 67

"Stay a week... or stay a lifetime.", from the portfolio Thongs: Experience the Luxury Included, 2010
Color offset lithograph with embossing on paper
22⅛ × 15 in.
p. 67

Unspoiled, Uncommon, Unpretentious, from the portfolio Thongs: Experience the Luxury Included, 2010
Color offset lithograph with embossing on paper
22⅛ × 15 in.
p. 66

Bato Disik, 2013
Sugar, resin, saltwater
Site-specific installation
Variable dimensions
pp. 32, 81

How Sweet it is, 2013
From the series I wanna Be Loved
Set of four works
C-print, embossing, and archetypes
22 × 30 in.
p. 69

Pick a straw, 2013
From the series I wanna Be Loved
Set of four works
C-print, embossing, and archetypes
22 × 30 in.
p. 68

Shacking up, 2013
From the series I wanna Be Loved
Set of four works
C-print, embossing, and archetypes
22 × 30 in.
p. 69

Sun Your Buns, 2013
From the series I wanna Be Loved
Set of four works
C-print, embossing, and archetypes
22 × 30 in.
p. 68

Crowning IV, 2014
Collage and ink
14 × 11 in.
Private collection, courtesy of Carolyn L. Miller
p. 70

Crowning V, 2014
Collage, ink, and color pencil
14 × 11 in.
p. 71

Blueprint, I, 2016
Embossed watercolor paper
22 × 15½ in.
p. 64

Blueprint, II, 2016
Embossed watercolor paper
22 × 15½ in.
p. 64

Blueprint, III, 2016
Embossed watercolor paper
22 × 15½ in.
p. 65

Untitled, 2016
Cyanotype on 140 lb. watercolor paper
22½ × 30 in.
p. 42 (top left)

Untitled, 2016
Cyanotype on 140 lb. watercolor paper
22½ × 30 in.
Cover, p. 42 (bottom left)

Untitled, 2016
Cyanotype on 140 lb. watercolor paper
22½ × 30 in.
pp. 42–43 (top)

Untitled, 2016
Cyanotype on 140 lb. watercolor paper
22½ × 30 in.
pp. 42–43 (bottom)

Untitled, 2016
Cyanotype on 140 lb. watercolor paper
22½ × 30 in.
p. 43 (top right)

Untitled, 2016
Cyanotype on 140 lb. watercolor paper
22½ × 30 in.
p. 43 (bottom right)

Untitled, 2016
Cyanotype on 140 lb. watercolor paper
22½ × 30 in.
p. 46 (top)

Untitled, 2016
Cyanotype on 140 lb. watercolor paper
22½ × 30 in.
p. 46 (bottom)

Untitled, 2016
Cyanotype on 140 lb. watercolor paper
22½ × 30 in.
Collection of the Butler Nance Family
p. 49 (top right)

Untitled, 2016
Cyanotype on 140 lb. watercolor paper
22½ × 60 in.
pp. 44–45

Untitled, 2016
Cyanotype on 140 lb. watercolor paper
22⅝ × 60 in.
p. 48 (bottom)

Untitled, 2016
Cyanotype on 140 lb. watercolor paper
22⅝ × 60 in.
p. 49 (bottom)

Untitled, 2016
Cyanotype on 140 lb. watercolor paper
22½ × 30 in.
p. 48 (top right)

Untitled, 2016
Cyanotype on 140 lb. watercolor paper
45 × 30 in.
p. 49 (top left)

Untitled, 2016
Cyanotype on 140 lb. watercolor paper
45 × 30 in.
p. 48 (top left)

Pure, 2017
Black soap, dry sink, towels, candles,
scissors, pitcher, bottle, and jewelry
48 × 24 × 20 in.
Collection of the Museum of
Contemporary Art, North Miami. Gift of
Jody Post. AX number 2024.01.01
p. 79

Sea Change, 2017
Cyanotype on watercolor paper
Site-specific installation
pp. 40–41

Spectre, 2017
Cyanotype on watercolor paper
Site-specific installation
Variable dimensions
pp. 50–51

Proverbs, 12:22, 2018
Sugar, beads, rice, herbs, spices,
and paper
Site-specific installation
Variable dimensions
pp. 6, 80

Untitled, 2018
Collage, glitter, and beads on handmade
birthing cloth paper
12 × 9 in.
Private collection
p. 61

Untitled XII, 2018
Collage and watercolor on handmade
paper from birthing clothes and red
raspberry tea
12 × 9 in.
The Suzie Wong Collection, Jamaica
p. 61

An Unrequited Love, 2019
Multichannel installation
1 minute 53 seconds
pp. 8–9, 77

Endosymbiotic Theory, 2019
Brass, glass, and sugar
56 × 23 in.
City of San Diego Civic Art Collection;
Purchase through a gift of Thomas O.
Rasmussen, 2021.16
p. 78

Sisters of Two Waters I, 2019
Collage, glitter, and beads on handmade
paper
18 × 12 in.
Collection of Jasmine Wahi
p. 60

Sisters of Two Waters II, 2019
Collage, glitter, and beads on handmade
birthing cloth paper
17½ × 11½ in.
Davis Museum at Wellesley College,
Wellesley, MA; Museum purchase, Nancy
Gray Sherrill, Class of 1954, Collection
Acquisitions Fund
p. 60

Toadstool Leather, 2019
Cyanotype and sugar
45 × 60 in.
p. 47

Colostrum I, 2020
Collage, ink, rhinestones, pins, and beads
on paper handmade from traditional
birthing cloth
Framed: 22 × 17 × 2 in.
Collection of Diane Allen
p. 52

Colostrum II, 2020
Collage, ink, rhinestones, pins, and beads
on paper handmade from traditional
birthing cloth
Framed: 22 × 17 × 2 in.
Collection of Bob and Erika Williams,
Yonkers, NY
p. 52

Colostrum IV, 2020
Collage, ink, rhinestones, pins, and beads
on paper handmade from traditional
birthing cloth
Framed: 22 × 17 × 2 in.
Collection of Stephanie and Timothy
Ingrassia
p. 52

Colostrum VII, 2020
Collage, ink, rhinestones, pins, and beads
on paper handmade from traditional
birthing cloth
17 × 13 in.
Collection of Leslie and William McMorrow
pp. 21, 52

Colostrum VIII, 2020
Collage, ink, rhinestones, pins, and beads
on paper handmade from traditional
birthing cloth
17¾ × 12¼ in.
Collection of Leslie and William McMorrow
p. 53

Vex VII, 2020
Collage, ink, and beads on paper
handmade from traditional birthing cloth
22 × 16½ in.
Collection of Laurie K. Silverman
pp. 30, 56

Vex VIII, 2020
Collage, ink, and beads on paper
handmade from traditional birthing cloth
22 × 16½ in.
Collection of Kim Vernon
p. 57

Vex XI, 2020
Collage, ink, and beads on handmade
paper
29 × 21¾ in.
Davis Museum at Wellesley College,
Wellesley, MA, Museum purchase, Nancy
Gray Sherrill, Class of 1954, Collection
Acquisitions Fund
pp. 34–35, 56

Vex XX, 2020
Collage, ink, and beads on paper
handmade from traditional birthing cloth
17 × 13 in.
Collection of Bahia Ramos
p. 55

Colostrum IX, 2021
Collage, ink and beads on paper
handmade from traditional birthing cloth
20 × 16 in.
Collection of Carol Cole Levin
p. 53

Colostrum XIII, 2021
Collage, ink and beads on paper
handmade from traditional birthing cloth
20 × 16 in.
Collection of Laura and Frank Baker
p. 53

Colostrum XIV, 2021
Collage, ink, rhinestones, pins, and beads
on paper handmade from traditional
birthing cloth
17 × 12 in.
Collection of Schwanda Rountree
p. 53

Colostrum XVII, 2021
Collage, ink, rhinestones, pins, and beads
on paper handmade from traditional
birthing cloth
17 × 12 in.
Collection of Thomas Rhoads
p. 54

Sula Never Competed; She Simply
Helped Others Define Themselves, II,
2021
Collage, gold ink, shells, pins, and beads
on paper handmade from traditional
birthing cloth
Framed: 55¼ × 70½ × 2¾ in. (Diptych)
Collection of Jill Davis
p. 59

Sula Never Competed; She Simply
Helped Other Define Themselves, III, 2021
Collage, gold ink, shells, and beads on
paper handmade from traditional birthing
cloth
Framed: 55¼ × 35¼ × 2¾ in.
Collection of Amanda Silverman
p. 58

Sula Never Competed; She Simply
Helped Other Define Themselves, VII,
2021
Collage, gold ink, shells, pins, and beads
on paper handmade from traditional
birthing cloth
Framed: 55¼ × 35¼ × 2¾ in.
Collection of Renita and Eric Woodson
pp. 17, 58

"If they put an iron circle around your
neck I will bite it away", 2022
Resin, pigments, beads, shells, crystals,
paper pulp, coral, beads, and stones
Site specific installation
pp. 13, 96–97

However The Image Enters Its Force
Remains Within My Eyes, III, 2023
Paper made from Anna Atkins:
Cyanotypes book published by Taschen,
methyl cellulose, and cyanotypes on Kozo
paper
24½ × 19½ × 1½ in.
p. 39

However The Image Enters Its Force
Remains Within My Eyes, V, 2023
Paper made from Anna Atkins:
Cyanotypes book published by Taschen,
methyl cellulose, and cyanotypes on Kozo
paper
24 × 19 × 2¼ in.
pp. 28, 38

However The Image Enters Its Force
Remains Within My Eyes, VI, 2023
Paper made from Anna Atkins:
Cyanotypes book published by Taschen,
methyl cellulose, crystalized sugar, and
cyanotypes on kozo paper
29½ × 22 × 2½ in.
Angelina Darrisaw, Brooklyn, NY
p. 37

However The Image Enters Its Force
Remains Within My Eyes, VII, 2023
Paper made from Anna Atkins:
Cyanotypes book published by Taschen,
methyl cellulose, crystallized sugar, and
cyanotypes on kozo paper
29½ × 22¾ × 2½ in.
p. 36

However The Image Enters Its Force
Remains Within My Eyes, VIII, 2023
Paper made from **Anna Atkins:
Cyanotypes** book published by Taschen,
methyl cellulose, and cyanotypes on kozo
paper
24½ × 18¾ × 2¼ in.
p. 36

The Load is Heavy, and My Back is
Tired I, 2023
Collage, gold ink, pins, and beads on
paper handmade from traditional birthing
cloth
50 × 30 × 2 in.
p. 62

The Load is Heavy, and My Back is
Tired II, 2023
Collage, gold ink, pins, and beads on
paper handmade from traditional birthing
cloth
50 × 30 × 2 in.
p. 62

The Load is Heavy, and My Back is
Tired IV, 2023
Collage, gold ink, pins, and beads on
paper handmade from traditional birthing
cloth
50 × 30 × 2 in.
p. 63

The Wailing Room, 2024
Sugar, sound
Site-specific installation
pp. 14, 84–85

"...there is no me. There is I and I, which
is you too. You and I intertwined.", 2024
17 pulped paper sculptures
115½ x 104 in.
pp. 14, 84–85

Alisha Wormsley
Children of NAN: Mothership, 2018
Digital film
42 minutes 2 seconds
Courtesy of the artist
p. 96

Curriculum Vitae
Andrea Chung

Born 1978, Newark, NJ
Lives and works in San Diego, CA

Education

Maryland Institute College of Art (MICA), Baltimore, MD
MFA, 2008

Parsons School of Design, New York, NY
BFA Illustration, 1999

Solo and Two Person Exhibitions

2024   *Andrea Chung: Between Too Late and Too Early*,
mid-career survey at the Museum of Contemporary
Art, North Miami, Miami, FL
The Weight of Memories, Tyler Park Presents, Los
Angeles, CA

2022   *Andrea Chung: if they put an iron circle around your
neck I will bite it away*, James Michael Kohler Arts
Center, Sheboygan, WI
Andrea Chung, Art Gallery of Ontario, Toronto, ON,
Canada

2021   *We Was Girls Together*, Tyler Park Presents, Los
Angeles, CA
The Children of Oshun and Yemaya, Centre [3] for
Artistic + Social Practice, Hamilton, ON, Canada

2020   *Focus*, The Armory Show, New York, NY

2019   *...Only to meet nothing that wants you*, Klowden Mann,
Culver City, CA

2018   *The Mess You Made*, Hawthorn Contemporary,
Milwaukee, WI
You broke the ocean in half to be here, Manetti Shrem
Museum of Art, UC Davis, Davis, CA

2017   *You broke the ocean in half to be here*, Museum of
Contemporary Art San Diego, San Diego, CA

2016   *Pride and Prejudice*, New Image Art, Los Angeles, CA

2013   *Corporeal Contours: Firelei Báez and Andrea Chung*,
Community Folk Art Center, Syracuse University,
Syracuse, NY

Selected Group Exhibitions

2024   *Constellations: Racial myths, land, and labour*, Esker
Foundation, Calgary, AB, Canada
Golden: Fifty Years of New Classics, Museum of
Contemporary Art Arlington, Arlington, VA
*Resonant Earth: Contemporary Perspectives on Land
and Body*, Moody Center for the Arts at Rice University,
Houston, TX
Nineteenth-Century Photography Now, Getty Center,
Los Angeles, CA
Spirit in the Land, Pérez Art Museum Miami, Miami, FL
*Multiplicity: Blackness in Contemporary American
Collage*, Museum of Fine Arts, Houston, TX;
The Phillips Collection, Washington, D.C.

2023   *Multiplicity: Blackness in Contemporary American
Collage*, Frist Art Museum, Nashville, TN
Kept Alive Within Us, Art Gallery of Guelph, Guelph,
ON, Canada
Spirit in the Land, Nasher Museum at Duke University,
Durham, NC

2022   *everything slackens in a wreck*, Ford Foundation
Gallery, New York, NY
Breathe into the Past: Crosscurrents in the Caribbean,
Colorado Springs Fine Art Center at Colorado
College, Colorado Springs, CO

2021   *Fragments of Epic Memories*, Art Gallery of Ontario,
Toronto, ON, Canada; Minneapolis Institute of Art,
Minneapolis, MI
*One song is very much like the other, and the boat
is always from afar*, Guangdong Times Museum,
Guangdong, China
LANDS END, For*Site, Cliff House, San Francisco, CA
Beyond, the Sea Sings, Times Art Center Berlin, Berlin,
Germany
Forward Flux: Unshuttering LA, Getty Center, Los
Angeles, CA
Picturing Motherhood Now, Cleveland Museum of Art,
Cleveland, OH

2020   *Wayfinding*, Phillips Academy Addison Gallery,
Andover, MA
Focus Projects, The Armory, curated by Jamilah
James, New York, NY

2019   *Untitled*, Klowden Mann, Miami, FL
Extended Self: Transformations and Connections, Hyde Park Art Center, Chicago, IL
HOME: narratives of time and belonging, presented by Klowden Mann, New York, NY
A NonHuman Horizon, LACE, Los Angeles, CA
The Other Side of Now, Pérez Art Museum Miami, Miami, FL
Coffee, Rhum, Sugar, & Gold, Museum of African Diaspora, San Francisco, CA
The Sea is History, Museum of Cultural History, Oslo, Norway
Process, Ithaca College, Ithaca, NY

2018   *Being Here With You/Estando aquí contigo: 42 Artists from San Diego and Tijuana*, Museum of Contemporary Art San Diego, San Diego, CA
Build a Longer Table, Metro Arts public project curated by Nicole Caruth, Nashville Department of Public Health, Nashville, TN
Biomythography: Reflexive Remix, University of La Verne Harris Art Gallery, La Verne, CA

2017   *Prospect.4: The Lotus in Spite of the Swamp*, New Orleans, LA
Pacific Standard Time – Circles and Circuits: Chinese Caribbean Art, Chinese American Museum and California African American Museum, Los Angeles, CA
BLACK + BROWN PEOPLE | WHITE PROBLEMS, Samsøñ, Boston, MA
Impressions: Andrea Chung, Kenyatta A. Hinkle and Robert Pruitt, Mesa College, San Diego, CA
Kingston Biennial, Kingston, Jamaica

2016   *indivisible: spirits in the material world*, curated by William Cordova, Prizm Art Fair, Miami, FL
Jamaican Pulse: Art and Politics from Jamaica and the Diaspora, Royal West of England Academy, Bristol, England
Jamaican Routes, Punkt Ø / Galleri F15, Oslo, Norway

2015   *Bienal del Sur*, Caracas, Venezuela
Venturing Out of the Heart of Darkness, The Gantt Center, Charlotte, NC

2012   *Jamaican National Biennial 2012*, The National Gallery of Jamaica, Kingston, Jamaica
Outward Reach, Art Museum of the Americas, Washington, D.C.
LIFT Project, curated by Kimberli Gant, Art House, Austin, TX

2010   *There is No Looking Glass Here*, 60 Wall Street Gallery, Deutsche Bank, New York, NY
Ain't I A Woman?, Museum of Contemporary African Diasporan Art, Brooklyn, NY

Black Artist as Activist Exhibition, Corridor Gallery, Brooklyn, NY

2008   *Transformers: More Than Meets The Eye*, curated by Derrick Adams, The Gateway Gallery, Maryland Institute College of Art, Baltimore, MD
Off Color, curated by Hank Willis Thomas and Kalia Brooks, Rush Arts, New York, NY; Corridor Gallery, Brooklyn, NY
PepperPot: Multi Media Installation, Meaning, and the Medium in Contemporary Art, curated by Pamela Phatsimo Sunstrum, Sonja Haynes Stone Center at UNC Chapel Hill, Chapel Hill, NC

Awards and Honors

2014 Joan Mitchell Foundation, Painters and Sculptors Grant Program

2008–2009 US Fulbright Scholar Fellow, Mauritius

Selected Bibliography

Bishop, Jacqueline. "Andrea Chung's Love Affair With Process and Materials." *Huffington Post Arts & Culture*, July 7, 2014.

Black, Matthew J. "Andrea Chung's Powerful Work is as Sweet as It Looks." *Locale Magazine*, November 2017.

Chen, Scarlett. "Pacific Standard Time turns to one overlooked group in Latin America: Asian immigrants." *Los Angeles Times*, December 22, 2017.

Chung, Andrea. "A Day Off from Dementia." *Small Axe* 29, vol. 13, no. 2 (June 2009): 135–142.

Davis, Ben. "See Highlights From the Just-Opened Prospect 4 Triennial in New Orleans." *Artnet*, November 2017.

Goffe, Tao Leigh. "Sugarwork: The Gastropoetics of Afro-Asia After the Plantation." *Asian Diasporic Visual Cultures and the Americas* 5, no. 1–2 (2019): 31–56.

Jacobson, Louis. "Reviewed: Outward Reach" at Art Museum of the Americas." *Washington City Paper*, August 3, 2012.

Johnson, Paddy. "Pleasant Surprises in the Swamp at Prospect, the New Orleans Triennial." *Hyperallergic*, November 22, 2017.

Mensah and the Museum of African Diaspora. *Coffee, Rhum, Gold & Sugar: A Postcolonial Paradox*. Cameron Books, 2019.

Meyer, Deborah R. "Sugar and Spice and Animation." *Chapel Hill News*, March 5, 2008.

Paul, Annie. "Not Slavish Reproductions." *ARC Magazine*, no. 2, April 2011.

Pearce, Marsha. "Ready for Takeoff? Lacerated Fantasies of the Caribbean Paradise in the Décollage Art of Andrea Chung." In *Travel and Imagination*, edited by Garth Lean, Russell Staiff, Emma Waterton. Ashgate, 2014.

Pearce, Marsha, and Maria Elena Ortiz. *The Other Side of Now*. Pérez Art Museum Miami, 2019.

Pelican Bomb. "Prospect.4 exhibitions are full of surprises – like Easter eggs." *New Orleans Times Picayune*, November 29, 2017.

Samudzi, Zoe. "A Caribbean Present Steeped in a Colonial Past." *Hyperallergic*, July 29, 2019.

Schoonmaker, Trevor. *Prospect.4: The Lotus in Spite of the Swamp*. Prestel, 2017.

Smyth-Johnson, Nicole. "2017 Jamaican Biennial." *Miami Rail*, February 2017.

Thompson, Krista. "The Evidence of Things Not Photographed: Slavery and Historical Memory in the British West Indies." *Representations* 113, no.1 (Winter 2011): 39–71.

Wendt, Selene. *The Sea Is History*. SKIRA, 2019.

Wimberly, Dexter, Larry Ossei-Wong, Steve. "Andrea Chung: You Broke the Ocean in Half to be Here." *Asian Diasporic Visual Cultures and the Americas* 5, no. 1–2 (2019): 219–223.

Wood, Sura. "Whose Paradise." *Bay Area Reporter*, May 14, 2019.

Collections

Art Gallery of Ontario

Cleveland Clinic Art & Medicine Institute, the Carter Collection

Crocker Art Museum

Davis Museum at Wellesley College

Harvard University

J. Paul Getty Museum

Minneapolis Institute of Art

Museum of Contemporary Art San Diego

NOVA Foundation

Rhode Island School of Design Museum

Smith College

University of Texas at Austin

Contributor Biographies

Eddie Chambers

Eddie Chambers gained his PhD from Goldsmiths College, University of London in 1998. He has curated a number of exhibitions, having worked with artists such as Denzil Forrester and Frank Bowling. He joined the Department of Art and Art History at the University of Texas at Austin in 2010 where he is now holder of the David Bruton, Jr. Centennial Professorship in Art History. His books include *Things Done Change: The Cultural Politics of Recent Black Artists in Britain* (2012), *Black Artists in British Art: A History since the 1950s*, (2014, reissued 2015), and *Roots & Culture: Cultural Politics in the Making of Black Britain* (2017). His most recent book is *World is Africa: Writings on Diaspora Art* (2021). He is the editor of the forthcoming *Routledge Companion to African Diaspora Art History*.

Aruna D'Souza

Aruna D'Souza writes about modern and contemporary art, intersectional feminisms, and diasporic aesthetics. Her work appears regularly in 4Columns, the *New York Times*, and in numerous artist's monographs and exhibition catalogues. *Whitewalling: Art, Race, & Protest in 3 Acts* was named one of the best art books of 2018 by the *New York Times*. Recent editorial projects include Linda Nochlin's *Making It Modern: Essays on the Art of the Now* (2022) and Lorraine O'Grady's *Writing in Space, 1973–2019* (2020). She cocurated the retrospective *Lorraine O'Grady: Both/And* at the Brooklyn Museum in 2021. She is the recipient of the 2021 Rabkin Prize for art journalism and a 2019 Andy Warhol Foundation Arts Writers Grant. She was appointed the Edmond J. Safra Visiting Professor at the National Gallery of Art in 2022 and the 2022–23 William Wilson Corcoran Professor of Community Engagement at the Corcoran School of the Arts and Design, George Washington University. Her most recent book, *Imperfect Solidarities* was published in 2024.

Adeze Wilford

Adeze Wilford is a curator at the Museum of Contemporary Art, North Miami, where she has organized *Leah Gordon: Kanaval* (2022), *Lonnie Holley: If You Really Knew* (2023), and *The South Florida Cultural Consortium* (2023). She was an assistant curator at the Shed, where she organized *Howardena Pindell: Rope/Fire/Water* (2020*)*, and an inaugural joint curatorial fellow at the Studio Museum in Harlem and the Museum of Modern Art, New York. She organized *Vernacular Interior* (2019) at Hales Gallery, *Excerpt* (2017) at the Studio Museum, and a film series, *Black Intimacy* (2017), at MoMA. Other curatorial projects include *Harlem Postcards* (2016–17) and *Color in Shadows*, the 2016 Expanding the Walls exhibition at the Studio Museum. She has contributed scholarship to various catalogues and magazines, including *Young, Gifted and Black: A Generation of New Artists* (2020), *Black Refractions* (2019), and *Art in America*, and served on the Queens Museum Board. She graduated from Northwestern University with a BA in art history and African American studies.

Acknowledgements

Andrea Chung: Between Too Late and Too Early is made possible with support from the Funding Arts Network. Special thanks to El Espacio 23 for supporting the artist's residency.

The catalogue is made possible with partial support from Rosie Gordon-Wallace and Roy Wallace.

MOCA North Miami is generously funded by the North Miami Mayor and Council and the City of North Miami; the Miami-Dade County Department of Cultural Affairs and the Cultural Affairs Council, the Miami-Dade County Mayor and Board of County Commissioners; and the John S. and James L. Knight Foundation. Additional support is provided by the Fine & Greenwald Foundation and the Sol Taplin Charitable Foundation. Founding support for the MOCA Sustainability Fund provided by the Green Family Foundation Trust. Major support provided by Shirley and William M. Lehman, Jr. We also thank our Board of Trustees, Curator's Circle, and MOCA Members for their meaningful support.

Artist Acknowledgments

I would like to thank Adeze for seeing in me what I couldn't at the time. Your belief in me is something I hold close. To my friends and chosen family, thank you for your love and support. Tara, Samira, Pamela, Rachel, Chris, Jeffreen, Zoe, Amy, Deborah, Lise, David and Karen, Ebony—thank you for your friendship and support. To Frances Barth, thank you for teaching me the importance of community. Aruna and Eddie, thank you for your words. Krista, for your constant inspiration. Mommy, thanks for loving me the way you do. Finally, to Jasaun and Kingston, without your love and support, none of this would be possible. Kingston, you are my everything. To the diaspora, please keep telling our stories so that our children may know.

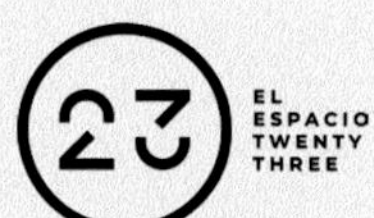

City of North Miami

Alix Desulme, EdD	*Mayor*
Mary Estimé-Irvin	*Vice Mayor, District 3*
Scott Galvin	*District 1 Councilman*
Kassandra Timothe, MPA	*District 2 Councilwoman*
Pierre Frantz Charles, MEd	*District 4 Councilman*
Anna-Bo Emmanuel, Esq., FRA-RA	*Interim City Manager*

Staff List

Chana Budgazad Sheldon	Executive Director
Akilah Child	Director of Communications
Amanda Covach	Director of Education and Community Engagement
Sara Ryan	Director of Development
Adeze Wilford	Curator
Fola Akinde	Museum Associate
Karla Argyropoulos	Executive Assistant
Andrew Arocho	Museum Associate
Lauren Baccus	Public Programs Manager
Sarah Compere	Museum Associate
Stephie Geffrard	Museum Associate
Antonio Guerrero	Maintenance Technician
Kimari Jackson	Curatorial Assistant
Shekinah Johnson	Development Assistant
Marceau Livette	Security Chief
Eric Mendoza	Graphic Designer
Fabienne Merritt	Content Manager and Copywriter
Tiquon Miller	Finance Associate
William Miranda	Building Manager
Sara Uhlig Perez	Membership and Donor Relations Manager
Tainisel Rodriguez	Guest Experience and Interim Operations Manager
Matt Roza	Exhibitions Manager
Claudia Santana	Marketing Manager
Felix St. Hilaire	Museum Associate

Andrea Chung: Between Too Late & Too Early

is published in conjunction with the exhibition curated by
Adeze Wilford and presented at the Museum of Contemporary Art,
North Miami, November 6, 2024–April 6, 2025

Published by

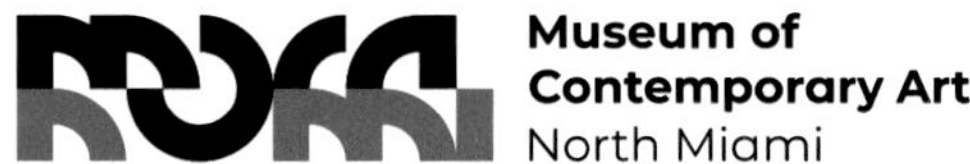

Museum of
Contemporary Art
North Miami

Museum of Contemporary Art, North Miami
770 NE 125th Street
North Miami, FL 33161
Mocanomi.org

© 2024 Museum of Contemporary Art, North Miami

Editor: Adeze Wilford
Managing Editor and Production: Todd Bradway
Design: Melanie Archer
Copy Editor: Flatpage
Printed and bound by GHP, West Haven, CT

Printed on McCoy Silk 100 lb.
Typeset in Roslindale and Aeonik

ISBN: 979-8-9871852-3-0
Library of Congress Control Number: 2024945929

Distributed by
ARTBOOK | D.A.P.
75 Broad Street, Suite 630
New York, NY 10004
Artbook.com

Printed in the United States of America

Captions
Front cover: Untitled, 2016. Detail
Back cover: The Load is Heavy, and My Back is Tired
I, 2023. Detail
p. 4: "Here Sandals has created our newest resort
and ultra-luxurious testament to Jamaica's storied
past, as well as a stunning tribute to the glories of
Europe", from the portfolio Thongs: Experience the
Luxury Included, 2010. Detail

Photo Credits
Zachary Balber: pp. 14, 15, 40–41, 43 (bottom right),
49 (top right), 50–51, 53 (bottom right), 54–55,
56 (bottom left), 64, 65, 68, 69, 84–95
Elon Schoenholz: pp. 17, 28 (right), 36–39, 58, 59
Oriol Tarridas: pp. 8-9, 77
Michael Underwood: pp. 21, 30, 34–35, 42–43 (top
left, bottom left, top middle, bottom middle, top
right), 44–45, 47, 48 (top left), 49, 52, 53 (top left, top
right), 56 (top left, top right), 57, 60 (right), 61, 75 (top
right), 78, 79, 84–95
Angel Xotlanihua: pp. 62, 63

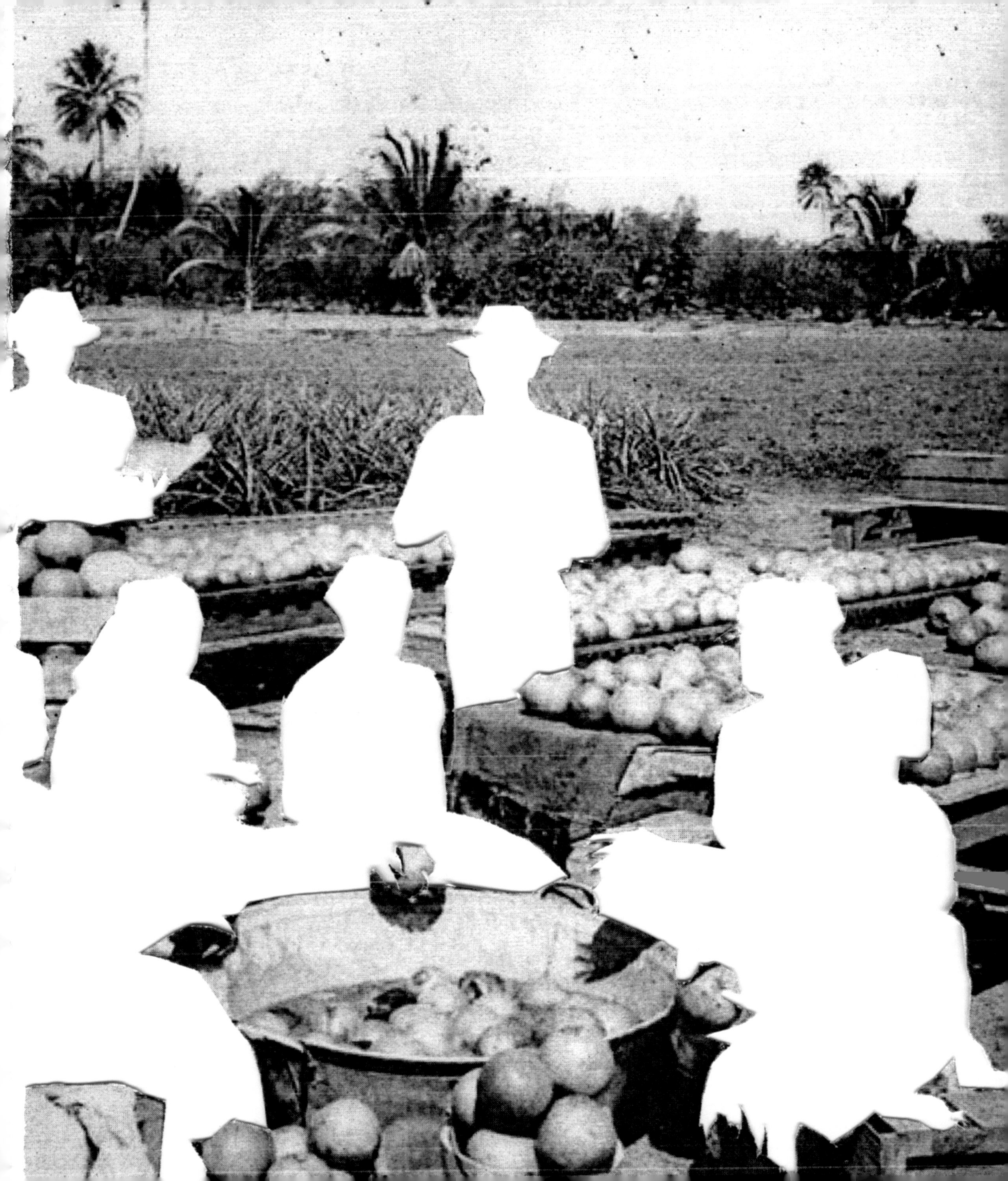

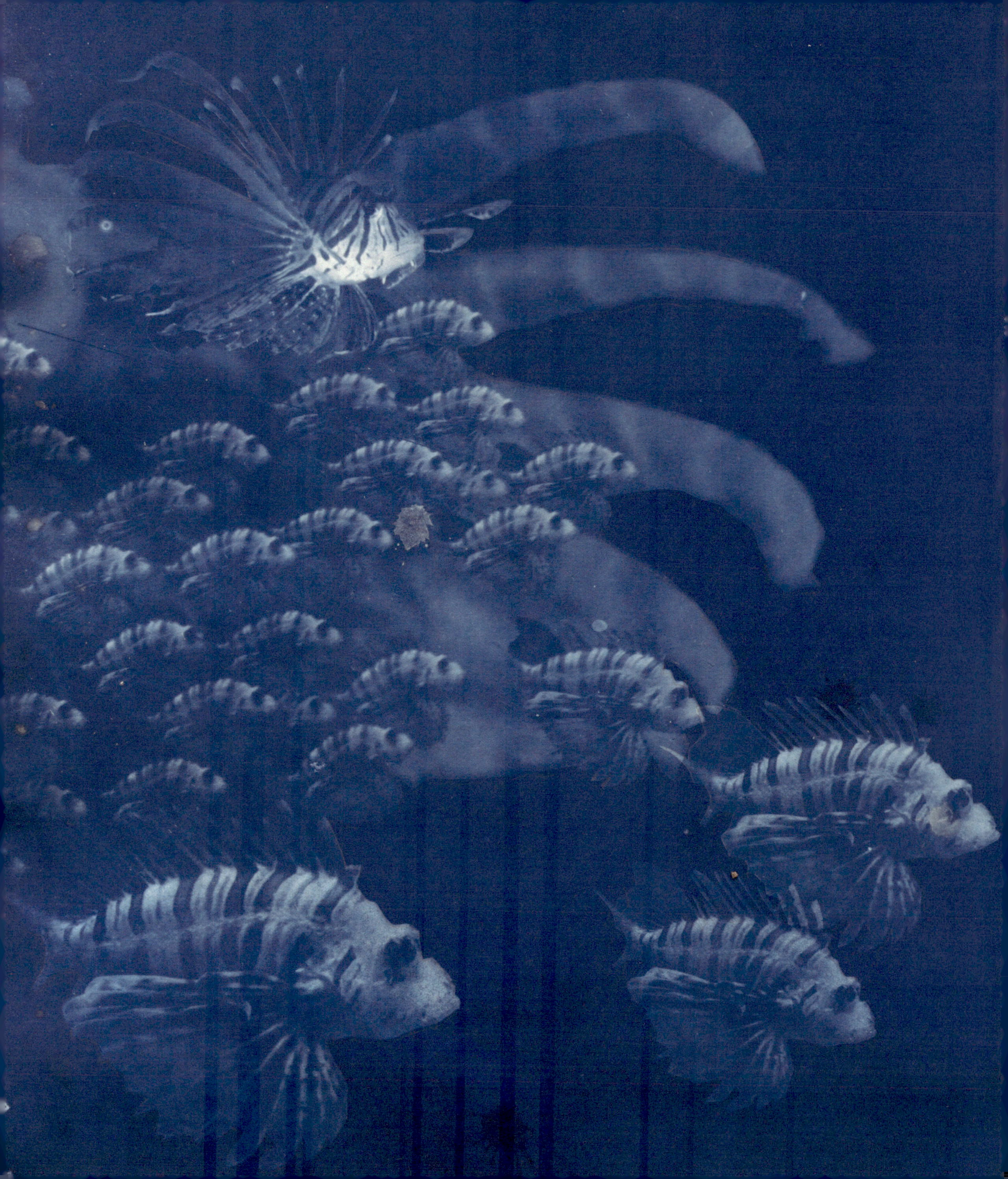